The Meek and the Militant

The Meek and the Militant

Religion and Power Across the World

Paul N. Siegel

Haymarket Books
Chicago, Illinois

First published by Zed Books in 1986
This edition published by Haymarket Books in 2005

Haymarket Books
PO Box 180165
Chicago, IL 60618
www.haymarketbooks.org

Cover design by Eric Ruder
Cover photo of a girl praying in a church in Belgrade © Reuters

Library of Congress Cataloging-in-Publication Data
Siegel, Paul N.
The meek and the militant : religion and power across the world /
Paul N. Siegel.
p. cm.
Includes bibliographical references and index.
ISBN-13: 978-1-931859-24-0 (13-digit)
ISBN-10: 1-931859-24-8 (10-digit)
1. Religions. 2. Communism and religion. I. Title.
BL85.S43 2005
200—dc22
2005020041

2 4 6 8 10 9 7 5 3 1

Printed in Canada

Contents

Foreword

Religion, religious institutions, religious movements, religious ideas and, sadly, religious bigotry, remain powerful forces in the modern world. One has to look no further than the United States over the past few years for confirmation of this claim. Since the fateful attacks on the World Trade Center and the Pentagon on September 11, 2001, the Bush administration has spent much of its energy whipping up anti-Muslim and anti-Arab sentiment in order to push the so-called "war on terrorism." Despite repeated official denials that Islam is the enemy, the administration's list of "terrorist organizations" consists overwhelmingly of Islamic and Arab organizations.[1] Meanwhile, at home, the Justice Department rounded up and/or deported thousands of Arabs and Muslims for minor immigration violations and imprisoned indefinitely hundreds of others.[2] Out of all these, only one person has been charged with having any connection to the September 11 attacks, and in his case the evidence is purely circumstantial.

At the same time as he was overseeing this orgy of racial profiling, the administration's first Attorney General, John Ashcroft, reportedly told a Christian fundamentalist radio broadcaster that Islam is "a religion in which God requires you to send your son to die for him."[3] Religious figures close to the Republican Party have joined in the attacks. In October 2001, Christian evangelist Franklin Graham, who gave the benediction at George Bush's first inauguration, and son of Billy Graham, called Islam "a very evil and wicked religion."[4] The following February, evangelist Pat Robertson told his television audience that Islam "is not a peaceful religion that wants to co-exist. They want to coexist until they can control, dominate and then if need be destroy."[5]

The Bush administration has given quiet encouragement to the bigots. In April 2003, Franklin Graham was invited to preach at the Pentagon. A few weeks earlier, Bush himself brought 141 evangelical Christians to the White House for a private briefing on the Iraq War. According to the *Washington Post*, "Those invited included Jerry Falwell, who apologized last year for calling the prophet Muhammad a 'terrorist,' and broadcaster Marlin Maddoux, who has proclaimed an 'irrefutable connection' between Islam and terror."[6] Comments like these have directly fanned the flames of bigotry. After Ashcroft's remarks on the radio show were publicized, for example, the Arab American Institute received a flood of hate messages. One e-mail message was headed "Ashcroft is 100 percent correct," and concluded, "Kill the Godless Arabs!"[7]

Anti-Muslim and anti-Arab bigotry, however, has come not only from politicians and the Christian right. Supposedly respectable scholars have added their voices to the attacks. In an interview with the online magazine *Salon*, former Harvard University professor Daniel Pipes (now director of the right-wing Middle East Forum) accused Muslims of wanting to create an Islamic state in the United States, even though he admitted he had no evidence for his claim. "I can sense it," he told the magazine. "Look, I have a filter. I've studied Islam and Islamism for 30 years. I have a sense of how they proceed and what their agenda is like." Wanting to see a Muslim president of the United States, said Pipes, is "like saying I want a fascist president."[8] For contributions such as these, Bush appointed Pipes in 2003 to the board of directors of the U.S. Institute for Peace, a body set up by the U.S. Congress in 1984 "to promote international peace and the resolution of conflicts among the nations and peoples of the world."[9]

The academic demonization of Islam is perhaps most famously exemplified by Samuel Huntington's 1996 book *The Clash of Civilizations* and the *Remaking of World Order*, which declares a fundamental conflict between "Western values" and an amorphous "Confucian-Islamic connection." According to Huntington, Muslims are "convinced of the superiority of their culture, and obsessed with the inferiority of their power." As the late Edward Said observed, despite the fact that Huntington ignores "the internal dynamics and plurality of every civilization," the September 11 attacks have "been turned into proof of Huntington's thesis." Politicians like Italian Prime Minister Berlusconi "have used Huntington's ideas to rant on about the West's superiority, how 'we' have Mozart and Michelangelo and they don't."[10] "We," of course, must ignore the great contributions of the Islamic world to mathematics, science, architecture, art, literature and philosophy, which laid the basis for modern European civilization in the first place.

Huntington's book is important, though, because it articulates the worldview that underpins what is basically the Bush administration's explanation for the September 11 attacks and its justification for its policy of permanent war. On this account, the attacks were the result of pure evil—the work of irrational religious fanatics who hate freedom, democracy and prosperity, and who took to the extreme ideas that are embedded in Islam itself. The only reasonable response is thus a military one, since the Islamic fanatics can't be stopped in any other way. An alternative explanation—that U.S. government policies and military intervention around the world for many decades are themselves a key part of the problem, and that the attacks on the World Trade Center and the Pentagon, however unjustifiable, were precipitated by Washington's attempts to dominate the globe—can then be safely ignored.

Since the end of the Cold War and the collapse of the Soviet Union, the U.S. ruling class has been casting around for a new justification for military intervention around the world. It has tried the "war on drugs." It has tried presenting its interventions as humanitarian. Now it thinks that it has found the perfect answer: a war on fanaticism, fundamentalism and terrorism that can continue indefinitely—carried out with fanatical zeal by a U.S. administration that believes that God is on its side and that is prepared to use devastating levels of state terror to achieve its goals.[11]

The myth that Islam is a peculiarly fanatical and intolerant religion can be traced back to the Crusades over 900 years ago, and has been common in the West since at least the nineteenth century. The truth is that Islam is like every other religion—an enormously flexible ideology that has been interpreted in many different ways at many different times. As Paul Siegel points out in his chapter on the social roots of Islam, at the height of Islamic civilization a thousand years ago, when Christians in Europe were engaging in forced baptisms, "there were no religious persecutions or forced conversions" by Muslims. "Jews found life much easier under Islamic rule than under Christian rule, for the Muslims had the tolerance of enlightened people who did not care particularly that the benighted remained in their ignorance."

In modern times, Islam has produced its fair share of fundamentalist fanatics[12]—but the same is true of other major religions. In the United Staes, Christian fundamentalists blow up abortion clinics and assassinate doctors.[13] Jewish fanatics planted bombs and carried out massacres to found the state of Israel, and Jewish settler fundamentalists today regularly carry out murderous attacks against Palestinians in the occupied territories.[14] In India, Hindu nationalists have carried out brutal massacres of Muslims.[15] All religions also contain more progressive currents that present reformist, or even revolutionary ideas in religious terms. Just as some religious figures in Latin America developed "liberation theology" in an attempt to reconcile Catholicism and Marxism,[16] there have also been attempts to develop an Islamic liberation theology—for instance, in Iran in the 1970s and in South Africa today.[17] The intellectual coherence of these efforts is beside the point. What they illustrate is that religion is a social phenomenon. Far from being unchanging, religious doctrines reflect the historical circumstances and the class interests of their adherents, and are shaped and reshaped as those circumstances and interests change.

No serious political activist can ignore the role of religion in contemporary world affairs, and for anyone seeking an understanding of religious ideologies and their historical roots there is no better starting place than Paul Siegel's *The Meek and the Militant*. Siegel shows than there is much more to the Marxist understanding of religion that the familiar expression "the opiate of the masses." Religious institutions and ideas have often acted as a bulwark for inequality and oppression in class societies, but religion has also sometimes been the vehicle for resistance to injustice, from the early Christians to the modern civil rights movement and the opposition of Buddhist monks to U.S. imperialism in Vietnam. Siegel mentions many more examples in his sweeping survey of the origin and development of the world's major faiths from a class perspective. He shows that it is necessary to grasp the social relations that underlie religion, together with the development of the productive forces that gave rise to them, in order to understand the complex roles that religion plays in society. Also very useful is Siegel's discussion of the attitude of Marxist parties to religion. There is much to be learned from what he says even if, like the present writer, one disagrees with some of the details.

This is not a book about current affairs. Its focus is largely theoretical and historical. But anyone who takes the time to grapple with the theory and the history will be in a better position to make sense of the many urgent contemporary questions—from imperialism and war, to world poverty, to women's rights—with which religion continues to intersect.

Phil Gasper for Haymarket Books
August 2005

References

Gilbert Achcar. The Clash of Barbarisms: September 11 and the Making of the New World Disorder. New York: Monthly Review Press, 2002.

Tariq Ali. The Clash of Fundamentalisms: Crusades, Jihads and Modernity. New York: Verso Books, 2002.

Tapan Basu, Pradip Datta, Sumit Sarkar, Tanika Sarkar and Sambuddha Sen. Khaki Shorts and Saffron Flags: A Critique of the Hindu Right. Hyderabad, India: Orient Longman, 1993.

Joel Beinin and Joe Stork, eds. Political Islam: Essays from Middle East Report. Berkeley, CA: University of California Press, 1996.

Sara Diamond. Not by Politics Alone: The Enduring Influence of the Christian Right. New York: The Guilford Press, 1998.

Farid Esack. Qur'an Liberation and Pluralism. Blue Ridge Summit, PA: National Book Network, 1997.

John Green, Mark Rozell and William Clyde Wilcox, eds. The Christian Right in American Politics: Marching to the Millennium. Washington DC: Georgetown University Press, 2003.

Thomas Hansen. The Saffron Wave. Princeton, NJ: Princeton University Press, 1999.

Samuel Huntington. The Clash of Civilizations and the Remaking of World Order. New York: Norton Books, 1996.

Christophe Jaffrelot. The Hindu Nationalist Movement in India New York: Columbia University Press, 1998.

Esther Kaplan. With God on Their Side: How Christian Fundamentalists Trampled Science, Policy, and Democracy in George W. Bush's White House. New York: New Press, 2004.

Gilles Kepel, 2002: Jihad: The Trail of Political Islam (Cambridge, MA: Harvard University Press).

Michael Löwy, 1996: The War of Gods: Religion and Politics in Latin America (New York: Verso Books).

Phil Marshall, 1988: Revolution and Counter-Revolution in Iran (Chicago: Bookmarks).

Olivier Roy, 2004: Globalized Islam: The Search for the New Ummah (New York: Columbia University Press).

Israel Shahak and Norton Mezvinsky, 2004: Jewish Fundamentalism in Israel (London: Pluto Press).

Notes

1. Quoted online at http://www.state.gov/s/ct/rls/fs/2001/6531.htm.
2. "Deportee Sweep Will Start With Mideast Focus," *Washington Post*, February 8, 2002; "The Disappeared," *The Independent* (UK), February 26, 2002.
3. "Alleged Remarks on Islam Prompt an Ashcroft Reply," *Washington Post*, February 14, 2002. Ashcroft later issued a carefully worded statement saying that the reported comments "do not accurately reflect what I believe I said."
4. "Christian Leader Condemns Islam," http://stacks.msnbc.com/news/659057.asp. In an NBC interview the following month, Graham stood by his remarks.
5. "Robertson Calls Islam a Religion of Violence, Mayhem," *Washington Post*, February 22, 2002.
6. Dana Milbank, "White House Notebook: An Answer? Out of the Question," *Washington Post*, April 22, 2003.
7. *Washington Post*, February 14, 2002.
8. "'Islamism is Fascism,'" online at http://www.salon.com/news/feature/2001/11/09/pipes/index_np.html.

9. Because of opposition from some U.S. Senators, Pipes was appointed while the Senate was in recess and thus had to step down at the beginning of 2005 at the start of a new Congress.

10. Said, "The Clash of Ignorance," *Nation*, October 22, 2001. For a sharp demolition of Huntington's thesis see M. Shahid Alam, "A Critique of Samuel Huntington: Peddling Civilizational Wars," online at http://www.counterpunch.org/alampeddle.html (February 28, 2002).

11. On the ways in which the ideology and actions of the U.S. government mirror those of the terrorist groups it opposes, see Achcar 2002 and Ali 2002. However, as Achcar notes, this does not mean that the two sides are equal. "[B]arbarism can never be an instrument of 'legitimate self-defense'; it is always illegitimate by definition. But this does not change the fact that when two barbarisms clash, the strongest, the one that acts as the oppressor, is still the more culpable. Except in cases of manifest irrationality, the barbarism of the weak is most often, logically enough, a reaction to the barbarism of the strong." (p.67) On the role of Christian fundamentalist ideology in the administration's domestic policy, see Kaplan 2004, although the author tends to underemphasize the material interests that underlie the rhetoric.

12. Many authors prefer the term "Islamism" to "Islamic fundamentalism," but as Gilbert Achcar points out, "The English word fundamentalism...defined as 'the desire to use religion to solve all social and political problems and, simultaneously, to restore full obedience to dogma and ritual,' has the great advantage, unlike 'Islamism,' of emphasizing the fact that this way of using religion is not a unique attribute of Islam. Catholic, Protestant, Jewish, Hindu, etc., fundamentalisms also exist, though of course each fundamentalism has its specificities." (Achcar 2002, p.110 n.28) On Islamic fundamentalism, see Achcar 2002, Ali 2002, Beinin and Stork 1996, Kepel 2002 and Roy 2004.

13. On the Christian Right in the U.S. see Diamond 2000 and Green et al. 2003.

14. On Jewish fundamentalism see Shahak and Mezvinsky 2004.

15. On Hindu fundamentalism see Basu et al. 1993, Hansen 1999 and Jaffrelot 1998.

16. Siegel briefly discusses the "theology of liberation" in chapter 10. For a more detailed study, see Löwy 1996.

17. In Iran, leading members of the Mojahedin guerilla organization attempted to integrate Islam and Marx. See Marshall 1988, pp.65–67. On Islamic liberation theology in South Africa, see Esack 1997.

Dedicated to the memory of Thomas Münzer (c. 1489–1525), religious fighter for freedom, and of Thomas Paine (1737–1809), anti-religious fighter for freedom.

Preface

Everyone knows that Marx wrote "religion is the opium of the people," but all too frequently this aphorism is regarded as exhausting what he and Engels had to say on the subject. In fact, they presented a penetrating critique of religion that explains its origin and persistence. They showed also how religion has not only historically acted as a bulwark of the social order, but how some forms of religion under certain circumstances have been, at least for a time, a revolutionary force. Their comments on the role of religion in history, which illuminate the complexity of the phenomenon, have been borne out by the studies of modern historians.

It is also well known that Lenin, like Marx and Engels, was an ideological opponent of religion, but it is not so well known that he welcomed into the ranks of the Bolshevik Party religious believers and even priests who accepted its political program. Nor is it generally known that the Bolsheviks in the years before Stalin's rule guaranteed the freedom of religion, giving dissident religious sects rights which they did not have under the Tsar, and that, although they deprived the Russian Orthodox church of the special privileges it enjoyed in Tsarist Russia, they undid the ties which made it a servile creature of the state.

These seeming paradoxes are in actuality a logical consequence of the Marxist critique of religion. Marxists are uncompromising ideological opponents of religion, but this does not mean that they cannot work with religious believers for common political purposes. While, unlike bourgeois politicians, who seek to be all things to all people, they are honest and forthright about their views, they fight religion not primarily through abstract ar-

1

gumentation (although such theoretical propaganda has its place) but through the class struggle, which is the best educator.

If readers who are religious believers find the tone of my exposition of the Marxist critique of religion in Part I too sharp, I would reply that my sharpness in attacking what I deem to be intellectual error does not necessarily mean that I bear hostility to those who subscribe to it, certainly not to those of them who are seeking to build a just social order, with whom I have a sense of solidarity. Christians say that one must hate the sin but love the sinner; but intellectual error can be as pernicious as moral error and must be opposed as well. Marxists, however, are unlike the dwindling number of bourgeois atheists and agnostics in the tradition of Robert G. Ingersoll and Clarence Darrow who find the root of all evil to be religious obscurantism, not the social system from which religious obscurantism grows.

In subordinating the ideological struggle against religion to the class struggle, Marxists do not give up their principles. Their principled collaboration with religious believers engaged in class struggle is not at all the same as the flirtation of the Italian Communist Party leaders with the Vatican, in the course of which they have temporized on the issues of the separation of church and state and of the liberalization of divorce and abortion. Such political practice is a perversion of Marxism, just as is the making of churches the creatures of the state in the Soviet Union and China.

It is time, therefore, to review the classical Marxist analysis of religion in order to understand what it says and what it does not say. Such a review will enlighten religious believers and others who are sincerely concerned with understanding the Marxist view of religion.

But the Marxist analysis of religion has more than an abstract theoretical purpose. In exhibiting religion's social roots, it aids us in the understanding of past society and, through the understanding of past society, of present society, which has evolved from it, raising fundamental questions and indicating suggestive answers.

The great Indian, Chinese, and Arab civilizations were in their day far more powerful than the European civilizations of the time. India gave birth to Hinduism, which remained indigenous to it, and to Buddhism, which died in India but spread through Asia, including China. Arabia gave birth to Islam, which spread through the Middle East and parts of Asia, Africa, and Europe. What do the rise and fall of these great civilizations and the development of their religions have to say to European and American civilization and its religions? Is there such a thing as exhausting the potentialities of a social system? On the other hand, can the dependent countries of the world today take the road of capitalist development? Is it religion that is blocking them from taking that road, or are there more underlying forces standing in the way?

R.H. Tawney's famous *Religion and the Rise of Capitalism* showed the interrelationships between English Puritanism of the sixteenth and seventeenth centuries and burgeoning capitalism, the social system that was to spread from England to other parts of the world. Today world capitalism is in decline—which does not mean, of course, that it does not retain considerable strength and is not capable of doing considerable damage and indeed of even destroying the world before it suffers definitive defeat. At the peripheries of world capitalism, the weakest parts of the system, socialist revolutions have occurred, and in the last seventy years post-capitalist societies—despite immense difficulties and aberrations, which have created their own problems—have continued to grow in number and strength. How has religion been affected in the three main sectors of the world—the advanced capitalist countries, the dependent countries of the so-called Third World, and the post-capitalist countries—and how in turn is religion acting as an ideological force in the class struggle in these sectors?

An appreciation of religion's roots in the past, of its growth and development, and of the change in its social soil enables us to arrive at the answers to many puzzling questions concerning present-day religion. Why has church membership long been in decline in the advanced capitalist countries of Europe but remains great and is indeed growing in the United States? What accounts for the strength of the evangelical and fundamentalist Religious Right in the United States?

Why, on the other hand, has an important part of the Catholic Church in the United States and other countries become liberalized politically and theologically? Are the present divisions in the Catholic Church the result of Vatican II, or did Vatican II occur as a result of changes in the Catholic Church that were creating divisions within it?

Why has Israel, which likes to call itself the only democracy in the Middle East, failed to effect the kind of separation between religion and the state that has been regarded as one of the hallmarks of bourgeois democracy? Why have liberal American-Jewish supporters of Israel, who have called for continued separation between church and state in the United States, failed to call for such a separation in Israel?

What accounts for the "new face" of Buddhism? How did Buddhist monks, who are supposed to be unconcerned with the things of this world and to regard all life as sacred, come to participate in the armed struggle against imperialism and to play an important role in the politics of Asia after the Second World War?

How did Hinduism, which talks of historical change as being of little significance, come to play a similar role in India? Why do Hindu communalists, members of a religion long said to be the most tolerant of religions, engage in pogroms against members of other religions?

What accounts for the "resurgence" of Islam? What is the source of the differences between Muslims who say that it is necessary to "rethink Islam in modern terms" and Muslim fundamentalists?

Why has the "theology of liberation" grown so strong in Latin America? Why are nuns and priests killed in El Salvador, a country named after Jesus Christ, the Savior, while there are four priests in the revolutionary government of Nicaragua?

The answers to these and other such questions will better enable us to understand our world. Understanding it will better enable us to change it.

This book, it will be seen, covers a vast field. In writing what is essentially a synthesis and popularization of work done in the many areas of this field, I have been indebted to the following, who have read those portions of the first draft dealing with their areas of scholarly expertise and given me the considerable benefit of their criticism: Ismail Hosseinzadeh, George Novack, Robert G. Olson, and Stuart Schaar.

I am also indebted for helpful aid and encouragement to George Breitman, Cliff Conner, Dianne Feeley, and Evan Siegel, who likewise read portions of the manuscript. Paul Le Blanc gave me useful bibliographical information. Robert Molteno, of Zed Books, in urging me to expand the scope of the book helped to improve it. I am grateful to all of them. The usual author's absolution of his manuscript's readers from responsibility for errors of fact and interpretation is more than ever necessary here, since in some instances I have not followed advice that was offered to me. But even where I have not followed it, that advice caused me to think about the problems involved.

PART I

The Marxist Critique of Religion

CHAPTER ONE

French Enlightenment Materialists' View of Religion

The French Materialist Ancestors of Marxism

Marx and Engels saw the French Enlightenment philosophers as being among their intellectual ancestors.[1] Engels paid tribute to them as follows:

> The great men who in France were clearing the minds of men for the coming revolution themselves acted in an extremely revolutionary fashion. They recognized no external authority of any kind. Religion, concepts of nature, society, political systems, everything was subjected to the most merciless criticism; everything had to justify its existence at the bar of reason or renounce all claim to existence.[2]

Elsewhere he spoke of "the splendid French materialistic literature of the past century" in which "French thought made its greatest achievement in form and content" and added that "considering the level of science at that time, it is still infinitely high today as far as content is concerned and has not been equaled as to form."[3] Where workers were influenced by religion, he advised the translation and dissemination of this literature. Lenin also advocated its translation in annotated editions, which would point out what had become obsolete and indicate the advance in the scientific criticism of religion since the eighteenth century.

As an approach to the Marxist view of religion, therefore, it is well to begin with the ideas of the French Encyclopedists, which Marx and Engels for the most part took for granted as common knowledge. The reader should, however, remember that they believed the Encyclopedists to be subject to the limitations of their epoch and therefore one-sided. Marxism remade the materialism of the Encyclopedists by giving it a dialectical instead of a mechanical character and by applying it to the study of social phenomena. The Marxist critique of religion is, therefore, much richer and more complex than the French materialist critique that was its starting point. It accepts but qualifies the Enlightenment accusations against religion. Although the sanctioning of tyranny by the Bible pointed to by the Encyclopedists has been used by churches for centuries, and cannot be explained away or disregarded by those who believe the Bible to be the word of God, the Bible also contains other concepts, which have likewise been appealed to by rebellious religious movements for centuries.[4] So too, although the Enlightenment dictum that religion fosters ignorance is basically correct, it fails to perceive that the fantasies of religion may be intertwined with genuine knowledge.[5]

The French materialists, although strongly against all organized religion ("crush the infamy" was Voltaire's motto), were for the most part deists, believing in a divine creator but denying scriptural revelation. Holbach and Diderot, however, carried their materialism to the point of atheism. The atheist work of the French materialists can perhaps be most profitably examined through Holbach's *Good Sense: or Natural Ideas Opposed to Supernatural.* This is a re-editing for popular purposes of his two-volume *System of Nature.* Though poorly organized, repetitive and declamatory, it strikingly presents in its aphorisms the Enlightenment accusations against religion, most specifically Christianity. I shall abstract some of the main points, adding some elaborations made by their nineteenth and twentieth century rationalist heirs and make use of my own illustrations. The Enlightenment accusations against Christianity apply most particularly to fundamentalist Christianity, which takes the Bible as the literal Word of God. Modernist liberal Christianity represents a retreat from such attacks in an attempt to hold a more defensible ground, but many of Holbach's shafts carry far and continue to fall on the modernist position. We shall see later how this position, which does not take the Bible literally to be accepted in all its details, is vulnerable to Marxist attack.

Religion Sanctions Tyranny

The Encyclopedists subjected the Bible to devastating criticism: they showed that it contained concepts that we today regard as barbarous, and that it sanctioned tyranny. "We find in all the religions of the earth," says Holbach,

> "a God of armies," a "jealous God," an "avenging God," a "destroying God," a "God" who is pleased with carnage and whom his worshippers consider it as a duty to serve to this taste.... Man...believes himself forced to bend under the yoke of his god, known to him only by the fabulous accounts given by his ministers, who, after binding each unhappy mortal in the chains of prejudice, remain his masters or else abandon him defenseless to the absolute power of tyrants, no less terrible than the gods, of whom they are the representatives upon earth.[6]

In speaking of "all religions on earth," Holbach is over-generalizing from the Bible. That the God of the Bible, however, is pleased with carnage is indeed evident to anyone who reads the Bible with a mind not put to sleep by uncritical reverence. The Lord commands the Israelites to seize the lands occupied by other peoples, promising he will aid them in their battles. "All the people will see what great things I, the Lord, can do," he boasts to Moses.

> I will drive out the Amorites, the Canaanites, the Hittites, the Perizzites, the Hivites, and the Jebusites, as you advance. Do not make any treaties with the people of the country into which you are going.... Instead, tear down their altars.... I, the Lord, tolerate no rivals." (Exodus 34:10–14)[7]

"When you capture cities in the land that the Lord your God is giving you," he says elsewhere (Deuteronomy 20:16), "kill everyone."

The Israelites indeed considered it their duty to serve this jealous God to his taste. Before going into battle with the Canaanites, they "made a vow to the Lord: 'If you will let us conquer these people, we will unconditionally dedicate them and their cities to you and will destroy them.' The Lord heard them and helped them conquer the Canaanites. So the Israelites completely destroyed them and their cities, and named the place Hormah." (Numbers 21:2–3). The pious editors of the Good News Bible explain that anything unconditionally dedicated "belonged completely to the Lord and could not be used; it had to be destroyed" and that "Hormah" means in Hebrew "destruction."

Just as he aided his chosen people provided that they sacrificed to him other peoples who worshipped different tribal deities, so did he aid his prophets when their dignity (and that of the Lord they served) was offended. The cruelty of the prophet Elisha would be appalling if we could take the naively told tale of his encounter with some children seriously:

> Elisha left Jericho to go to Bethel, and on the way some boys came out of a town and made fun of him. "Get out of here, baldy!" they shouted. Elisha turned around, glared at them, and cursed them in the name of the Lord. Then two she-bears came out of the woods and tore forty-two of the boys to pieces. (2 Kings 2:23–24)

The moral of the story is clear: that'll teach the kids a lesson!

At times, however, the Israelites did not quite match their God in ferocity. When they killed all the men of the Midianites, plundered their belongings, burned to the ground their cities, and took prisoner their women and children, Moses, who had been instructed by the Lord to punish the Midianites, exclaimed: "Why have you kept all the women alive?... Kill every boy and kill every woman who has had sexual intercourse, but keep alive for yourselves all the girls and all the women who are virgins" (Numbers 31:15–18). The Lord evidently approved of Moses's commandment, for, far from upbraiding him, he gave him detailed instructions on how the loot was to be divided, with a specified portion of the cattle, donkeys, sheep, and virgins going to the Lord himself (Numbers 31:25–30).

What does the giving of the virgins to God mean? Modern students of the Bible state that while the Old Testament condemns human sacrifice in some passages, in other passages it sanctions this practice;[8] this is one such passage. Another passage is Leviticus 27:28–29:

> No one may sell or buy back what he has unconditionally dedicated to the Lord, whether it is a human being, an animal, or land.... Not even a human being who has been unconditionally dedicated may be bought back; he must be put to death.

Before Jephthah went into battle, he vowed to the Lord:

> If you will give me victory over the Ammonites, I will burn as an

> offering the first person that comes out of my house to meet me, when I come back from the victory. I will offer that person to you as a sacrifice.

On returning home, the victorious Jephthah was met by his own daughter.

He exclaimed: "I have made a solemn promise to the Lord, and I cannot take it back." "He did what he had promised the Lord, and she died still a virgin" (Judges 11:30–31, 35, 39). In the light of these passages it is clear that the Midianite virgins given to the Lord were sacrificed as burnt offerings, as were the cattle, donkeys, and sheep.

And what did Moses mean by telling the Israelites to take the other virgins for themselves? Thomas Paine, the great American-revolutionary propagandist and deist, a disciple of the Encyclopedists, took it to mean the rape of these virgins and denounced the inhumanity of the purported Word of God. He was disputed by Richard Watson, the Bishop of Llandaff and Regius Professor of Divinity at Cambridge University, who came to the defense of the faith. Paine's interpretation, said the bishop, was the wicked construction of an infidel. "Prove this," he fervently exclaimed, denouncing Paine as "thou child of the devil," "and I will allow that the Bible is what you call it—a book of lies, wickedness, and blasphemy."[9] All that was meant, he held, was that the young women were taken as slaves. This, in the view of the worthy bishop, preserved the moral reputation of the Bible.

Although he was a professor of divinity with a chair endowed by the king himself, while his opponent was only a rebel with a grammar school education, the bishop overlooked the words of Moses in Deuteronomy 21:10–14:

> When the Lord your God gives you victory in battle and you take prisoners, you may see among them a beautiful woman that you like and want to marry.... She is to stay in your home and mourn for her parents for a month; after that, you may marry her. Later, if you no longer want her, you are to let her go free. Since you forced her to have intercourse with you, you cannot treat her as a slave and sell her.

Thus God is made to sanction rape and concubinage provided that the woman is "mercifully" permitted to mourn for a month for the parents massacred at his behest by the army of her captor, and that she is released after her captor has tired of her.

Not all the Israelite leaders were as meticulous about obeying God's bloody instructions as was Moses. The prophet Samuel told Saul,

> Now listen to what the Lord Almighty says.... Go and attack the Amalekites and completely destroy everything they have. Don't leave a thing: kill all the men, women, children, and babies; the cattle, sheep, camels, and donkeys. (1 Samuel 15:1–3)

However, Saul held out on the Lord, keeping some things for himself. Although he "killed all the people," he "spared [King] Agog's life [presumably, to gain ransom] and did not kill the best sheep and cattle" (1 Samuel 15:9), consequently, Samuel came back from the dead to tell Saul that he was being beset by the Philistines because he had incurred God's wrath: "You disobeyed the Lord's command and did not completely destroy the Amalekites and all they had. That is why the Lord is doing this to you now" (1 Samuel 28:18).

God was the King of Kings who ruled by terror. So ferocious was he that he slew a man who, while the sacred Covenant Box was being transported, in stumbling inadvertently touched it (2 Samuel 6:6–8). The laws that he gave to Moses for observance by the people of Israel, including the payment of a tax for upkeep of a tent for the Lord's presence, a tax each man was to render as "a price for his life" (Exodus 30:12), were presented with the most gruesome threats against those who dared to violate them.

> The Lord said, "If you will not obey my commands, you will be punished.... I will bring disaster on you—incurable diseases and fevers that will make you blind and cause your life to waste away.... If after all this you still continue to defy me and refuse to obey me, then in my anger I will turn on you and again make your punishment seven times worse than before. Your hunger will be so great that you will eat your own children." (Leviticus 26:14–29)

The servile subjects of despots love to tell them not only how great they are but how merciful they are in mitigating their rigors towards their favorites, and despots gratefully accept this flattering estimate of themselves. Such was the God of the Israelites:

> I, the Lord, am a God who is full of compassion and pity, who is not easily angered and who shows great love and faithfulness.... But

> I will not fail to punish children and grandchildren to the third and
> fourth generation for the sins of their parents. (Exodus 34:6–7)

One is reminded of the tough business executive who tyrannizes over his "white-collar slaves" and then tells them, "OK, you guys. You've had it pretty soft up till now, but I'm tired of your fooling around. No more Mr. Nice Guy!" The God of the New Testament talks even more about love and mercy, but he nevertheless announces in Old Testament style a divine devastation of Jerusalem that will strike babies as well as their parents. "For those will be The Days of Punishment," says Jesus

> to make come true all that the Scriptures say. How terrible it will
> be in those days for women who are pregnant and for mothers
> with little babies! Terrible distress will come upon this land, and
> God's punishment will fall on this people. (Luke 2:22–23)

The God of the New Testament, moreover, introduces a new and even greater terror: eternal torment after death. "The Son of Man," says Jesus, "will send out his angels...and they will throw them [all sinners] into the fiery furnace, where they will cry and gnash their teeth" (Matthew 13:41–42). Paul states that "the Lord Jesus" will "appear from heaven with his mighty angels, with a flaming fire, to punish those who reject God and do not obey the Good News about our Lord Jesus. They will suffer the punishment of eternal destruction" (2 Thessalonians 1:7–9). Those who do not accept Christ's deity are therefore consigned to everlasting hell-fire. In short, rejoice in the good news—or go to hell!

This doctrine was accepted for centuries—as it still is accepted by millions of fundamentalists—while at the same time the mercy and goodness of God was extolled. We may, however, ask the simple question: what would we think of a father who, whatever the misdeeds of his children, punished them by exposing them to flames even for a moment? And yet we are told that "our Heavenly Father" tortures eternally the human beings for whom he is so concerned!

The Catholic Church, regarding itself as the ministry of Christ, claimed to hold in its hands the keys to the next life. Only through its sacraments could one achieve heaven. Though the Protestant movement broke this monopoly, it delivered humanity, as Holbach says, to "the absolute power of tyrants." During the period of absolute monarchy the king was regarded as the image and symbol of God, his deputy on earth. No matter how tyrannical he might be, rebellion against him was a heinous sin, a violation of the divinely established order. "I will always side with him," said Luther, "however unjust, who endures rebellion and against him who rebels, however justly." So too Calvin stated: "If we are cruelly vexed by an inhuman prince or robbed and plundered by one prodigal and avaricious—let us remember our own offences against God which doubtless are chastised by these plagues."[10] The American rebels against George III were, of course, denying this theory of the divine right of kings, claiming that a people may "alter" or "abolish" a government which has violated its "inalienable rights." Their leaders, in good part deists and freethinkers,[11] drew for their arsenal of ideas from Enlightenment rationalism.[12]

Religion Fosters Ignorance

According to the thinkers of the Enlightenment, religious terrors rise from ignorance and feed upon that ignorance, paralyzing thought. "How could the human mind," asks Holbach (*Good Sense*, ix), "make any considerable progress while tormented with frightful phantoms and guided by men interested in perpetuating its ignorance and fears?"

The religious prohibition of knowledge is expressed in God's command to Adam that he eat not of the tree of the knowledge of good and evil. Eve, however, "thought how wonderful it would be to become wise" (Genesis 3:6). God's response is that of the despot who fears that the enlightenment of his subjects threatens his power. "Then the Lord God said, 'Now the man has become like one of us and has knowledge of what is good and what is bad. He must not be allowed to eat fruit from the tree of life, and live forever'" (Genesis 3:22).

So too he is fearful when the people are building the tower of Babel to reach the sky: "This is just the beginning of what they are going to do. Soon they will be able to do anything they want" (Genesis 11:6). He meets the threat of human beings acquiring knowledge by destroying their means of communication (their common language) and setting them at odds with each other, using the traditional device of despots, "divide and conquer."

The idea that too bold an inquiry into the ways of nature was dangerous became a part of Christian thinking. In the Middle Ages, physicians, for instance, were looked at suspiciously, especially if they were followers of Avicenna and Averroes, the famous Islamic philosophers and medical authorities. Although medicine was in a primitive state, the very fact that men regarded disease as something other than the possession by demons or inflictions from God, as it was regarded in the Bible, made them somewhat dangerous characters. Hence, the proverb "Where there are three physicians, there are two atheists." John of Salisbury, the English scholastic philosopher, condemned physicians who "attribute too much to Nature, cast aside the Author of Nature."[13]

In the Renaissance the theme of the dangers of the search for knowledge was sounded in the legend of Faust, the scholar who sold his soul to the Devil to gain a knowledge of black magic. This was a period when science was struggling to emerge from magic and was confounded with it. The legend, based on tales of a wandering necromancer, Georg Faustus, who was confused with Johann Fust, an early printer and therefore regarded by many as another dubious character, expresses both the fascination of the new vistas that were opening up and the fears of venturing forth toward them.

The Catholic Church sternly forbade scientific explorations and theories of nature that threatened its authority and dogma. Galileo was forced on pain of death to recant his belief that the earth moves around the sun. His finding of sunspots was denounced for showing that God's work has imperfections. It was forbidden to teach this discovery of the telescope in Catholic universities. In some of them the prohibition lasted for centuries.[14] Works supporting the theory of Copernicus and Galileo that the earth moves round the sun remained until 1835 on the Church's index of books that the faithful were forbidden to read. This honor Copernicus and Galileo shared with Cervantes, Descartes, Pascal, Swift, and Stendhal.

The Catholic Church was not alone in opposing the new astronomy as being in conflict with the Bible. "This fool," said

Luther of Copernicus, "wishes to reverse the entire science of astronomy; but sacred Scripture tells us that Joshua commanded the sun to stand still, and not the earth." Calvin quoted: "The world also is established, that it cannot be moved" (Psalms 93:1) and exclaimed: "Who will venture to place the authority of Copernicus above that of the Holy Spirit?"[15]

Both Catholic and Protestant authorities burned heretics at the stake, providing martyrs in the history of free thought. Giordano Bruno, who championed Copernicus and advocated the study of nature without regard to authority, was executed for, among other things, speculating about life on other planets in an infinite universe. For, it was pointed out, if Christ appeared on earth to be crucified for the sins of man, must he not have been moved to undergo the same torment on countless other planets? We would then have a God who exists only to suffer eternally and a humanity that has no unique place in the scheme of things. So too Servetus, the physician and philosopher who came close to anticipating Harvey in discovering the circulation of blood, was consigned to flames in Calvin's Geneva. One charge brought against him was that in his work on geography he attacked the verity of Moses.

Burning at the stake as a punishment for intellectual differences received sanction from God's use of hell-fire for the same reason. "Bloody Mary," the sixteenth century Catholic English queen, stated: "As the souls of heretics are hereafter to be eternally burning in hell, there can be nothing more proper than for me to imitate the Divine vengeance by burning them on earth."[16] Burning at the stake was not confined to a few eminent heretics: it has been estimated by many authorities that from the fifteenth to the seventeenth centuries several million people, mostly women, were burned to death for witchcraft. The persecution of alleged witches may have had its origin in the efforts to stamp out the remnants of paganism among the common people.[17] Started by the Catholic Church, it was revived and intensified by Protestants. The search for witches was carried out with a zeal that made every village old woman readily suspected of being an agent of the Devil. Many of the victims seem to have been the practitioners of an empirical folk medicine that was in opposition to the professional physicians, who relied on ancient authorities and were subjected to religious controls.[18] The witch-hunting craze lasted into the eighteenth century, when John Wesley, the founder of Methodism, citing Exodus 22:18, "Thou shalt not suffer a witch to live," and other biblical texts, stated that "the giving up of witchcraft is in effect the giving up of the Bible."[19]

The "warfare between science and religion," as it was called by the rationalist successors to the Enlightenment philosophers, continued into the nineteenth century, when the findings of geologists were opposed because they contradicted the Bible. Darwin's theory of evolution was vociferously resisted for the same reason. In the twentieth century Tennessee's law forbidding the teaching of the doctrine of evolution occasioned the famous Scopes trial, in which William Jennings Bryan, denying that man had ape-like ancestors, was made a monkey of by Clarence Darrow. Confronted by Darrow with such embarrassing questions as how did Cain get his wife since the Bible says that the only people on earth at the time were Adam, Eve, Cain, and Abel, and how could the sun have been made on the fourth day of creation, as the Bible says, if we are to accept its statement that "The morning and the evening were the first day,"[20] Bryan could only stubbornly reiterate his faith.

Today religionists, having suffered this defeat, take a different tack. The doctrine of creation, they claim, should be by law accorded "equal time" with the doctrine of evolution in the schools. What this means is that biologists in textbooks and teachers in schoolrooms must present as equally valid as the theory of evolution a doctrine which they do not consider as valid at all. It is similar to the terms under which Galileo, before the papacy clamped down upon him, was given permission to write about the Copernican theory, provided that he presented it as a "mathematical possibility" like the Aristotelian theory, which had the authority of Scripture to support it.

Just as the evidence of the telescope was set aside, so the mountain of evidence verifying the theory of evolution is set aside (here, at least, it is true that faith moves mountains) on the ground of the continuing differences among scientists concerning the mechanics of evolution. Since the theory of evolution does not give the absolute knowledge claimed by religion (science always makes new refinements, advancing to new complexities), it is dismissed as "only a theory," as the Copernican theory was dismissed as only a mathematical supposition. But this dismissal is not an openness to new knowledge but a means of disregarding present knowledge, through which we advance to new knowledge. It asserts that no scientific doctrine is to be taken as gospel (which no scientific philosopher would ever do) in order to take the Gospel as science.[21]

Matter Is Eternal: The Universe Needs No Gods

The fearsome gods of religion, Holbach held, were merely the products of men's terrified imaginations in the face of a universe not understood and that constantly visited calamities upon them. Religion tried to explain both the calamities and the order of nature by reference to these gods. But in reality "the phenomena of nature prove the existence of a God only to some prejudiced men, who have been early taught to behold the finger of God in everything whose mechanism could embarrass them. In the wonders of nature the unprejudiced philosopher sees nothing but the power of nature, the permanent and various laws, the necessary effects of different combinations of matter indefinitely diversified." "Nature, you say, is totally inexplicable without a God. That is to say, to explain that you understand very little, you have need of a cause which you understand not at all" (26, 27). The remedy for man's ignorance is not to attribute that which is unknown to God but to seek to discover the laws of nature.

Religion has, bit by bit, had to give up explanations of natural phenomena by reference to supernatural causes. In Shakespeare's time, only a few centuries ago, it was held that madness was possession by demons and that earthquakes and plagues were the visitations of God's wrath. Luther stated: "The heathen write that the comet may arise from natural causes, but God creates not one but does not foretoken a sure calamity."[22] When science, however, was able to predict the movements of comets, prevent plagues, and warn against earthquakes, these things could no longer be attributed to the will of God. Yet there are residual religious habits of thought manifested in the public prayers of clergymen calling for God's mercy in times of natural disasters, in insurance policies which refer to such disasters as "acts of God," and in the statement of Anita Bryant that the California drought of 1978 was a punishment for the rampant homosexuality in San Francisco. Here, as always, there is the biblical assumption that a "just" God makes use of a collective punishment that falls upon the innocent as well as upon the "guilty."

In reality, said Holbach (28–31),

> Matter has...the power of self-motion; and nature, to act, has no need of a mover.... To be astonished that a certain order reigns in the world is to be surprised that the same causes constantly produce the same effects. To be shocked at disorder is to forget that when things change or are interrupted in their actions the effects can no longer be the same.

What seems to us (because it is unusual or because it is disturbing to humanity) to be disorder is as much the result of natural law as anything else. Natural laws describe how matter moves as a result of all the factors involved, thus enabling us, with a knowledge of these factors, to predict what will happen or, by changing the factors, to change the process; they are not simple statements that what has happened in the past will happen in the future.

A prolonged dry spell does not mean that God is angry at Californians any more than California's customary climate means that God prefers Californians to New Yorkers. And if, despite limited successes in "seeding" clouds, we have not yet got very far in influencing the weather, it would seem that we are more likely to do so by continuing climatological research than by outlawing homosexuality. After all, if Anita Bryant's explanation of the California drought is correct, since the drought ceased without homosexual lifestyles having been altered, God himself quickly gave up in his efforts to do something about the existence of gays.

It has been argued that natural laws imply the existence of a lawgiver, but this is to confuse natural law with human law. Human laws are edicts that may or may not be obeyed. Natural laws, however, must be obeyed, for they are in reality not edicts but descriptions of how things actually operate. As such, they do not presuppose a lawgiver.[23]

It has also been argued that there must have been a creator of the universe who started things going. This is the so-called first cause of things. From this the argument leaps to the conclusion that this creator must be all wise, all knowing, and all good, which by no means follows. But, in any event, the argument for God making use of the idea of the first cause of things is meaningless. "The word 'cause' denotes a relation between things and is inapplicable if only one thing is concerned. The universe as a whole has no cause, since, by definition, there is nothing outside it that could be its cause."[24] To ask "Who made the universe?" or "How did the universe come to be?" is as meaningless as to ask "Could there be a father who never had a child?"

If it is legitimate to say that the universe must have been made, then it is legitimate to say that the creator too must have been made, and the first cause of things turns out not to be the first cause. Those who claim that it is not legitimate to ask such a question about the Creator are retreating from logic to dogma. When they assert that God is his own cause, their assertion is, as the twentieth-century philosopher of science Ernest Nagel states, "simply an unclear statement of the grounds upon which scientists regard as unintelligible the *initial* 'why' as to the world's existence."[25]

Everything in the universe has an origin that can be traced, but the universe itself is the totality of things, not simply a thing whose origin needs to be explained. The notion that an infinity of successive states is logically impossible is true only if we insist that it must be completed, that is, that it must have had a beginning, which is the very point at issue. But such an insistence would be mistaken.

> The infinity of time, in both directions, offers no difficulties to the understanding. We know that the series of numbers has no end, that for every number there is a larger number. If we include the negative numbers, the number series has no beginning either; for every number there is a smaller number. Infinite series without a beginning and an end have been successfully treated in mathematics; there is nothing paradoxical in them. To object that there must have been a first event, a beginning in time, is the attitude of an untrained mind.[26]

If we assume nevertheless that the universe was created by God, we must ask of what did he make the universe if nothing existed prior to creation? Something cannot be made of nothing: this is a contradiction in terms.

> Power—*no matter how much*—has nothing to do with being able
> to bring into existence self-contradictions such as square-circles
> [figures which are both squares and circles at the same time] and
> Creation Ex Nihilo [creation out of nothing].... All the Power a
> God could ever have would not be able to bring something (mat-
> ter) into existence out of Nothing.[27]

This would be a self-contradiction similar to the statement that God in his omnipotence can create a rock that is so heavy that he himself cannot lift it. Omnipotence, if it is to have any meaning, cannot include such self-contradictions but must refer to logical possibilities.

If God, however, made the universe from existing matter, then there is no need for a God. If we do not object to the idea of God being eternal, we cannot object to the idea of matter being eternal. Matter, which our observation shows is constantly changing in accordance with its laws, itself generates life, including intelligent life, which continues to change in accordance with the law of natural evolution.

The materialistic statement that the universe produces life without any form of divine action is borne out by recent work in biochemistry. In the pages of the *Christian Science Monitor*, of all places, its natural science editor, Robert C. Cowes, spoke (November 7, 1978) of the "growing conviction" among scientists "of the inevitability and probable universality of life" and stated that the Nobel Prize-winning chemist Melvin Calvin summed up "the scientific consensus" in his words, "Life is a logical consequence of known chemical principles operating on the atomic composition of the universe."[28] It is this conclusion, drawn from, among other studies, experiments simulating primitive earth conditions, and the observations of astronomers suggesting that a small but significant number of bodies in the universe have conditions suitable for life, which have prompted the sending out of government-subsidized radio signals into outer space in a search for extra-terrestrial forms of intelligent life.

In addition to the First Cause argument, theologians have made use of two other main arguments: the argument from design and the argument from universal agreement. The world is so marvelously ordered, it is said, that we must assume that it was created in accordance with a purpose. To this Holbach replies,

"What is order to one being is disorder to another." Order and purpose are human concepts meaningless in the universe outside of man: the teleological-guided universe is a human projection.

A favorite analogy used by those invoking the argument from design was that of a man who found a watch in a desert. He would know from the intricate mechanism that someone must have made it even if he saw no other evidence of human beings about him. So it is as we observe the vastly greater and more intricate mechanism that is the universe. But, as Holbach's contemporary, the skeptical philosopher Hume, pointed out, the analogy does not hold: we cannot infer purpose in the universe from a comparison with man-made objects. The man in the desert was able to infer the existence of other human beings in the area because he had seen other watches or other objects similar to watches made by men, but none of us have seen gods making universes.[29] As the American philosopher Charles Peirce said in an oft-quoted sentence, "Universes are not as plentiful as blackberries."

In the teleological-guided universe a comet approaching the earth has a purpose: to warn of an impending calamity. The presumption is that there is an intelligence governing the universe akin to human intelligence. Science, in abandoning this presumption, has discovered the laws governing the motion of comets and is able to predict them. The notion of divine purpose does not contribute to an understanding of the universe.[30]

Holbach illustrates the point that purpose is a human imposition upon the universe by telling the story of a holy man of the East who, drinking the water, eating the dates, and contemplating the beauty of an oasis in the desert, exclaimed: "O Allah! How great is thy goodness to the children of men!" But then, as he was proceeding to Mecca, he observed a wolf battening on the corpses of a battlefield, and by the power of his wisdom he understood what it was saying. It was addressing itself to God and exclaiming: "By an effect of thy Providence, which watches over thy creatures, these destroyers of our race cut one another's throats and furnish us with sumptuous meals. O Allah! How great is thy goodness to the children of wolves!" Human beings who believe that the universe was created for their benefit and thank God at mealtimes for the food that men have grown by making use of the forces of nature, have as little reason to do so as had this wolf.

To those who expatiated on the wonders of the human body, each part of which was adapted to perform its function, Holbach pointed to its defects and breakdowns. He was anticipating Helmholtz, the nineteeth century investigator of optics who, in response to the commonly voiced theistic economium on the eye as a mechanism, said that if he had been the Creator he would have been chagrined to have produced so faulty an instrument. We might also point out that the appendix serves no purpose— unless, that is, like Voltaire's Dr. Pangloss, who claimed that the nose was made in order to hold spectacles, we assume that it exists for the purpose of enabling surgeons to make money. In fact, modern biology has shown that the appendix is a vestigial organ from an earlier stage in the evolutionary process in which man, like other animals, was adapted to cope with his environment. The fact that the peripheral vision of horses is much superior to that of human beings does not mean that God preferred horses to human beings or that he was punishing human beings for the fall of Adam; it means that horses are more dependent than human beings on sight and speed in coping with dangers. On the other hand, human beings through the development of their intelligence were able to invent microscopes and telescopes, improving their vision a million-fold.

Finally, with regard to the theistic argument that all peoples, from the most savage to the most civilized, have believed in gods or a God and that the idea of a deity must therefore be an intuitively perceived truth, Holbach answers that, until science proved otherwise, there was a universal belief that the sun moved around the earth. This did not, however, make this commonly held belief correct. The "inward sense" of God is simply an idea that was transmitted from the time of the childhood of the human race, which, however, is growing in knowledge and is in the process of giving up its childish, irrational fantasies.

Contradictions in Theism

"We are gravely assured," says Holbach (69–70),

> that the non-existence of God is not demonstrated.... Is there anything more incompatible with every notion of common sense than

to believe that a supremely good, wise, equitable, and powerful being presides over nature and by himself directs the movements of a world full of folly, misery, crimes, and disorders, which by a single word he could have prevented or removed?

If we believe in an omnipotent God, then we must logically hold him responsible for the evils in the universe. The more charitable hypothesis would seem to be that there is no God. The religionist, however, seeks to escape from this dilemma in various ways, including the invoking of fearful consequences for those who seek to raise the question. One is reminded of the terrible grim humor of a story concerning a group of Jews at Auschwitz. Talking about the horrors around them, they agreed that since God permits such evil to exist he himself must be evil. But the very next day they were punished for their blasphemy: they were taken to the gas chambers.

One theistic answer to the problem of evil is that what seems to be evil really is good because it serves a higher purpose in the divine scheme of things. Just as a painting requires shadows to heighten the effect of brilliant color, so pain, suffering, and other evils are necessary for the sake of a higher good. But this answer is unwarranted speculation: one might just as well argue that what seems to be good is really evil. Moreover, since humanity cannot see the larger picture, it makes humanity suffer for the sake of God's aesthetic satisfaction. Voltaire in *Candide* made the final devastating comment on the contention that we live in "the best of all possible worlds." No matter what agonizing experiences Candide goes through, the fatuous philosopher Dr. Pangloss is always there to explain that what seems to be bad is really ultimately good.

It may be that some evil is logically necessary, but surely there is a huge amount of evil which is not, evil whose existence is incompatible with the notion of an omnipotent, benevolent God. If human beings have to have a sense of pain to avoid physical dangers, does this mean that humanity has to suffer the horrors of war in order to appreciate the blessings of peace? If it were necessary to have the absence of color in order to appreciate color, would not a tiny spot of blackness do for the purpose of making contrasts? Must human beings be plunged into the terrible cold darkness of despair to appreciate the comfort of light and warmth? To argue that they must is to argue like the man who beat his head against the wall because it felt so good when he stopped.

One version of the idea that evil serves a higher good is that in which the world is seen as a kind of moral gymnasium in which we strengthen our characters by wrestling with evil. But what purpose is served if a baby is born idiotic, insane, or blind? Do these afflictions minister to the building of character? Moreover, it is difficult to see how the existence of hookworm, which makes children listless and apathetic, and of infant malnutrition, which dulls the mind so that the capacity for understanding moral choices is impaired, strengthens character. Religionists will argue that such afflictions teach the parents the stoic acceptance of God's will. Even if we assume this is good for the parents—and many will say that such acceptance is itself intellectual dullness and a kind of spiritual hookworm—it does not take into account the welfare of the children.

The moral gymnasium theory is derived from the doctrine of free will, the old answer to the problem of evil in a world created by a beneficent God. Evil came about, it was said, when Adam and Eve transgressed by disobeying God's commandment. As a result of this transgression not only were their descendants born with a propensity to evil but nature itself was disordered so that instead of living in a blissful Eden we live in a world of droughts, hurricanes, and earthquakes. This is what Malcolm X, referring to the blaming of Blacks for their own situation, called making the victim out to be the criminal. If evil only came into the world as a result of Adam and Eve's transgression, how did they come to commit the sin of disobedience in the first place? Furthermore, before Adam and Eve ate of the tree of the knowledge of good and evil, how could they know that it was evil to disobey God?

God is often represented as behaving with a strange arbitrariness toward the sin-prone descendants of Adam and Eve. "There, but for the grace of God, go I." But why does God confer his grace upon one person and withhold it from another? Aside from the charge of capriciousness, there is also the question of God's method of ordering the world so that it is not conducive to the practice of virtue. Suppose a man has a son who every now and then goes off on an alcoholic binge during which he mistreats his wife and children. Should the man constantly press liquor upon his son with the idea that he is giving him an opportunity to strengthen his character? What is the likelihood of this method succeeding, and what are the consequences of failure for the wife and children? Would it not be better to seek to keep liquor out of his son's way, give him moral support in facing up to his problem, and encourage him to search out the origins of his behavior with scientific help, thereby enabling him the better to cope with his behavior pattern? A wise and loving father would do so even if it risked the son's concluding from his self-analysis that his father bore a share of the responsibility. But our Heavenly Father is represented as acting in a way that we would condemn on the part of our fellow human beings.[31]

Frequently, such objections are met with the statement that the reasons of God are beyond human wisdom. But to say this is to limit the power of God, for what we are saying is that for an ultimately beneficent purpose that we cannot explain God has made use of evil. But the need to use evil to attain good implies a limited power, for otherwise the doer would not have had to make use of evil.[32] The same is true of the presumption that there must be an after-life in which we are recompensed for our suffering in this world. If God has to rectify the injustice in this world in the next world, he is not all-powerful in this one. But then, as Hume said, if we go solely by experience, we have no reason to believe that another existence will be any better than this one.[33]

Man's "Immortal Soul"

The materialist, however, denies the existence of an after-life in which consciousness of self, intelligence, and memory survive death. If we assign a soul to ourselves, says Holbach, should we deny it to animals, who have to a limited degree intelligence and memory and whom he finds, morally speaking, superior to tyrants? Do the souls of the babies who die when they are one day old survive, but the souls of chimpanzees, who are much more intelligent than day-old babies, do not? If we allow chimpanzees to have souls, at what point in the scale of life do we stop? With the ameba? If the souls of day-old babies survive, what kind of consciousness do they have after death since their intelligence and memory were so little developed before death? At what point in the evolutionary process did man acquire an immortal soul? Was it conferred upon him as a kind of graduation present when he became homo sapiens? And at what point in gestation do human beings acquire a soul? At the time of the first stirrings in the womb, as the Catholic Church said from the twelfth to the nineteenth century, or at the time of conception, as it now says?

In truth, we have as little reason to believe that human beings have immortal souls as we have to credit animals with them. Without the body there can be no life of any kind, just as the Cheshire cat's grin could not exist (except in the imaginings of Lewis Carroll) without the cat. As Holbach phrases it, "To say that the souls of men will be happy or unhappy after the death of their bodies is in other words to say that men will see without eyes, hear without ears, taste without palates, smell without noses, and touch without hands or skin." And so too without the brain, the seat of intelligence and memory. We know that injury to the brain may produce a coma, a state of prolonged unconsciousness. If damage to a portion of the brain wipes out memory and consciousness, how can memory and consciousness survive the total destruction of the brain in death?[34]

Faith and the Mystical Experience in Revealed Religion

It is often affirmed that Christianity involves a faith that is superior to reason. Its truth can be felt; it cannot be explained. To the assertion of faith Holbach retorts (72–73):

> The Deity has revealed himself with so little uniformity in the different countries of our globe that in point of religion men regard one another with hatred and contempt.... If this religion were the most important concern of men, the goodness of God would seem to demand that it should be to them of all things the most clear, evident and demonstrative.

The statement of the religionist that he believes despite reason is psychologically interesting, but how can it convince others? Are we to believe *all* absurdities? If not, how shall we choose which absurdity to believe?[35]

The faith of the "born again" preacher is often peddled as if it were a patent medicine: "Why not try God? He'll make a new man of you!" But of all the faiths on the market, which one shall we buy? The Muslim believes that an angel appeared to Muhammad, the Catholic believes that angels appeared to Joan of Arc, the Mormon believes that an angel appeared to Joseph Smith. None of them believes in the visitations accepted by the others. While the sophisticated Protestant is not inclined to accept such miraculous visitations in our time, he does believe that an angel appeared to Mary. Since each faith claims to be the true religion, the skeptic will answer the question "Which faith shall I select?" by saying, "God knows—and he'll have to show me before I buy."

Instead of showing himself to human beings all over the world in a manner which is "clear, evident, and demonstrative" such as the perception that three times one is three (trinitarian Christianity says on the contrary that as far as the deity is concerned three times one is one), the God of the revealed religions has shown himself to only a few individuals whose word all of us are expected to accept. As Holbach's associate, Diderot, said, "The pretended facts with which all religion is supported are ancient and wonderful, that is to say, the most suspicious evidence possible to prove things the most incredible; for to prove the truth of the Gospel by a miracle is to prove an absurdity by a contradiction in nature."[36]

The primitive credulousness, the myth-making propensity, and the disregard for the verification of alleged fact of the authors of the Bible are manifest. They accepted "miracles"—violations of nature's laws—as readily as did their superstitious contemporaries and predecessors. A student of comparative religion points out:

> [Jesus's] death is marked by an eclipse, as was alleged to have been the case with Julius Caesar, Augustus, and Drusus, although no eclipse is recorded by the historians, and if, as it was related, the crucifixion occurred at the Jewish Passover, the moon was full and a solar eclipse was impossible.... Jesus turned water into wine, as did Dionysus on January sixth of every year; and multiplied loaves of bread, as did Elijah. He walked on water like Orion, Poseidon's son. He raised men from the dead, as did Elijah and Elisha—this feat had once been so common that Aristophanes in *The Frogs* (ca. 405 BC) made Dionysus say of Hermes and of

Hermes's father, that performing resurrections was a family profession. He gave sight to the blind by application of his spittle, the
remedy which Thoth had used to restore the eye of Horas, and
one which was used all around the Mediterranean by medicine
men and had even been used successfully and to his great fame by
the Emperor Vespasian.... He healed the leper, the lunatic, the
deaf and dumb, as did Askelepios.[37]

So readily did the early Christians accept miracles that they did
not deny those which were allegedly performed by the heathens.

They owned that the Pythian Apollo prophesied correctly and told
what Croesus was doing though hundreds of miles away: that Cas-
tor and Pollux appeared [as spirits who led the Romans to victory]
at Regillus, and that Tuccia carried water in a sieve. ["All these absurdities are spoken of by Tertullian as true: *Apology*, cap. 22."]
Their only resource was to declare that these wonders were done
by the agency of demons, in which they, like the Jews and the heathens, undoubtedly believed.[38]

So too the second-century Christian apologist, Justin Martyr,
answered those who compared the story of Jesus's birth with
that of the birth of Perseus, whose mother was said to have
been visited by Zeus as a "shower of gold," by "what was with
him a favorite and unanswerable argument, that Satan had anticipated Christianity and imitated it in advance in the pagan
cults: 'When I am told that Perseus was born of a virgin, I realize that here again is a case in which the serpent and deceiver
has imitated our religion.'"[39]

The modern believer in the New Testament miracles of the
virgin birth, the resurrection from the dead, and the rest, is only
slightly less credulous than the early Christians. He does not accept the pagans' myths but accepts those of his own religion. But
there is no more reason to believe the one more than the other.
As Hume pointed out in his essay on miracles, the greater the im-
probability of something the more evidence is necessary if we are
to accept it. If someone were to swear that he had seen a man
walking on ocean waves, reasonable people would not accept
that as readily as if he swore that it had rained hard yesterday in
his city. The accounts of miracles do not hold up if we consider
the notorious unreliability of eyewitness testimony, especially by
those who were at the time under the influence of excitement, the
power of suggestion, and the effect of mass hysteria.

It is to the power of suggestion upon hysterics that modern "miracles" such as the "cures" at Lourdes are to be attributed. Freud found that hypnotism was often able to effect spectacular cures of hysterical symptoms, but these cures did not last long. The symptoms were either temporarily masked or converted to other symptoms. This was why he gave up hypnotism for psychoanalysis. The "faith cure," which can be achieved by faith in medical science by the use of placebos as well as by faith in religion, is similar to the apparent cure effected by hypnotic suggestion.

The claims of revealed religion have been defended not only on the basis of alleged miracles or by an appeal to authority but on the basis of what is alleged to be a direct communion with God. This communion gives a sense of peace and assurance, and this blissful feeling is said to be convincing evidence of God's existence. But this is to say: "It makes me feel good; therefore, it is true." Not only is this dubious logic but the same could be said by the user of amphetamine, which likewise gives an enhanced feeling of well-being that is, however, as fleeting as the soothing perception of the divine presence. Communion with God, moreover, can only be experienced, we are told, if one really and truly believed. In the same way, the medium at a seance insists that the spirits she is summoning will not come if there is a skeptic present: apparently, these spirits are shy beings, easily put out. But this is scarcely proof; rather is it the "wish fulfillment" and regression to infantilism in which one believes one's self to be under the protection of an all-powerful authority figure that Freud characterized religion as being.

The regression to the infantile state, when the world was scarcely more than a blob and the self scarcely differentiated from it, is the basis of the mystical experience.[40] This experience, as described by the mystics, insofar as they have been able to articulate it, is one in which the inspired individual rises above the ordinary everyday world and the self to perceive a higher reality in which everything forms a single inseparable whole. In perceiving this higher reality one realizes that evil is an illusion, for the differences and conflicts of the ordinary everyday world are transcended. This perception, say the mystics, is valid knowledge.

If we were to accept this view as true, then there is no point in trying to improve the conditions of life or indeed in doing anything at all, for all is the same in the higher reality. But this experience cannot be verified as truth. A scientific experiment can be repeated and so verified, but the mystical experience is fitful and given only to a few people. Various means such as isolation, prolonged wakefulness, fasting, breathing exercises, peyote and other drugs, and concentration on the monotonous repetition of words have been used to induce it. These result in an abnormal physical and psychological state.

The evidence derived from such a state is not trustworthy. The person suffering from delirium tremens may be convinced of the reality of the pink elephants he sees, but there is no reason for anyone else to believe in them. The same is true of the perceptions of those who have had too little food or too little sleep: lightheadedness is not a means of ascending to a higher reality.[41] We can only concur with J.H. Leuba, the psychologist who studied religious mysticism: "Experiences named 'mystical'…are all explicable *in the same sense, to the same extent* and *by the same general scientific principles* as any other fact of consciousness."[42]

CHAPTER TWO

The Marxist View of Religion

Dialectical Materialism and Its Criticism of French Materialism

"The materialism of the last century," says Engels, was predominantly mechanical, because at that time of all natural sciences only mechanics, and indeed only the mechanics of solid bodies—celestial and terrestrial—in short, the mechanics of gravity, had come to any definite close.... This exclusive application of the standards of mechanics to processes of a chemical and organic nature—in which processes the laws of mechanics are, indeed, also valid but are pushed into the background by other, higher laws—constitutes the first specific but at that time inevitable limitation of classical French materialism. The second specific limitation of this materialism lay in its inability to comprehend the universe as a process, as matter undergoing uninterrupted historical development.... Nature, so much was known, was in eternal motion. But according to the ideas of that time, this motion turned, also eternally, in a circle and therefore never moved from the spot; it produced the same results over and over again.... This same unhistorical conception prevailed also in the domain of history.... Thus a rational insight into the great historical interconnections was made impossible, and history served at best as a collection of examples and illustrations for the use of philosophers. (*On Religion*, 231–33)

For dialectical materialism, on the other hand, change is not merely repetitive. Things undergo qualitative transformation in their interactions with one another. "The motion of matter is not merely crude mechanical motion, mere change of place, it is heat and light, electric and magnetic tension, chemical combination and dissociation, life and, finally, consciousness" (171).

These are different forms of motion.

Matter is not merely acted upon from outside; it is impelled by inner opposing forces. In the struggle between these inner forces a gradual accumulation of changes brings about at a given point a sudden transformation. Water that is heated is at a certain definite temperature transformed into steam; water that is cooled is likewise at a precise temperature transformed into ice. The addition of a single crystal to a supersaturated solution of certain crystals will cause a precipitation. In biological evolution, an accumulation of small changes leads to the emergence of a new species.[2]

The solar system, the earth, the plants and animals on it, human societies came into existence in this way. Everything is in a process of evolution, of coming into being and passing away. The main features of this process can be summed up in a very general manner by a series of laws which were first formulated by Hegel: interpenetration and struggle of opposites; development through contradiction; the transformation of quantity into quality and vice versa; "breaks of gradualness"; new stages of development which contain in a different and higher form something of what has been destroyed ("the negation of the negation").

Diderot anticipated to some degree the evolutionary views of the next century.[3] However, because other eighteenth-century materialists saw the universe as a machine which repeats its movements, they were deists: a machine needs a "first impulse" from a prime mover to get it started. Whereas the God of the Bible was a Middle Eastern monarch who ruled over the universe with the might and wisdom with which Solomon ruled over his kingdom, the God of the deists was a British constitutional monarch who did not interfere with nature's laws and who, once having created the universe, presided over it but did not rule it. But as for Marxism, Engels commented, "in our evolutionary conception of the universe, there is absolutely no room for either a Creator or a Ruler; and to talk of a Supreme Being shut out from the whole existing world, implies a contradiction in terms" (295).

So too the eighteenth-century materialists saw human society not as lawfully developing in accordance with its own internal forces but as acted upon from the outside by superior individuals who exerted their ideas and their will upon the inert masses of people. They tended to look upon religion as a conspiracy of kings, priests, and aristocrats to "lull to sleep the people in fetters," as one of them put it,[4] a theory which Marxism, as we shall see, regards as an oversimplification. At the same time in an elitist spirit they feared what would happen if not merely the educated, but the masses, were to reject the notion of the God of Christianity. This was the point of Voltaire's quip "If God did not exist, it would be necessary to invent him."

"In the realm of history," said Engels (256), "the old materialism becomes untrue to itself because it takes the ideal driving forces which operate there as ultimate forces, instead of investigating what is behind them, what are the driving forces of these driving forces." In short, it takes the ideas by which people explain their actions to be the impelling force of history instead of seeking the material causes which bring about changes in their view of things.

Marxism holds that, just as coping with their environment leads, in animals, to the evolutionary development of natural organs through natural selection, so with humanity the labor process leads to the development of tools, humanity's artificial organs. The development of the forces of production, in which the means of production—the aggregate of tools socially organized—are an essential element, is the dynamic power of social development. Different social classes stand in different relationships to the mode of production, the productive forces plus the productive relations. The further development of the means of production, which disintegrated primitive collectivism and brought in class divisions, brings about the rise of new social classes, which after a gradual economic development effect a sudden transformation in society, a revolution.

Each ruling class, the class that owns the means of production, constructs an "ideology," a system of ideas expressive of its outlook on life that dominates its age. Other classes have different interests and ideas, but until they become revolutionary they normally tend to accept or at least adapt to the dominant ideology.

> A new social class does not come into existence with a ready-made view of the world corresponding to its real conditions and constitution. Quite the contrary. At the beginning this budding formation may have as distorted and inadequate a picture of the social setup

and its position and prospects in it as a child does of the world
around it. The class's distinctive conceptions have to be elaborated in
the course of its activities and evolution by specialists in that line.[5]

These "specialists," the ideologists of the class, generalize upon
the class's distinctive conceptions, which express the new needs
and interests rising from its new social circumstances, shaping
them into a new world-view.

In constructing an ideology, the ideologists of a class make
frequent use of the ideas of the past in accordance with the same
principle of economy of energy that distinguishes all production.
The process of the construction of an ideology is complex, in-
volving interaction between the diverse components of a class
and its ideologists; it is not fully conscious. Although an ideology acts as a rationalization of a class's social position and material interests, it is not mere hypocrisy but is sincerely trusted as
truth by its members. For instance, the Puritans among the bourgeoisie of the late sixteenth century, who were often denounced
as hypocrites by their opponents, generally had the genuine
strength of their belief which made it possible for them to gain
adherents and lead a revolution fifty years later.

On the "economic foundations" or "material base," the forces
of production and the sum total of the relations into which people
enter to carry on social production, there develops, then, an "ideological superstructure" constituted by the various systems of ideas
and cultural institutions of a society. The metaphor of base and superstructure is not to be construed to imply a static or one-way relationship between them. There is constant interaction among the
diverse aspects of a given socio-economic order. In the "ideological
superstructure" religion acts upon literature, art, political theory,
philosophy, and other kinds of ideological activity and is also
acted upon by them. But there is also action on the economic base
by ideological forces: the ideas that people have play a role in
shaping the form of society, as did the Puritan ideas of the English
revolutionary bourgeoisie in the seventeenth century. Ideology becomes a force in the class struggle, just as an individual's concept
of himself, even though mistaken, affects that person's actions.

Ideological activities, however, are not independent forces.
Although the people engaged in each form of ideological activity
operate in accordance with the traditions and special concerns

developed within that activity, these activities—even religion, which "stands furthest away from material life and seems to be most alien to it" (263)—are only relatively independent. All of these factors are different manifestations of the unified process of social development from which they have evolved. Amid all of the movements the most powerful movement acting upon them is the underlying economic movement. It is this underlying movement that *"ultimately* always asserts itself" (*Reader,* 202).[6]

The Marxist Analysis of the Origins of Religion

Marxism accepts the dictum of the earlier materialists, derived from Epicurus, that religion originated from the savage's awe and fear in the face of an inexplicable nature. However, making use of subsequent comparative mythology and its own sociological insight, it has elaborated and expanded upon this observation. "All religion...is nothing but the fantastic reflection in men's minds of those external forces which control their daily life," says Engels (*On Religion,* 147), "a reflection in which the terrestrial forces assume the form of supernatural forces. In the beginnings of history it was the forces of nature which were first so reflected and which in the course of further evolution underwent the most manifold and varied personifications among various peoples."

Using the findings of Edward Tylor, the founder of modern anthropology, Engels also called attention to the fact that the idea of a human being's immortal soul came from the dreams of primitive peoples, who thought that during sleep the soul left the body and had the experiences of which a person dreamed. They assumed that this soul would leave the body after death as it did in sleep. What Engels did not know and what modern anthropology has established is that this soul, when it left the body on death, was, since it had supernatural powers, generally feared.[7] Some primitive peoples are afraid of cameras because they believe that souls are thereby captured on photographs. Even in civilized countries today mediums present, as evidence of their powers in summoning the spirits of the dead, photographs allegedly showing these spirits' materializations, and books about poltergeists such as the *The Amityville Horror* gain enough credulous readers to become bestsellers.

In such dread and awe do primitive peoples hold the spirits of the dead that ancestors and outstanding persons are apotheosized into gods.[8] Contemporary anthropologists and students of comparative religion for the most part agree that both natural forces and the spirits of the dead were the origins of the gods.

> In the animistic stage of culture all nature was thought to be alive with souls.... The ancestral origin of some of the spirits and demons came to be forgotten, while others were remembered for a longer period of time.... Polytheism seems also to have stemmed from animism. The more important the object in the life of a people, the greater its divine soul was considered to be.... A mountain in Midian [Mount Sinai] contributed a Semitic god whose spiritualization has fathered at least three great religions. Among the Greeks, the Romans, the Indo-Aryans, the Teutons, and many other tribal groups, imagination in the course of time organized polytheism into a system and attributed a social life to the gods.[9]

Religion, therefore, is derived from the animism of primitive peoples, who do not differentiate themselves from the other things of nature, endowing them with spirits that have the thoughts and desires of human beings. Magic is the means by which the savage seeks to control these spirits either by inducing them to follow his example, squirting water from his mouth to cause rain, or by transferring their powers to himself, wearing a tiger's tooth to gain the tiger's strength.

Religion came into being with the advance from savagery to barbarism, when the passage from food-gathering to agriculture brought with it class society and an unproductive priesthood, just as in a higher stage of productive development the commercial centers of Greek civilization saw the birth of philosophy and in a still higher stage the industrial society of the seventeenth century saw the birth of modern experimental science. But the old persists amid the progress of the new. Religion continues although science advances, and it contains within it elements of magic.

Thus swine flesh may not be eaten by Jews or Muslims and cows may not be killed by Hindus, just as savages have taboos which forbid them to touch objects believed to be inhabited by supernatural beings or forces. The icon, the image of a saint or other sacred personage that is itself sacred, is similar to the fetish of the savage. Prayers, holy water, and priestly blessings are similar to the formulas, incantations, and rituals of magic.

The doctrine of transubstantiation of the Catholic Church, which holds that in the rite of the Eucharist the bread and wine are actually converted into the body and blood of Christ although they retain their external appearance, resembles the cannibalism of primitive peoples who believe that eating a man's flesh is a means of gaining his strength and courage. The "laying on of hands" in various Protestant sects is a quasi-magical means of allaying distress—a power formerly reserved for kings and saints, including the unsanitary Charles II, whose "royal touch" was supposed to be able to cure scrofula.

Both magic and religion have their origin in humanity's lack of control over nature. Religion, however, also reflects humanity's lack of control over the forces of society that resulted from class domination. This was first perceived by Engels, who pointed out that the students of comparative mythology in paying attention exclusively to the gods as imaginary reflections of the forces of nature overlooked one increasingly important factor in the evolution of religion. That was its connection with and conditioning by the loss of control over the forces of society with the advent of class distinctions and domination.

> Side by side with the forces of nature, social forces begin to be active—forces which confront man as equally alien and at first equally inexplicable, dominating him with the same apparent natural necessity as the forces of nature themselves.... At a still further stage of evolution, all the natural and social attributes of the numerous gods are transferred to *one* almighty god. (148)

How the "natural and social attributes of the numerous gods" were transferred to the God of the Old Testament is suggested by a recent student of comparative religion, Weston La Barre: "The priestly Jehovah himself is an odd syncretism of fertility- and place-daemons, fire- and volcano-god, Mesopotamian sky god and neolithic rain bull, shaman-husband [medicine-man cultivator] of the land, and many others besides."[10]

The Marxist Perception of Religion as Ideology

The Marxist perception of religion as ideology is not the same as the French materialists' view of religion as a conspiracy of the ruling class. This was not understood by Reinhold Niebuhr, one of the pre-eminent theologians of our time, who writes in his introduction to the Schocken edition of *Marx and Engels on Religion* that Marx and Engels's "appreciation of the socially radical peasants of the sixteenth century under Anabaptist religious leadership, revealed particularly in Engels' article on the Peasant Wars, is not quite in agreement with Marxism's central thesis that religion is a weapon always used by the established social forces." The function of an introduction to a book is to make the reader better acquainted with the author of the book and his ideas so that the reader comes to the book better oriented: it is, in short, to introduce, not traduce. But this statement, like other statements in Niebuhr's introduction, with which we shall deal later, only misleads the reader.

Niebuhr's statement is applicable to the Enlightenment philosophers' view of religion as conspiracy. That was an unhistorical approach to religion. The philosophers rightly regarded the Catholic Church of their time as the enemy of progress and consequently looked upon religion as ministering exclusively to reaction at all times and in all respects. This was too one-sided an appraisal of the phenomenon.

In accord with the method of dialectical materialism Marx and Engels gave a much more concretely historical explanation of the role of religion through the ages that took into account its contradictory functions. Although the primary function of religion was to sanctify repressive institutions, because it dominated people's thinking about the world and society around them, rebellious moods and movements among the oppressed in pre-bourgeois times—and even after—tended spontaneously to acquire a religious coloration and heretical cast. The aims and aspirations of social agitators were expressed through traditional religious ideas adapted to the need and demands of the insurgent masses.

There is, therefore, no sort of contradiction, as Niebuhr suggests, between the perception that German Anabaptism served the socially radical peasants and the perception that religion is a weapon used by the established social forces: religion—in different forms, of course—can be a weapon used by opposing sides. The reinterpretations of religious ideas have accompanied deep-going changes in social relations that have given rise to sharp class conflicts.

In fact, this is clearly stated, although obtusely disregarded by Niebuhr, in the very passage in Engels's *The Peasant War in Germany* from which Niebuhr got his metaphor of religion as a weapon. There were three opposing forces in Luther's time, says Engels, analyzing the social classes in each, "the *conservative Catholic* camp," "the camp of *burgher-like moderate Lutheran* reforms," and the *"revolutionary party"* of Münzer, the Anabaptist leader (103).

> Luther had put a powerful weapon into the hands of the plebeian movement by translating the Bible. Through the Bible he contrasted the feudalized Christianity of his day with the unassuming Christianity of the first century, and the decaying feudal society with a picture of a society that knew nothing of the complex and artificial hierarchy. The peasants had made extensive use of this instrument against the princes, the nobility, and the clergy. Now Luther turned it against them, extracting from the Bible a real hymn to the God-ordained authorities such as no boot-licker of absolute monarchy had ever been able to achieve. (108)

Nor did Marx and Engels regard German Anabaptism as a special exception, as Niebuhr implies. If he only had read with some care the book he was introducing, he would have found that they saw rebellious movements of the oppressed as taking their own distinctive religious forms from the earliest days of Christianity. "Christianity was originally a movement of oppressed people: it first appeared as the religion of slaves and emancipated slaves, of poor people deprived of all rights, of peoples subjugated or dispersed by Rome" (316). "Revolutionary opposition to feudalism lasted throughout the Middle Ages. It took the shape of mysticism, open heresy, or armed insurrection.... The heresies gave expression partly...to the opposition to feudalism of the towns that had outgrown it (the Albigenses, Arnold of Brescia, etc.), and partly to direct peasant insurrections (John Ball, the Hungarian teacher in Picardy, etc.)" (ibid., 99). In those two varieties of medieval heresy "we see, as early as the twelfth century, the precursors of the great antithesis between the burgher and peasant—plebeian oppositions, which caused the failure of the Peasant War" (100).

> At that time the plebeians were the only classes that...stood outside both the feudal and the burgher associations. They had neither privileges nor property.... This explains why the plebeian

opposition even then could not confine itself to fighting only feudalism and the privileged burghers; why, in fantasy at least,...it
questioned the institutions, views and conceptions common to all
societies based on class antagonism.... In this respect, the chiliastic
dream visions of early Christianity offered a very convenient start-
ing-point.... This sally beyond both the present and even the future could be nothing but violent and fantastic. (102)

The "chiliastic dream-visions of early Christianity"—the
idea of the second coming of Christ, which would bring a thousand years of the Kingdom of God on earth—inspired, then, the
struggles of the poor and the oppressed for centuries. This sheds
a new light on Marx's "Religion is the opium of the people."
This is generally taken to mean that religion is a drug that enables the masses to bear their misery by losing themselves in
dreams that deprive them of the capacity to revolt. This is the
conception, as we have seen, of the Enlightenment philosophers, and it is undoubtedly a good deal of what Marx meant,
but it is not all that he meant. Immediately preceding his famous sentence is the sentence "*Religious* distress is at the same
time the *expression* of real distress and the *protest* against real
distress" (42). Opium dreams can rouse to protest and struggle,
can stimulate as well as stupefy. Opium, however, is never conducive to realistic perception, and it is precisely because communism could not be achieved at that time, because the struggle
for it could only be an anticipation of the future, that the yearning for it took the form of fantasy.

But even the revolutionary English bourgeoisie of the seventeenth century used religion—although not in so "violent and
fantastic" a form—to provide "the self-deceptions" that the adherents of the revolution needed in order to "conceal from
themselves the bourgeois limitations of the content of their
struggles and to keep their enthusiasm on the high plane of the
great historical tragedy." "Cromwell and the English people,"
therefore, "borrowed speech, passions, and illusions from the
Old Testament for their bourgeois revolution. When the real
aim had been achieved, when the bourgeois transformation of
English society had been accomplished, Locke supplanted
Habakkuk [the book of the Old Testament dealing with the triumph of divine justice over evil]."[11]

With the rise of the bourgeoisie there came the development of science, which furthered industry; seventeenth century Calvinism, the religion of the revolutionary English bourgeoisie, paved the way for science,[12] and the bourgeoisie and science soon went beyond religion.

> The flag of religion waved for the last time in England in the seventeenth century, and hardly fifty years later appeared undisguised in France the new world outlook which was to become the classical outlook of the bourgeoisie, *the juristic world outlook*. It was a secularization of the theological outlook. Human right took the place of dogma, of divine right, the state took the place of the church.... And because competition, the basic form of trade of free commodity producers, is the greatest equalizer, equality before the law became the main battle cry of the bourgeoisie. (270–71)

The idea of the "inalienable rights" of man, which fired the imaginations of the American and French revolutionists, was, however, a rationalization of the bourgeoisie, just as Puritanism had been a religious rationalization of the English revolutionists. "The sale and purchase of labor-power...is in fact a very Eden of the innate rights of man. There alone rules Freedom, Equality, Property."[13] Ostensibly, both capital and labor enter into a contract as free agents in which they exchange on an equal basis that which is the possession of each, money and labor. In reality, since the worker must starve if he does not sell his labor-power, he is under constraint to be exploited. Capitalists and workers are theoretically equal before the law, but that equality received its best comment in the famous sentence of Anatole France: "The law in its majestic equality forbids the rich as well as the poor to sleep under bridges, to beg in the streets and to steal bread."

However, if the bourgeoisie in its revolutionary heyday gave up religion for a secularist ideology, in the nineteenth century it returned to religion although it could not summon up the old fervor. The British bourgeoisie had been terrified by the Jacobins and the sansculottes of the French Revolution and attributed the whole nasty affair to the spread of irreligion. "By 1795," says Bertrand Russell, "almost all the well to do in England saw in every unbiblical [geological] doctrine an attack upon property and a threat of the guillotine. For many years British opinion was far less liberal than before the Revolution."[14]

Soon enough, however, the English bourgeoisie did not stand alone in its acceptance of religion. With the growth of socialism "British respectability," says Engels, triumphed over "the free thought and religious laxity of the Continental bourgeois."

> Nothing remained to the French and German bourgeoisie as a last resource but to silently drop their free thought, as a youngster, when sea-sickness creeps upon him, quietly drops the burning cigar he brought swaggeringly on board; one by one, the scoffers turned pious in outward behavior, spoke with respect of the Church, its dogmas and rites, and even conformed with the latter as far as could not be helped.... Religion must be kept alive for the people—that was the lonely and last means to save society from utter ruin. (312–13)

That Engels is correct in seeing the Continental bourgeois turn to religion as a consequence of the growth of socialism is attested to by so eminent an historian and so sympathetic a friend of religion as Arnold Toynbee:

> Towards the close of the 19th century, a section of the French bourgeoisie that had been anti-clerical or agnostic or atheist since at least as far back as the time of the French Revolution reverted to a profession of Roman Catholic orthodoxy in a more or less cynical mood, because they had come to think that the Roman Catholic Church's deeply ingrained conservatism was now making the Church a bulwark of private property in an age in which socialism was on the march.[15]

Thus the European bourgeoisie, after having in its most progressive sections rejected the drug of religion, became its "pushers." The Enlightenment thinkers' view of religion as a cynical ruling-class conspiracy was—although "pushers" are themselves often drug addicts—closer to reality at this time than during the Enlightenment itself.

Since the French Revolution, however, religion has become, said Engels, speaking of the advanced capitalist countries of Europe (his statement must be qualified when one speaks of the predominantly peasant countries in the periphery of world capitalism),[16] "incapable of serving any progressive class as the ideological garb of its aspirations" (266). The working class has no need of the illusions of religious ideology or any other kind of ideology to make its revolution. Marx's materialistic concept of history, the world outlook of the politically conscious workers, has in fact served to dispel such illusions, bringing about for the first time a consistent concordance between the aims of a revolutionary class and its general outlook, free of religious and other ideological obfuscation.

Marxism and Modernist Christianity

Among the religious illusions which Marxist materialism dispels are those of modernist Christianity, a modification of the earlier Christianity attacked by the French materialists.

As a result of the advance of science Christians had to surrender bit by bit what had been regarded as essential elements of their faith. The warfare between science and religion took place in the sixteenth and seventeenth centuries on the front of astronomy and in the nineteenth century on the fronts of geology and biology. Fighting on these fronts was fierce, but the successive retreats of the Christians enabled believing scientists to continue to adhere to the religion of their time as that religion became modified. Today, as at most times in the last three hundred years, it is said that science and religion have established a peace,[17] although Protestant fundamentalists and some Catholic theologians are still fighting a rearguard action. Scientists on such fronts as biochemistry and psychology, where such matters as the origin of life and the indivisibility of mind and body are involved, continue, however, to wrest territory from theology.

Engels, surveying the process taking place in his own time, observed ironically:

> God is nowhere treated worse than by the natural scientists who believe in him.... One fortress after another capitulates before the march of science, until at last the whole infinite realm of nature is captured for science, and there is no place left in it for the Creator... What a distance from the old God—the Creator of heaven and earth, the maintainer of all things—without whom not a hair can fall from the head! (192–93)

Just as Henry IV said of his conversion to Catholicism to gain the throne, Paris is worth a mass," so the contemporary theologian can say "Maintenance of the church is worth the sacrifice of the old God."

Not only has religion retreated before the onslaught of nat-

ural science; it has retreated before the advance of the philologi-
cal study of the Bible. Using methods literary scholars have used
on other texts, Biblical scholars have shown that the Bible was
written over a period of more than fourteen centuries, the earliest parts going back to before 1200 BC, the latest having been
written in the middle of AD 200. The first five books of the Old
Testament, which had been attributed to Moses, were actually
written by several people at different times in an order that was
not the same as the order in the Bible. Thus at least three people
wrote Genesis, the first chapter of which was written some centuries after most of the second chapter. So too the gospel of the
New Testament, which had been believed to be eyewitness accounts by Jesus's disciples, have been found to be compilations
of oral tradition that had accumulated over a period of time.[18]

Liberal theologians have accepted these findings but have
continued to regard the Bible as in some sense the word of God
even though it is not a direct communication from Moses who
got it straight from Jehovah or a recital of events by the disciples of Christ who had witnessed them. This kind of liberal
theology was already present in the time of Marx and Engels.
Engels speaks of "that latitudinarian criticism" of the Bible
"which prides itself upon being unprejudiced and thoroughgoing, and, at the same time, Christian. The books are not
exactly revealed by the holy ghost, but they are revelations of
divinity through the sacred spirit of humanity, etc." (205).

Characteristic of this liberalism is the article on the Bible by
the theologian Sanday in the *Encyclopedia of Religion and Ethics.*
"Given a spiritual interpretation of the universe," writes Sanday,

> assuming that behind the world of phenomena there is a supreme
> spirit which has brought it into being, there has been a wide-spread
> belief that this Spirit desires to be known, and has caused itself to
> be known, by the most intelligent of its own creatures.... The
> whole idea of Spirit "speaking to" spirit is, of course, metaphor....
> But if we are to suppose that God has "spoken to" man, how
> should He speak?... Surely it is very credible that the method of
> communication chosen might well be through the influence of the
> higher Spirit upon the lower, not in equal degree upon all individu-
> als but pre-eminently upon some. That is the way in which the
> Bible appears to describe the relation of God to man.... When we
> come to consider him [man] as a religious being, we find...that his

career has been on the whole one of gradual and progressive advance.... If we look steadily upon the contents of the Bible from this point of view of "an increasing purpose," they seem quite worthy to have come from God.... There are certainly some ways—many ways—in which the Bible is not infallible, and therefore not in the strict sense authoritative. More and more the authority of the Bible has come to be restricted to the spheres of ethics and religion. But more and more it is coming to be seen even within these spheres, allowance must be made for difference of times.

Sanday rejects the old anthropomorphic God who spoke to Moses, as the Bible says, "just as a man speaks with a friend" but did not permit him to see his "face," only his "back"—it must have made communication awkward—since no one could see the face of God and live (Exodus 33: 11, 20–23). The idea of spirit speaking to spirit is only a metaphor since speech implies a larynx and a material body. Nevertheless God supposedly exerted his "influence" on the authors of the Bible although how he communicated ideas without language ("Ideas do not exist apart from language," as Marx pointed out)[19] is not specified.

The message of the Bible which is the result of God's communication to a few choice spirits is said to be becoming increasingly clear in the course of man's spiritual evolution, which is part of the divine plan. Its authority is now seen to be restricted to ethics and religion—that is, to the enunciations of the commandments of the God whose existence Sanday had begun by assuming, not proving. What it has to say about the things which are contradicted by natural science are to be regarded as the crudities adapted to the ignorance of the men whom God "influenced," not as eternal truths.

This is the doctrine of accommodation by which the absurdities of the Bible are explained by the need of God to accommodate himself to the limited intelligence of man. The trouble with this explanation is that it makes God accommodate himself much too much: the supposed concession to man's limited intelligence is really a stumbling block in the way of the progress of that intelligence. Blind belief in the Bible has been the prime source of obscurantist resistance to the acquisition of knowledge concerning the universe and humanity. Not only was it used to forbid the teaching of Copernican astronomy, to engage in witch hunts, and to oppose the concept of biological evolution, in our day it has been used by South African Boers to defend apartheid and by Mormons to exclude Blacks from the priesthood, thereby consigning them to a lower place in the Celestial Paradise, that is, to a segregated heaven. It really seems as if an all-wise God could have done better.

Even in the spheres of ethics and religion the modernist theologian concedes that allowance must be made for differences in times. This spares him the embarrassment of defending such things as the commands that men who will not obey their parents should be stoned to death (Deuteronomy 21:18–21), as should brides who are "proven" not to have been virgins on their wedding night by their not being able to exhibit blood-stained sheets (Deuteronomy 22:15–20). But what then remains after such allowances have been? The answer given by the modernist theologian is that the Ten Commandments and the Sermon on the Mount teach us a morality that is true for today and always and is so sublime that it must have in some sense come from God.

Engels, on the other hand, rejects "every attempt to impose on us any moral dogma whatsoever as an eternal, ultimate, and forever immutable moral law" (*Reader*, 252). In rejecting moral absolutes Engels anticipates what the great anthropologist Sir James Frazer found from his study of many cultures: "The old view that the principles of right and wrong are immutable and eternal is no longer tenable. The moral world is as little exempt as the physical world from the law of ceaseless change, of perpetual flux."[20] But, although there are no moral absolutes, ends and means are dialectically interconnected, with ends determining means and with the achievement of an end becoming the means of achieving a further end. Since, for instance, the liberation of the working class can only come about through the workers themselves, socialism cannot be achieved by the deception and coercion practiced by Stalinist "leaders."[21]

Engels, unlike Frazer, sees the changes in morality as arising from the economic development of society:

> All former moral theories are the product, in the last analysis, of the economic stage which society had reached at that particular epoch. And as society has hitherto moved in class antagonisms, morality was always a class morality; it has either justified the domination and the interests of the ruling class, or, as soon as the

oppressed class has become powerful enough, it has represented the revolt against this domination and the future interests of the oppressed. That in this process there has on the whole been progress in morality, as in all other branches of human knowledge, cannot be doubted. But we have not yet passed beyond class morality. A really human morality which transcends class antagonisms and their legacies in thought becomes possible only at a stage of society which has not only overcome class contradictions but has even forgotten them in practical life. (252)

If we examine the Ten Commandments and the Sermon on the Mount, we find that they do not constitute in truth an immutable and acceptable moral dogma. The Second Commandment, for instance, which announces that God will "tolerate no rivals," states: "I bring punishment on those who hate me and on their descendants to the third and fourth generations" (Exodus 20:5). Would liberal theologians defend this vengefulness upon the grandchildren and great-grandchildren of criminals as a guide to human conduct today?

The Tenth Commandment states: "Do not desire another man's house; do not desire his wife, his slaves, his cattle, his donkeys, or anything else that he owns" (Exodus 20:17). Here the existence of slavery is accepted as moral, and women are regarded as possessions similar to cattle. The low place of women is manifestly derived from the same patriarchal culture of a nomadic tribe which caused Lot, the upright man of God, to offer his two daughters to the wicked men of Sodom if they would not rape the two male strangers who were Lot's guests (Genesis 19:7–8). Among nomads in a desert country hospitality is all-important, but women do not count for much.

The commands "Do not steal" and "Do not commit murder," derived from Hammurabi's codification of the Babylonian laws that had come down to him from earlier times, are more enduring moral precepts, necessary for the normal functioning of civilized society. Because of social tensions and class contradictions, however, these precepts cannot be absolute and will be at times regarded differently, especially by opposing classes.

The Bible relates, for instance, how Joseph, favored by God, was able to foretell years of famine and advised the pharaoh to accumulate a large store of grain. When the famine came, the people of Egypt and Canaan were forced by hunger to give their livestock and their land to Joseph, acting as the pharaoh's governor, and to become the pharaoh's slaves in return for food. They bound themselves and their descendants, moreover, to give the pharaoh one-fifth of the harvest they cultivated for him (Genesis 47:18–26). The Bible evidently regards this extortion as commendable conduct on the part of Joseph. Rebellious slaves, however, would have regarded it as a form of stealing, whereas if they were to have expropriated the land they or their forefathers had relinquished under duress this would have been regarded as stealing by the pharaoh and his underlings, including the privileged priests, who had not been required to give up their land and who received allowances from him.

Moreover, as Engels points out, "Do not steal" is not an eternal moral law. Stealing presupposes the prevalence of private property and its concepts of ownership. "In a society in which the motive for stealing has been done away with, in which therefore at the very most only lunatics would ever steal, how the preacher of morals would be laughed at who tried solemnly to proclaim the eternal truth: Thou shalt not steal" *(Reader,* 252).

The Arctic explorer Vilhjalmur Stefansson, who observed at close range the Stone Age Eskimos of Coronation Gulf from 1906 to 1918, tells in fact of such a society, a society of primitive communism.

> The system which I watched breaking down under the combined influence of Christianity and the fur trade was on its economic side communism. Natural resources and raw materials were owned in common, but made articles were privately owned.... You don't have to accumulate food, apart from the community's store; for you are welcome to all you reasonably need of the best there is. You do not have to buy clothes; for they will be made for you by some woman member of your family or by some woman friend.... You do not have to accumulate wealth against your old age; for the community will support you as gladly when you are too old to work as it would if you had never been able to work at all—say because you had been blind from infancy.[22]

In this society the Judeo-Christian injunction "Do not steal" did not have any meaning—or at least it did not until Christianity and capitalism disrupted the old ways.

Even less than the injunction forbidding stealing has the injunction forbidding killing been an absolute, even to the faithful. Catholics thought that they were performing a religious duty in killing every Huguenot in sight on St. Bartholomew's Eve. Although the Huguenots presumably differed with them on this doctrinal point, Protestants were nevertheless not always averse to killing. Luther felt the same way about the German peasants during their uprising as the French Catholics did about the Huguenots. "They must be knocked to pieces, strangled and stabbed, covertly and overtly, by every one who can, just as one must kill a *maddog!*" he exhorted (*On Religion*, 107).

The churches, of course, have always condoned mass murder, using the doctrine of the "just war." Coincidentally, each church has found the war conducted by its own state to be a just one. While the Kaiser in World War One spoke of "*Gott und mich,*" the English poet Rupert Brooke summoned his countrymen to fight "for God, King and Country." Each regime is confident that the old "God of Battles" is on its side. On the other hand, the war which the ruling class of the imperialist nations presented as a holy war, the Russian Bolsheviks rejected as a capitalist war, calling upon the working people of all countries to oppose it. Different classes, different moral criteria and conclusions.

The Sermon on the Mount is no more a moral doctrine whose superiority proves that it is a revelation of God than is the Ten Commandments. If the test of truth is experience, then the morality of the Sermon on the Mount has been refuted by life. As Marx said,

> Does not every minute of your practical life give the lie to your theory? Do you consider it wrong to appeal to the courts when you are cheated? But the apostle writes that that is wrong. Do you offer your right cheek when you are struck upon the left, or do you not institute proceedings for assault? Yet the Gospel forbids that.... Are not most of your court proceedings and the majority of civil laws concerned with property? But you have been told that your treasure is not of this world. (35)

The claim that the doctrine is so lofty that it cannot be realized in life is only an expression of underlying contempt for it: ideas which are so pure that they are sullied by contact with reality are not worth anything. One pays lip service to them, but they are not a guide for one's conduct; they are sterile abstractions.

In reality, the Sermon on the Mount expressed a doctrine

that enabled the oppressed of the Roman Empire to find consolation for their lot. To those who suffered constant humiliation it preached the glory of submission.[23] The psychologist Bruno Bettelheim, who was imprisoned in a Nazi concentration camp, has revealed the shocking fact that some of the prisoners there were so broken that they fell in love with their guards. This is the sick masochism of the slave who loves those who abuse him. The slave who struggles against his slavery, however, thereby frees himself of his slave psychology.

Far from showing moral superiority, the Sermon on the Mount expresses the sneaking resentment of those who are wretched but cannot give vent to their sense of injustice.

> Happy are you who weep now; you will laugh! Happy are you when people hate you, reject you, insult you, and say that you are evil, all because of the Son of Man! Be glad when that happens and dance for joy, because a great reward is kept for you in heaven.... But how terrible for you who are rich now; you have had your easy life! How terrible for you who are full now; you will go hungry! How terrible for you who laugh now; you will mourn and weep! (Luke 6:21–25)

Is there not a suppressed vindictiveness here that is masked by the statement "Love your enemies, do good to those who hate you, and pray for those who mistreat you" (Luke 6: 27–28)? To his followers Christ says, "Pray for your enemies, and you will go to heaven, but your enemies, who are now laughing, will weep and wail in hell." To his opponents he says, as we might put it in the vernacular employed by the Good News Bible, "That's all right, bud—go ahead and laugh. You'll get yours some day. He laughs best who laughs last."

The palming off on God of one's own unacknowledged desire for justice leads to a patent self-contradiction. "Do not judge others," says Christ, "and God will not judge you; do not condemn others, and God will not condemn you; forgive others, and God will forgive you.... The measure you use for others is the one God will use for you" (Luke 6:37–38). But he had just before said of God, "He is good to the ungrateful and the wicked. Be merciful just as your Father is merciful" (Luke 6:35–36). In saying that if you are unforgiving God will be unforgiving to you, he is contradicting the statement that God is merciful to the wicked. God, the model for mercy, whom humanity is urged to imitate, is himself vengeful. In actuality, the revelations that purportedly come from God are merely an expression of human desires and dreams.

Marxism and Agnosticism

In the eighteenth century religious disbelief often took the form of deism, belief in a God which denied scriptural revelation or established religion; in the nineteenth century it often took the form of agnosticism. The word "agnosticism" was invented by Thomas Henry Huxley from the Greek *agnost(os)* ("not known, incapable of being known") to refer to the doctrine that it is impossible to gain knowledge concerning the existence or non-existence of God. Engels said of agnosticism:

> What, indeed, is agnosticism but, to use an expressive Lancashire term, "shamefaced" materialism? The agnostic's conception of nature is materialistic throughout. The entire natural world is governed by law, and absolutely excludes the intervention of action from without. But, he adds, we have no means either of ascertaining or of disproving the existence of some Supreme Being beyond the known universe.... Thus, as far as he is a scientific man, as far as he *knows* anything, he is a materialist; outside his science, in spheres about which he knows nothing, he translates his ignorance into Greek and calls it agnosticism. (*On Religion*, 295–98)

Humanity, however, will never acquire a complete knowledge of the universe, which is inexhaustible. Dialectical materialism holds that every scientific theory is only a rough approximation of reality, an approximation which becomes more and more close to the truth as scientific knowledge advances, but that this greater closeness to the truth is that only compared to the previous theory. But, says Engels, quoting Spinoza on the obscurantist argument for believing on the basis of ignorance, "*Ignorantia non est argumentum*" (193). Ignorance, whether we translate it into Greek or Latin, is not an argument for God. In the dialectic of humanity's enlargement of its understanding of nature, ignorance becomes in the process of time knowledge, which has, however, a new though lesser element of ignorance in it. If we explain what is at the moment unknown by reference to God, we are blocking the way to new discoveries. The development of our understanding of nature, then, is in contradiction with the idea of God. This is implicitly recognized by the agnostic in practice although in theory he leaves open the possibility that there is a God, whom, however, we shall never get to know.

Such a theoretical possibility serves no purpose but a mischievous one. If, for instance, carried away by Bardolotry, I were to claim *A Midsummer Night's Dream* as a new Bible that reveals to us the actual existence of Oberon, Titania, and their court, opponents to this claim could not absolutely disprove it. Since the fairies are invisible to ordinary mortals' eyes, the fact that trustworthy witnesses have not seen them is not proof that they do not exist. Moreover, it could be argued against opponents of our new Bible, that, as the Eleventh Edition of the *Encyclopedia Britannica* says in its article "Fairy," "one of the most interesting facts about fairies is the wide distribution and long persistence of the belief in them." Here we have an example of that *consentium gentium*, that common agreement by peoples everywhere, by which theologians set such store as an argument for God.

However, since there is no evidence at all that Oberon and Titania exist except as creatures of the imagination, since it is easy enough to see how they and their court are derived from the real-life Renaissance monarch and his court, and since the belief that bad weather occurs as a result of domestic quarrels between them gets in the way of our study of how the weather changes and how we may control it, it would seem proper to dismiss the notion of the actual existence of Oberon and Titania out of hand and to say that the person who takes this fairy tale for reality is like that ass Bottom and his crew, who confuse the play they are putting on with real life. The same is true of the belief in God. We may add that mistaking fiction for reality is not conducive to appreciating the artistry of the fiction as well as to understanding reality—and that this is true for both the Bible and *A Midsummer Night's Dream*.

Engels and Freud on Religious Alienation

What Marx and Engels had to say about religion anticipates remarkably what Freud says about it in *The Future of an Illusion* although Freud knew very little about Marxism. Religion, states Freud, is a "wish fulfillment" that was "born from man's need to make his helplessness tolerable" and "was built up from the material of memories of the helplessness of his own childhood and the childhood of the human race. It can be clearly seen that the possession of these ideas protects him in two directions—against the dangers of nature and Fate, and against the injuries that threaten him from human society itself."[24] So, it will be recalled, did Engels speak of the gods as reflecting the "forces of nature" and "social forces" which were "alien" and "inexplicable" and which humanity called upon to protect it, not to destroy it.

"Religion," Freud goes on, "is comparable to a childhood neurosis." Freud is, however, "optimistic enough to suppose that mankind will surmount this neurotic phase, just as so many children grow out of their similar neurosis."[25] So too Engels wrote, echoing Ludwig Feuerbach (from whom he and Marx profited although they found that Feuerbach's materialism did not go far enough):

> Religion is essentially the emptying of man and nature of all content, the transferring of this content to the phantom of a distant God who then in his turn graciously allows something from his abundance to come to human beings and to nature.... Man has in religion lost his own existence, he has renounced his humanity, and now is aware (since through the progress of history religion has begun to totter) of its emptiness and lack of content. But there is no salvation for him, he can once more win his humanity, his essence only through a basic overcoming of all religious assumptions and a decisive, honest return not to "God," but to himself. (*Reader*, 234–38)

Prostrating themselves before the God of their own creation, human beings are alienated from themselves and their fellows. The protection they gain from this God is at the cost of the integrity of the self. Just as with a child submitting to a domineering and capricious father, submission to God only increases insecurity by creating dependence on an arbitrary force and fosters a suppressed rebelliousness against Big Daddy that adds to fears of retaliation. It is only when humanity has finally freed itself from this dependence that it can be free.

"By withdrawing their expectations from the other world and concentrating all their liberated energies into their life on earth," says Freud, human beings "will probably succeed in achieving a state of life in which life will become tolerable for every one and civilization no longer oppressive to any one."[26]

The Marxist adds that this will only be accomplished when the present society, which brings the evils of unemployment, inflation, and war, before which the masses of people are impotent, has been overthrown and a new society, in which social relationships are clear and unveiled and human beings are not alienated from the products of their labor, has been constructed.

It is true that in any kind of society human beings will still be subject to injury, disease, and death. But where these are seen to be the working of natural law, not arbitrary acts, they are endurable and in part remediable. "Necessity is *blind* only *in so far as it is not understood.*" Freedom does not consist in the dream of independence of natural laws, but in the knowledge of these laws, and in the possibility this gives of systematically making them work towards definite ends (*Reader*, 266).

Since, however, religion will vanish only after "the last alien force which is still reflected in religion" vanishes, it would be wrong for a revolutionary regime to prohibit the practice of religion. Thus Engels, attacking what he called the "Prussian socialism" of Dühring, who advocated just such a prohibition, said: "Herr Dühring...cannot wait until religion dies this, its natural, death.... He incites his gendarmes of the future against religion, and thereby helps it to martyrdom and a prolonged lease of life" (*On Religion*, 149).

Similarly, Freud wrote:

> It is certainly senseless to begin by trying to do away with religion by force and at a single blow. Above all, because it would be useless. The believer will not let his belief be torn from him, either by arguments or by prohibition. And even if this did succeed with some it would be cruelty. A man who has been taking sleeping draughts for tens of years is naturally unable to sleep if his sleeping draught is taken away from him.[27]

In the realm of religion at least there is no point to making a drug addict, whether of sleeping draughts or of opium, go "cold turkey." It is better to remove the conditions that have caused him to take up his habit.

CHAPTER THREE

Marxism and Religion Compared

The Charge That Marxism Is a Religion

One religious response to Marxism has been that Marxism itself is a religion. By saying this, religionists seek to blunt Marxism's attack on religion with a "you're another" argument: if religious belief is intellectually reprehensible, then you're a sinner too! It is also a charge made by secular liberals who would dismiss Marxism as being as obsolete for an educated man as religion is.

This description of Marxism, however, far from being sophisticated modern understanding, is merely an updating of the comment on atheism by the Parisian intellectuals of the 1840s, who, says Engels, "could conceive a man without religion only as a monster, and used to say to us: *'Donc, l'atheisme c'est votre religion!'*" (*On Religion*, 239). To say that atheism is itself a religion is manifestly a mere playing with words. In the sense of the popularly accepted use of "religion" as a belief in a God or gods—or in the broader definition of religion by the anthropologist Tylor that religion is "a belief in spirits"— atheism is of course a denial of religion. The paradox is achieved by implying another definition of religion such as "coherent world outlook." But this is to disregard the atheist claim that religion is a world outlook that makes use of fantasy.

Something else is implied by those who say that Marxism is really a religion: that Marxism is, as it charges religion with being, a self-deception and a dogma to be accepted on faith and on authority. Although the acceptance of authority as proof

59

without verification is especially characteristic of religion and is most widely practiced where religion dominates the thought of the time, it is, to be sure, not confined to religion. For instance, the classical authority of Galen was accepted by medieval medicine without an attempt to prove or disprove by experimentation what he had to say. It may be well, therefore, to examine the charge that Marxism is a religion more closely, especially since it is given color by the Stalinist perversion of Marxism. We can do so conveniently by examining the comments of Niebuhr, one of the chief exponents of this view of Marxism, in his introduction to *Marx and Engels on Religion.*[1]

As proof for his assertion that Marx in his fervor and dogmatism was unwittingly transformed from "an empirical observer into a religious prophet," Niebuhr quotes from Marx's youthful *The Holy Family*:

> There is no need of any great penetration to see from the teaching of materialism on the original goodness and equal intellectual endowment of men, the omnipotence of experience, habit, and education, and the influence of environment on man, the great significance of industry, the justification of enjoyment, etc., how necessarily materialism is connected with communism and socialism.

"Marx...pretends to draw self-evident deductions," Niebuhr comments

> from the mere presupposition of metaphysical materialism.... One can only regard this passage, and similar passages, as the ladders on which the empirical critic of the status quo climbed up to the heaven and haven of a new world religion.... Marx, as an empiricist, would have been just another learned man. As an apocalyptic dogmatist, he became the founder of a new religion, whose writing would be quoted as parts of a new sacred canon.

Niebuhr's comment is based on an egregious misreading of the text. Marx is not concerned with stating "all the propositions, dear to a revolutionary and apocalyptic idealist" (xi) as if they were "self-evident deductions from his materialistic philosophy and therefore needed no proof." He is stating the propositions held by the French materialistic social philosophers such as Condillac and Helvetius and asserting that they led historically to the Utopian socialism of Robert Owen and others. He introduces the passage quoted by Niebuhr with the statement that "the other branch of French materialism [the branch of Condillac and Helvetius that had its origin in Locke as opposed to the branch that had its origin in Descartes and led to natural science] leads direct to *socialism* and communism[2] and states immediately after the passage in question: "This and similar propositions are to be found almost literally even in the oldest French materialists. This is not the place to assess them" (x–xi).

It is evident from the statement "This is not the place to assess them" that Marx is not presenting these propositions as his own and does not necessarily agree with them. As a matter of fact, in his "Theses on Feuerbach," contained in the book which Niebuhr is introducing, Marx makes clear his differences with them:

> The materialist doctrine that men are products of circumstances and upbringing, and that, therefore, changed men are products of other circumstances and changed upbringing, forgets that it is men that change circumstances and that the educator himself needs educating. Hence, this doctrine necessarily arrives at dividing society into two parts, of which one is superior to society (in Robert Owen, for example). The coincidence of the changing of circumstances and of human activity can be conceived and rationally understood only as *revolutionizing practice* (70).

In short, the older non-dialectical materialism did not see the historical process in which people collectively seek to answer social questions only when these questions are thrust upon them. In this historical process human activity is both the product of social development and a cause of social development. In transforming its social environment, humanity transforms itself, but its transformation of society is limited by historical conditions, in the first place the level and power of the productive forces. Superior individuals cannot rise so high above their society as to make it realize an ideal plan of their devising.

Just as Niebuhr is mistaken in assigning the beliefs of the French materialists to Marx, so is he mistaken in calling him an empiricist who gave up his empiricism to construct a religious dogma. Empiricism as a philosophical outlook is opposed to rationalism, setting experience up against reason as the source of knowledge. Experience, thought Marx and Engels, is the test of theory, but it is not the sole source of knowledge. The "empirical, inductive method, exalting mere experience," says Engels (175), again in a selection in the book that Niebuhr is introducing, "treats thought with sovereign disdain and really has gone to the furthest extreme in emptiness of thought." "It is not the extravagant theorizing of the philosophy of nature" which is "the surest path from natural science to mysticism" but "the shallowest empiricism that spurns all theory and distrusts all thought" (186).

As George Novack phrases it,

> The Marxist theory of knowledge accepted...the empirical contention that all the contents of knowledge are derived from sense experience and the rationalist counterclaim that its forms were provided by the understanding.... The two factors, each of which had been the basis for independent and antagonistic philosophies, were transformed into interrelated aspects of a single process.... Experience gave birth to reflection whose results fructified and directed further experience. This conceptually enriched experience in turn corrected, tested, and amplified the results of reasoning—and so on, in a never ending spiral.[3]

Experience and reason, induction and deduction, engage in a constant interaction, engendering the dialectic of human thought that reflects the dialectic of nature and society.

Not only does Niebuhr see Marx as an empiricist who unconsciously departed from empiricism; he also sees him as an anti-Hegelian who is unconsciously entrammeled in Hegel's dialectical mode of thought: "the anti-Hegelian materialist speaks in terms of Hegelian dialectic to project a materialistic version of an even more traditional religious apocalypse" (xiii). But Marx was very conscious of his indebtedness to Hegel and "openly avowed" himself to be "the pupil of that mighty thinker." At the same time he differentiated his dialectic from that of Hegel:

> My dialectic method is not only different from the Hegelian, but is its direct opposite. To Hegel...the real world is only the external, phenomenal form of "the Idea." With me, on the contrary, the ideal is nothing else than the material world reflected by the human mind, and translated into forms of thought.... The mystification which dialectic suffers in Hegel's hands, by no means prevents him from being the first to present its general form of working in a comprehensive and conscious manner. With him it is standing on its head. It must be turned right side up again, if you would discover the rational kernel within the mystical shell. (*Reader*, 98–99)

Despite Marx's claim to have found and salvaged the rational kernel within the shell of Hegel's mysticism, his dialecticism has often been attacked as sheer Hegelian mumbo-jumbo. Dühring, the contemporary of Marx and Engels whose name continues to live only because Engels devoted a book to replying to him, said of Marx's discussion of the factors leading to capitalism's destruction: "Hegel's first negation is the idea of the fall from grace, which is taken from catechism, and his second is the idea of a higher unity leading to redemption. The logic of facts can hardly be based on this nonsensical analogy borrowed from the religious sphere."

To this Engels replied that "it is...a pure distortion of the facts by Herr Dühring, when he declares that...Marx wants anyone to allow himself to be convinced of the necessity of the common ownership of land and capital...on the basis of the negation of the negation."[4] The passage whose Hegelian terminology gave offence to Dühring was merely the summation of Marx's previous close analysis of capitalism's origin and development and of the forces within that will destroy it, as capitalism had destroyed the feudalistic mode of production. It is incumbent upon someone who disagrees with Marx to seek to refute that analysis, not to dismiss the summation of it with the statement that it is "based" on a "nonsensical analogy borrowed from the religious sphere," an analogy which the critic himself has conjured up.

Dialectics is not a magical incantation that has only to be uttered to produce an irrefutable truth. By using what Marx called scornfully "wooden trichotomies,"[5] one can "prove" anything—that is to say, nothing—arriving at any "synthesis" one wishes by choosing the right "thesis" and "antithesis." But the same is true of the syllogism. For instance, in the syllogism "All clergymen are persons of towering intellect; the Reverend Dimwit is a clergyman; therefore, the Reverend Dimwit is a person of towering intellect," the conclusion follows from the premises, but that does not make it correct. The laws of logic, whether those of Aristotelian or of dialectical logic, are of little use if concrete reality is disregarded. Nevertheless, although no systems of logic are foolproof, training in dialectical thinking, like training in Aristotelian logic, over which it is a great advance, is of value. Aristotelian logic thinks in fixed categories: if all A is B and all B is C, then all A is C. But dialectics observes

A, B, and C as they are in the process of changing so that it may cease to be true that all A are B or that all B are C.

For this reason dialectical thinking requires a higher degree of concreteness and comes closer to approaching the reality that is in a constant state of flux. Although conscious study is of value, dialectical thinking may, as is true of Aristotelian logic, be used by those who have not studied it: any cook knows that the addition of salt beyond a given point makes a decided qualitative difference. As Engels put it, "Men thought dialectically long before they knew what dialectics was, just as they spoke prose long before the term prose existed" (137).

Far from being mere mumbo-jumbo, dialectical materialism, says the historian of science Loren R. Graham, has produced among the scientists in the Soviet Union a philosophy of science that "is an impressive intellectual achievement" and "has no competitors among modern systems of thought." They have been able to produce this achievement, he says, "in sharp contrast to other Soviet intellectual efforts," because the repressive regime had for its own purposes to relax its controls over science after the interference with it under Stalin, with the consequence that the best minds went into scientific fields and because the esoteric character of their discussion as they sought to grapple with the implications of new scientific theories such as quantum theory and relativity further served as a defense against censorship. Although dialectical materialism "would never predict the result of a specific experiment," Graham is convinced that "in certain cases" dialectical materialism helped scientists "to arrive at views that won them international recognition among their foreign colleagues."[6] It helped them in arriving at these views by the orientation it gave them.

The theories at which these scientists arrived are not to be refuted by characterizing the scientists as dogmatists, as Niebuhr characterizes Marx. They can only be refuted by examining their scientific reasoning and observing how well they stand the test of experience. So too with Marx's theory of proletarian revolution. Critics like Niebuhr have spoken of it disparagingly as an apocalyptic dogma. But is not the twentieth century indeed the epoch of wars and revolutions that Lenin characterized it as being? At the beginning of the century bourgeois thinkers were imbued with the idea of uninterrupted progress within the existing social system. Revolutionary Marxists warned of impending catastrophes. Which were correct? Could anyone have envisaged more cataclysmic happenings than the enormous bloodshed of two world wars, the ravages of the great depression, the extermination program of fascism, the threat of nuclear annihilation?

But, the Niebuhrs say, Marx spoke of the inevitability of socialism. Socialism has not triumphed in the advanced capitalist countries, as he predicted. Are not the Marxists like the Christians, who have waited for two millennia for the Second Coming? If the Christians are waiting for Godot, are not the Marxists waiting for Lefty?

In reply, it may be said that "Lefty" (social revolution) did come—in Russia, China, Cuba, Yugoslavia, and other countries. That the revolution was delayed in advanced capitalist countries and came first to backward countries created unforeseen difficulties. But Marxism, far from being the "immutable dogma" that Niebuhr says it is (*On Religion*, viii), realizes more than any other doctrine that theory has to be constantly corrected to take account of a changing reality. "We do not in any way," said Lenin, "regard Marx's theory as something final and inviolable, we are convinced, on the contrary, that it only laid the cornerstone of the science which socialists *must push* further in all directions, if they do not wish to be left behind by life."[7]

So too Trotsky wrote on the occasion of the ninetieth anniversary of *The Communist Manifesto* that, although no other book can "even distantly be compared with the *Communist Manifesto*," this

> does not imply that, after ninety years of unprecedented development of productive forces and vast social struggles, the *Manifesto* needs neither corrections nor additions.... Revolutionary thought has nothing in common with idol worship. Programs and prognoses are tested and corrected in the light of experience, which is the supreme criterion of reason. The *Manifesto*, too, requires corrections and additions. However, as is evidenced by historical experience itself, these corrections and additions can be successfully made only by proceeding in accord with the method, which forms the basis of the *Manifesto* itself.[8]

"Revolutionary thought has nothing in common with idol

worship." Marxism has no sacred books to be consulted as Nostradamus or the Bible are consulted for predictions of what will happen.

> Prognosis outlines only the definite and ascertainable trends of the development. But along with these trends a different order of forces and tendencies operate, which at a certain moment begin to predominate. All those who seek exact predictions of concrete events should consult the astrologists. Marxist prognosis aids only in orientation.[9]

The great Marxist theoreticians, observing when a dialectical change, "a different order of forces and tendencies," has made itself manifest, have applied Marxist method to develop Marxist doctrine: witness Lenin's theory of imperialism and Trotsky's theory of permanent revolution. The consequence has been that, although Marxists have made many mistakes, the best of them have been far better oriented than bourgeois observers, who have pooh-poohed Marxism in "good times," when they have declared that capitalism has solved its problems, and have warned against the dangers of Marxism in "bad times."

It may also be said that revolutionary Marxists do not *wait* for "Lefty." They believe, as Marx said, that the liberation of the proletariat is the task of the proletariat itself, not that of a messiah who will appear at some future date. They seek to educate the working class in the course of its struggle concerning the need for a new social order that will be built by it in virtue of its position in capitalism. When Marx spoke of the inevitability of socialism, he did not mean that it will come as a gift from above but that, since one's outlook on life is shaped by material conditions, the working class will eventually be driven by the conditions of capitalism in decline to search for and find the way to build a new society through its abolition. Even if one cannot make exact predictions of concrete events, there is every reason to hold to this general, long-range perspective, which provides the guidelines for strategic orientation. Yet one must also add that Engels spoke of the choice for humanity as being "socialism or barbarism." It must be admitted that the immense destruction capable of being wrought by existing nuclear weapons makes the possibility of barbarism far more real that it was in Engels's day if the pressing problems of human society are not soon solved. Those who would dismiss Engels's words as "apocalyptic dogma" are blinding themselves to reality.

Marxism vs. Stalinist Scholasticism

Niebuhr is entirely wrong when he says that the "dogmatic atrophy" of Marxism is "not a corruption" of it. He is, however, right when he speaks of the writings of Marx, Engels, and Lenin having been made into a "sacred canon" by the "priest-kings" (xiv) of the Soviet Union and the People's Republic of China. But this is a perversion of Marxism, not a continuation of it. Just as it is foreign to the spirit of Marxism, which regards the entire universe as being in the process of change, to consider itself to be an "immutable dogma," so it is foreign to it to engage in a scholastic citation of authority.

Lenin described how Marx had been canonized by the Social Democrats, who in doing so robbed him of his revolutionary essence. After the death of great revolutionists, he wrote,

> attempts are made to convert them into harmless icons, to canonize them, so to say, and to surround their *names* with a certain halo for the "consolation" of the oppressed classes and with the object of duping the latter, while at the same time emasculating the *essence* of the revolutionary teaching, blunting its revolutionary edge and vulgarizing it.[10]

Ironically, this is what happened to Lenin himself at the hands of the conservative Stalinist bureaucracy. Lenin, wrote Trotsky, "was 'only' a man of genius, and nothing human was alien to him, therein included the capacity to make mistakes."[11] Stalin, however, made Lenin out to be a god so that he himself might be proclaimed the son of god.

This perversion of Marxism can be best explained by the use of the Marxist method itself. "Just as original Christianity, as it was spreading into pagan countries," says Isaac Deutscher, Stalin's Marxist biographer,

> absorbed elements of pagan beliefs and rites and blended them with its own ideas, so now Marxism, the product of western European thought, was absorbing elements of the Byzantine tradition, so deeply ingrained in Russia, and of the Greek Orthodox style.... The abstract tenets of Marxism could exist, in their purity, in the brains of intellectual revolutionaries, especially those who had

lived as exiles in western Europe. Now, after the doctrine had really been transplanted to Russia and come to dominate the outlook of a great nation, it could not but, in its turn, assimilate itself to that nation's spiritual climate, to its traditions, customs, and habits.[12]

The reaction to the revolution caused by the failure of other revolutions in Europe and the pressure of world imperialism upon a backward country produced a specially privileged bureaucracy, which revived the "traditions, customs, and habits" that had been repressed by the revolution. The "deification of Stalin," as Trotsky said, expressed this bureaucracy's need of "an inviolable arbiter, a first consul if not an emperor."[13] The reaction was aided greatly by the physical destruction in the 1930s of large numbers of revolutionists in whose brains the tenets of Marxism had existed.

Leninism was thus replaced by Stalinism.

It was perhaps natural that the triumvir [Stalin] who had spent his formative years in a Greek Orthodox seminary should become the foremost agent of that change.... He presented Lenin's doctrine, which was essentially sociological and experimental, as a series of rigid canons and flat strategic and tactical recipes for mankind's salvation.... He supported every contention of his with a quotation from Lenin, sometimes irrelevant and sometimes torn out of the context, in the same way that the medieval scholastic sought sanction for his speculations in the holy writ.[14]

In China, where the Communist party was educated in Stalinism, a similar deification of Mao took place. The masses of China were urged by Lin Biao, Mao's heir-designate, in his introduction to *Quotations From Chairman Mao Tse-tung*, the famous "little red book" which became the New Testament in China, to "study Chairman Mao's writings, follow his teachings, act according to his instructions and be his good fighters,"[15] as the masses had been urged by Paul to follow the teachings of Christ and to be his soldiers in the good fight. "In order really to master Mao Tse-tung's thought," Lin added, "it is essential to study many of Chairman Mao's basic concepts over and over again, and it is best to memorize important statements and study and apply them repeatedly. The newspapers should regularly carry quotations from Chairman Mao relevant to current issues for readers to study and apply." Lin himself, however, apparently did not memorize the statements of Mao sufficiently assiduously—or perhaps he mastered Mao's thought all too well—for he is said by the regime to have been killed in a plane crash while seeking to escape China after having led an unsuccessful struggle against the Chairman.

It is worth contrasting the injunctions of Lin on the rote memorization of Mao with those of Lenin on learning about communism. If the study of communism, said Lenin, speaking to a congress of the Russian Young Communist League in 1920

> consisted in imbibing what is contained in communist books and pamphlets, we might all too easily obtain communist text-jugglers or braggarts, and this would very often cause us harm and damage, because such people, having learned by rote what is contained in communist books and pamphlets would be incapable of combining this knowledge, and would be unable to act in the way communism really demands.... It would be a mistake to think that it is enough to imbibe communist slogans, the conclusions of communist science, without acquiring the sum total of knowledge of which communism itself is a consequence.... You can become a Communist only by enriching your mind with the knowledge of all the treasures created by mankind.... You must not only assimilate this knowledge, you must assimilate it critically. (*Reader*, 42–44)

Paul urged the study of the sayings and parables of Christ, rejecting the study of the heathen philosophers, including the Platonists and the Stoics to whom early Christianity was indebted; the Maoists urged the study of "the little red book," outlawing the study of Shakespeare, whom Marx read every year, and of Pushkin, who was Lenin's favorite author. Not so Lenin.

The successors of Stalin and Mao, intent on further modernizing their countries, found that the primitive worship of Stalin and Mao did not suit their purposes. The rigid dogmas were too much of a dead weight in the drive to meet the new needs of their societies. As Deutscher said of the contradictory process taking place in the Soviet Union after the death of Stalin, "Through the forcible modernization of the structure of society Stalinism had worked toward its own undoing and had prepared the ground for the return of classical Marxism."[16] A halting and hesitant reformation has taken place. If, however, the "cult of personality" has been denounced and the era of infallible popes is gone, there remains in power an episcopate, with its own kind of modified authoritarianism and dogmatism, to be overthrown.

The Spirit of Marxism and That of Early Christianity

Although the dogmatism of religion and its reverence for authority are alien to Marxism, there is, as Engels observed, a significant resemblance between the spirit animating Marxist revolutionists and that animating the early Christians.

> The history of early Christianity has notable points of resemblance with the modern working-class movement.... Both are persecuted and baited, their adherents are despised and made the objects of exclusive laws, the former as enemies of the human race, the latter as enemies of the state, enemies of religion, the family, social order. And in spite of all persecution, nay, even spurred on by it, they forge victoriously, irresistibly ahead. (*On Religion*, 316)

This spirit is far different from the predominant spirit of modern Christianity. More than a century and a quarter ago, Thomas Carlyle bewailed the emptiness of feeling of his age. But, observed Engels, "This emptiness and shallowness, this 'lack of soul,' this irreligion and this 'atheism' have their basis in religion itself." "So long...as the belief in this distant phantom [God] is strong and living, so long does man in his roundabout way arrive at some kind of content." But, with the crumbling of religious belief, "hollowness and lack of content" have become prevalent and "will continue so long as mankind does not understand that the Being which it has honored as God, was his own not yet understood Being" (*Reader*, 234–35). This has proved to be entirely true.

In the service of humanity, Marxists display the same fervor and self-sacrifice that the early Christians displayed in the service of God. Although humanity is a product of nature, humanity is the highest value for itself. As Marx said, "The criticism of religion ends in the teaching that *man is the highest being for man*, it ends, that is, with the categorical imperative to overthrow all conditions in which man is a debased, forsaken, contemptible being forced into servitude."[17]

So did the twenty-one-year-old Trotsky write at the beginning of the twentieth century, "If I were one of the celestial bodies, I would look with complete detachment upon this miserable ball of dust and dirt.... But I am a *man*. World history, which to you, dispassionate gobbler of science, to you, bookkeeper of eternity, seems only a negligible moment in the balance of time, is to me everything! As long as I breathe, I shall fight for the future." The fighter for the future, he went on, often finds that he is subjected to a "collective Torquemada," a Holy Inquisition intent on defending the sacred status quo. But, although he may be momentarily crushed, he rises again and "as passionate, as full of faith and as militant as ever, confidently knocks at the gate of history."[18]

The word "faith" here should not mislead us: it is not the same as religious faith. Religious faith has the sense of one of the *Webster's Third New International Dictionary's* definitions of "faith": "firm or unquestioning belief in something for which there is no proof." The faith of which Trotsky speaks has the sense of another of the *Webster's* definitions of the word: "something that is believed or adhered to, especially with strong conviction." The religionist says, "I believe because I accept the holiness of a book or the authoritativeness of a church"; the Marxist says, "I believe and accept wholeheartedly this outlook on life because I am rationally convinced by it." It is true, however, that the revolutionary Marxist believed with the same strength of feeling and readiness for self-sacrifice as the early Christians.

Almost forty years after the youthful Trotsky wrote his greeting to the twentieth century, the Trotsky who had experienced titanic events, had become an outcast with a few followers rejected by most countries of the world after having been the leader of a great nation, and had seen his children die before him, the victims directly or indirectly of the blows leveled at him, while he himself had been subjected to a campaign of calumny unprecedented in its scope, wrote his testament in the belief that he might die shortly. He speaks in it of his "happiness" in having been "a fighter for the cause of socialism," of which he had said two years before, "to participate in this movement with open eyes and with an intense will—only this can give the highest moral satisfaction to a thinking being."[19]

> If I were to begin all over again, I would...try to avoid making this or that mistake, but the main course of my life would remain unchanged. I shall die a proletarian revolutionary, a Marxist, a dialectical materialist, and consequently an irreconcilable atheist. My faith in the communist future of mankind is not less ardent, indeed it is firmer today, than it was in the days of my youth.... This faith in

man and in his future gives me even now such power of resistance
as cannot be given by any religion.[20]

Trotsky, to be sure, was a person of exceptional strength of
character. But it remains true that most avowed Christians
today do not have the inner strength that characterizes the revolutionary Marxist. As Trotsky himself wrote of the pre-war Bolsheviks, implicitly comparing them to the early Christians, who
sustained martyrdom as their master had done at Calvary,

> Whoever joined an organization knew that prison followed by exile
> awaited him within the next few months.... The professional revo-
> lutionists believed what they taught. They could have had no other
> incentive for taking the road to Calvary. Solidarity under persecu-
> tion was no empty word, and it was augmented by contempt for
> cowardice and desertion.... The young men and young women who
> devoted themselves entirely to the revolutionary movement, with-
> out demanding anything in return, were not the worst representa-
> tives of their generation. The order of "professional revolutionists"
> could not suffer by comparison with any other social group.[21]

To believe what one teaches and to act accordingly despite
personal hardships—this is the source of great strength. It is a
quality that seems so strange to many today that they regard
the possessors of it as religious fanatics. But it does not make
Marxism a religion.

PART II

The Social Roots of the Chief Western Religions

CHAPTER FOUR

Judaism: Its Origin and Development in Europe and Israel

Marxism and the History of Western Religions

Thanks to the influence of Marx and Engels, the history of religion can no longer be regarded as either a revelation of God's laws which humanity, not too successfully, is still struggling to observe, or as a progressive revelation of God's purpose which humanity, as it becomes more worthy, is increasingly coming to understand. Religion did not come down to humanity from on high but evolved from humanity's own social development. It has social roots, which the historian can study. This concept is more or less accepted by all modern historians, even if they are not consistent materialists, that is, Marxists.

Commenting on a passage of Engels's in which he describes Calvinism as the religion of the bourgeoisie, Christopher Hill, the foremost historian of English Puritanism, says: "All these ideas, of course, are familiar enough to historians today, thanks to the writings of Weber, Tawney and others. They have become almost commonplace. But they originally go back to Marx and Engels, and to no one else."[1] Even if Weber—who believed that the Protestant ethic engendered capitalism—put the cart before the horse, he did show the connection between horse and cart that prevents us from regarding the cart as miraculously pulled along by divine providence.[2]

In this section I shall briefly examine the social origins of the chief western religions that have been studied by Marxist and other historians. By understanding their social origins, we can better understand these religions today. We shall see that the historians validate Marx and Engels's perception of religion as serving the status quo and yet capable of expressing the aspirations of rebellious movements in the form of sects opposed to the churches aligned with the ruling classes. But the other-worldly aspect of religion makes these rebellious movements turn away from class struggle. Instead of learning the lessons of defeat to renew the struggle, they find solace in dreaming of heavenly bliss or in passively waiting for a messiah. Having laid down their weapons, they are co-opted and often transformed into their opposites through the influx of new members of different social classes. This process, epitomized in the evolution of early Christianity from a lower-class religion to the religion supporting the feudal structure, is repeated again and again. What Marx and Engels say of the Utopian socialist sects is applicable to the religious ones as well: "Although the originators of these systems were, in many respects, revolutionary, their disciples have, in every case, formed mere reactionary sects."[3]

The Nomadic Ancestors of the Israelites

The ancestors of the Biblical Israelites were in part semi-nomads who lived in tents "between the desert and the sown" (Jeremiah 2:2), where they raised domestic animals, and in part true nomads who lived in the desert. They were, therefore, governed by the two laws of the desert, blood revenge (Judges 8:18–21) and hospitality (Genesis 18:1–8).

The gods of the nomads, either spirits dwelling in objects of nature or tribal deities, had human characteristics; they even had sons by human women (Genesis 6:2, 4). In time the spirits inhabiting nature became identified either with Jehovah or his angels. The original dwelling place of Jehovah was Mount Sinai, where he showed himself to Moses (Exodus 3:1–6) and to Elijah (1 Kings 19:8–18). Jehovah continued to be "a mountain god" (1 Kings 20:33), the "mountain of the Lord" (Psalms 24:3), "his holy mountain" (Psalms 48:1) on which he dwelled (Isaiah 8:18; 18:7; 24:23), now becoming Mount Zion, where Solomon's temple was built.[4]

Jehovah, like other tribal gods, resembled an earthly king

who required the observance of prescribed ceremonies. In each instance one had to avoid what gave offense and to do what gave pleasure. Just as a slave was supposed on pain of death to be spotlessly clean when serving his master, as stated in a Hittite tablet comparing the service rendered to gods and men, so priests were commanded that when they went into the tabernacle "they shall wash with water, that they die not" (Exodus 30:20). Just as every visitor to Solomon brought him a present (1 Kings 10:25), so did Jehovah command: "None shall appear before me empty-handed" (Exodus 23:15; Deuteronomy 16:16). The offerings made to Jehovah were like the bribes offered to a ruler to influence his decision (cf. 1 Samuel 26:19). Animals were sacrificed to him on altars of earth, with the blood being drained off for him. This is the origin of the Jewish dietary law that meat must be salted and watered to be drained of blood (Leviticus 17:11–12): blood is a sacrifice to the deity and taboo to human beings.

> The horrible rite of human sacrifice, although rare, was not unknown among the early Semites.... In general, human sacrifice was offered only as blood revenge (Judg. 8:18–21; II Sam. 21:1–9) and as a result of the ban (I Sam. 15: 33).... A murder or accidental manslaughter is not primarily an injury to an individual but an outrage against the tribe and therefore against its chief, the tribal god, whose power is commensurate to the number of his worshippers and has consequently been diminished by one of them. Blood revenge is therefore an expiation, a human sacrifice intended to atone for an offense against the deity and to placate its anger. This appears clearly in II Sam. 21:1–9.... When all hope [in time of war] was lost unless the deity did its utmost, the ancient Semites had recourse to the ban—a vow to sacrifice to the deity on a tremendous scale all persons and property of the enemy if victory was gained (Num. 21:2; Josh. 6:17–19, 21: I Sam. 15:3, 9–23).[5]

The warlike bedouin life of the desert, which made tribal brotherhood a necessity, just as it made the assurance of a reciprocated hospitality a necessity, is the origin of blood revenge and of the vengeful god of the Israelites.

Under the leadership of Moses, the clans freed from Egyptian slavery were united in the worship of Jehovah, to whom the deliverance was attributed. Moses did not give the Israelites the doctrine that Jehovah is the one god in existence or the code of laws ascribed to him in the Pentateuch. The evidence, says Pfeiffer, points to a later stage of development as the time when these ideas had their inception. Thus the Ten Commandments refer to aspects of agricultural life in Canaan, the Biblical name for Palestine. But Moses did begin the conversion of Jehovah from a mountain god to the god of a people. For a considerable period, however, Jehovah was contradictorily both of these. He continued to dwell on Mount Sinai, but he also dwelled in numerous sanctuaries in Canaan (Judges 5:4; Deuteronomy 33:2; 1 Kings 19:8), where Israelites came to consult him. As Israel's god, he had to be where Israel was.[6]

The Influence of Canaanite Culture

As has happened many times in history, the superior culture of a conquered people triumphed over the culture of the conquerors, and the fierce nomadic Israelites absorbed the culture and elements of the religion of the agricultural people of Canaan. The Baals, the divine patrons of Canaanite agriculture, were first accepted as local deities whose efforts supplemented Jehovah's. Jehovah was the god of battles who helped the Israelites against their enemies, and the Baals were the gods of agriculture who gave them their produce. Jehovah, however, finally supplanted the Baals as the rainmaker (1 Kings 18:1) and agricultural benefactor (Hosea 2:8). He was now the god of the land of Canaan (1 Samuel 6:9), but his authority was only within that country. He was counterposed to other gods, foreign gods (Genesis 35:2; Joshua 24:20, 23), not false gods or idols.[7]

Canaanite culture, moreover, not only contributed to the attributes of Jehovah: it contributed to the agricultural festivals and the myths of the Israelites. Among these myths, ultimately derived from Babylonia, is that of the Flood and possibly those of the Garden of Eden and of the Tower of Babel.

The Reforming Prophets' Response to Palestine's Foreign Domination

Palestine was a crossroads: it bordered on the great Egyptian and Babylonian empires, and important trade routes ran through it. It was consequently always subject to foreign domination. This caused the Hebrew tribes to become more closely unified into a people. For a time, however, Israel was divided into two kingdoms, each threatened and sometimes dominated by a different neighboring power. As in nineteenth century Poland, which was also overshadowed by foreign great powers and fragmented, religion became the vehicle for nationalism. Just as the Catholic Church in Poland served as a bulwark against the Protestant Germans and the Orthodox Russians, so did the religion of the Israelites serve as a bulwark for them against their enemies, whose gods they hated not as fictions but as helpers of these enemies.

The military power of Israel was weakened by the growth of great estates and the consequent reduction of the number of independent peasants. Beginning about 750 BC, the message of successive "reforming prophets," who were opposed to the established priesthood, was that unless this process was arrested Israel would fall, and all classes would go down in a common ruin.

> You are doomed! You buy more houses and fields to add to those you already have. Soon there will be no place for anyone else to live, and you alone will live in the land. I have heard the Lord Almighty say, "All these big, fine houses will be empty ruins."... But you don't understand what the Lord is doing, and so you will be carried away as prisoners. Your leaders will starve to death, and the common people will die of thirst. (Isaiah 5:8–13)

Some of these prophets

> belonged to the oppressed classes; others, like Isaiah and Zephaniah, were members of the highest aristocracy, or, like Jeremiah, belonged to a financially independent family of provincial priests. This espousal by the more thoughtful members of the privileged classes of the case of the disinherited, forecast, as often afterwards, the downfall of the existing order.... The effectiveness of the message was determined by its reception by the masses to whom they preached on the streets and in the temples.... Before this sympathetic audience the prophets could cry out against religious and social wrongs.[8]

Like the Protestants and other religious reformers of later days, the prophets claimed that they were returning to the purity of religion of an idealized earlier time. They attacked, therefore, Canaanite rites and shrines that the Israelites had appropriated.

But what they stated was the religion of Moses contained an important new concept, that of the conditional covenant between Jehovah and Israel. Jehovah was now no longer a war god who helped his people under all circumstances. He was a partner who expected Israel to fulfill its part of the bargain by heeding his laws and who used the enemies of Israel to serve his purpose of chastisement. If, however, Israel would reform her ways and return to the religion of Moses, Jehovah would cease chastising her as a man chastises his wife (Hosea 2:8–17) and would restore her to his favor.

The Effects of the Babylonian Exile

The disasters which were so clearly impending happened: the northern kingdom of Samaria was conquered in 722 BC by the Assyrians, who followed their customary practice of exacting tribute from the rural dwellers and of transporting the city dwellers and aristocrats to their own country so that they could not lead an uprising. These exiles, the "ten lost tribes," were assimilated in the course of time.

Four generations later the same thing happened to the southern kingdom of Judea, when the inhabitants of Jerusalem, the members of the royal court, and the military men were exiled to Babylon, the new conqueror. In the interim between the defeats of the two kingdoms, however, religious-nationalistic fervor had built up in the threatened Judea. Moreover, this exile lasted for less than fifty years, terminating with the defeat of Babylon by the Persians. These exiles, therefore, were not completely assimilated into the foreign population, as had been the Samarian exiles. A portion of them returned to Judea, although most preferred to stay in wealthy Babylon rather than to return to ruined Judea.[9]

The Jews, while seeking to retain their national identity, were affected by their stay in the splendid city of Babylon, with its superior culture. Philosophy and ancient science developed in the great commercial centers of ancient civilization among those elements that had leisure. In the Greek trading cities these were wealthy landowners who were able to live in the city and were subject to its influence. In the trade centers of Egypt and Babylon, philosophy and science were cultivated by the temple priests. This connection with religion limited Eastern thought in a way in which it was not limited in Greece. The philosophical doctrine of materialism had its origin in Greece, not in the great empires of the East.[10]

Removed from daily agriculture, leisured city dwellers had less need for individual deities inhabiting the earth and perpetrating natural events. There was thus a tendency toward monotheism among both the Egyptian and Babylonian priesthood, but this tendency remained an occult doctrine except when Amehotep (Ikhnaton), in conflict with the powerful priesthood, sought to make it an official religion. In Babylon the tendency to monotheism was expressed by the doctrine that other gods were only different manifestations of the supreme god, Marduk, the creator of the universe.[11]

The Jews, who acquired their strict observance of the Sabbath and a good deal of their cosmology from the Babylonians, were no doubt influenced by the Babylonians' "latent monotheism." They were able to take to monotheism the more readily because, due to the backwardness of their industry and art, they had not made images of Jehovah or of the Baals. Where the images of gods are not fixed in the popular imagination, it is easier to develop the notion of one god.

The Israelites had, however, their fetishes, sacred objects associated with the deity or in which he was thought to dwell. One of these was the chest allegedly containing the tablets Moses received from Jehovah, which was put in the "Most Holy Place" of the Temple in Jerusalem. When the "Covenant Box" was brought to the Temple, which Solomon had constructed as "a place" for the Lord "to live in forever," the Temple "was suddenly filled with a cloud shining with the dazzling light of the Lord's presence" (1 Kings 8:10–12).

In the Babylonian exile the Jews from Jerusalem predominated, and the authority of their priests increased over that of the priests of the rest of Judah.

> Under the influence of Babylonian philosophy and their own national catastrophe...the efforts of the priests [of Jerusalem] to create a monopoly for their fetish took the form of an ethical monotheism in which Jahveh was no longer merely the particular tribal god of Israel but the only god in the world, the personification of the

> good, the sum and substance of all morality.... The erection of the
> Temple in Jerusalem, and then its preservation, became the watch-
> word, which brought the Jewish nation together. The priesthood of
> this temple had become the highest national authority of the
> Jews....Thus there was a remarkable amalgam of the high philo-
> sophical abstraction of a single omnipresent God...with the old
> primitive fetishism, which localized the god in a particular place.[12]

So too there was a contradiction between the idea of the God
of all humanity and that of the old tribal god. Although God was
the god of all mankind, the Jews, to whom he had revealed himself and who were especially favored by him, were the only ones
who knew it. This knowledge of their special mission, which set
them above the rest of humanity, providentially came to them
during the time of the exile. It was also during this time of desper-
ation that the idea of the Messiah, a savior sent by God to restore
the Jews to a renovated kingdom, came into being. Thus did the
Jews seek to compensate for the conditions of their exile.[13]

The Effects of the Scattering of the Jews

The Diaspora had started before the Babylonian captivity and
gathered momentum after the return from Babylon. It is estimated that even before Jerusalem fell to Rome, only about one-
quarter of the Jews remained in Palestine. Jerusalem was the
religious center for the Jews, to which they sent gifts and made
pilgrimages—as Muslims do to Mecca—but they were scattered
over the whole of the known world.

The fundamental reason for the Jewish emigration was the
mountainousness of the country and the loss of its strategic position with the development of shipbuilding and overseas commerce.

> The Jews in Palestine were the possessors of a mountainous coun-
> try, which at a certain time no longer sufficed for assuring its in-
> habitants as tolerable an existence as that among their neighbors.
> Such a people is driven to choose between brigandage and emigra-
> tion. The Scots, for example, alternately engaged in each of these
> pursuits. The Jews, after numerous struggles with their neighbors,
> also took the second road.... Peoples living under such conditions
> do not go to foreign countries as agriculturalists. They go there
> rather in the role of mercenaries, like the Arcadians of Antiquity,
> the Swiss in the Middle Ages, the Albanians in our day; or in the

role of *merchants*, like the Jews, the Scots and the Armenians.[14]

In a natural economy, where production is predominantly for immediate use and not for sale as commodities, says an historian of the origins of capitalism, "the first traders are foreigners."[15] These members of a precapitalist mercantile class arouse hostility in an agricultural society based on the production of use values. This hostility generates a sense of solidarity among the community of foreign traders, and a fierce attachment to their national and religious customs. Thus the Armenians, who are said to be "remarkable" for "their aptitude for business and for the enterprising spirit which led their ancestors, in Roman times, to trade with Scythia, China and India," are also said to possess "like the Jews, whom they resemble in their exclusiveness and widespread dispersion, a remarkable tenacity [that] has enabled them to preserve their nationality and religion under the sorest trials."[16] So too Henri Pirenne says of the preservation of their national character by the Germans living in Slavic countries: "The principal explanation [of this preservation] is the fact that among the Slavs they were the initiators and for long centuries *par excellence* the representatives of the urban life."[17] In preserving their national character they also preserved their Lutheranism in countries where the Eastern Orthodox Church was a state institution.

The "miracle of the Jew" is thus no miracle, but the most striking exemplification of a process by which other peoples have maintained their religions and their identities. "Judaism," as Marx said, "has survived not in spite of history, but by virtue of history."[18]

Commerce, and later usury, was a selective process through which Judaism was preserved. Jews of other classes were lost to Judaism. From the uprooted peasants and artisans of Jerusalem came Christianity, which spread to Jewish proletarians in other cities of the Roman Empire. Later, as Christianity changed in nature, Jews of different classes were converted to it or to Islam.

While Jewish history is the history of the preservation of Judaism, it is at the same time the history of the assimilation of large sections of Judaism. "In Northern Africa, in pre-Islamic times, great numbers of Jews were engaged in agriculture, but of these, too, the vast majority have been absorbed by the local population.... [Where the Jews] engaged in commerce and concentrated in towns, they formed agglomerations and developed a social life of their own, moving and marrying within their own community." Let us also recall the numerous conversions of Jewish landed proprietors in Germany in the Fourth Century; the complete disappearance of the Jewish warrior tribes of Arabia.... The law of assimilation might be formulated as follows: Wherever the Jews cease to constitute a class, they lose, more or less rapidly, their ethnical, religious and linguistic characteristics; they become assimilated.[19]

On the other hand, Judaism during the immediately pre-Christian and early Christian period was a proselytizing religion, and it gained many adherents, its identification with a far-flung and flourishing trading community having its attraction.[20]

Judaism in the Middle Ages

As a precapitalist mercantile class, the Jews in the ancient and early medieval world were a more or less tolerated cult, despite the hostility they engendered. Anti-Semitism existed in the Roman Empire, as we learn from Tacitus, Seneca, Juvenal, and Quintilian, but the emperors protected them, just as the kings of feudal Europe gave them special privileges (as well as imposing restrictions on them), permitting them jurisdiction over their own community. The reason is that the landowning class in a natural economy needs the merchant, although it despises him.

In the later Middle Ages the growth of cities and the creation of native merchants brought about the displacement of Jews from commerce. They became usurers, loaning money both to the nobility and the peasantry. As such they acted as sponges for the kings, who squeezed money from them while the Jews incurred popular enmity that manifested itself in outbreaks against them. With the further development of a capitalist sector within feudalism and the growing abundance of money, the nobility was able to free itself from its dependence on usury. The Jews were expelled from one country after another.

The hostility toward the Jews inevitably took a religious expression. They were accused of the strange crime of deicide, the killing of the immortal God who had come down to earth for the express purpose of being killed. They were also accused of the ritual murder of Christian children whose blood, it was alleged, they used for the making of unleavened bread during

Passover. Ritual murder of children was a charge that had originally been made by the Roman state against the early Christians
and that had been repeated by different Christian sects in their
mutual recriminations. It was revived and used against the Jews
in the twelfth century. Monasteries to which pilgrims repaired
to view the "relics" of child martyrs especially contributed to
the propagation of this belief.[21] Even when Emperor Frederick
II called together ecclesiastical dignitaries who gravely announced that Jewish dietary law forbade the partaking of the
blood of animals, let alone children, it was to no avail.

The government was concerned because it feared that, as
sometimes happened, the killing of Jews and the seizure of their
property by the aroused masses would not stop there but would
proceed to the lives and property of the nobility and the clergy.
The peasants who revolted in Alsace in 1525 voiced as their
battle cry "Chastise the clergy and the Jews."[22] It was such outbreaks that spurred European governments to expel the Jews.

Jews in the Modern World

The small number of Jews who remained in Western Europe was
for the most part integrated into the bourgeoisie. This process received a great impetus from the French Revolution, which
speeded up the giving of full rights of citizenship to Jews. Ceasing
more and more to be a special social group, Jews became increasingly assimilated through conversion, intermarriage, and the
adoption of a "reformed" Judaism which discarded the religious
observances such as the strict adherence to the Sabbath and to
the dietary laws that set Jews apart from the rest of society.

Judaism was kept alive, first, by the continued influx of
Eastern European Jews into Western Europe and the United
States and, second, by a revival of anti-Semitism late in the nineteenth century. In Eastern Europe, where capitalism was slow in
developing, the Jews had maintained their old position as a
mercantile class in a semi-feudal society. However, in the course
of time many of them found their way into the rural villages,
and from these came the new religious movement of hasidism.

> Although the livelihood of most of these Jews was derived from
> tax farming, the liquor trade and money lending, their attachment

to the soil and their intimacy with the earth-bound peasantry far exceeded those of any other medieval Jewish group.... Hasidism is, most of all, the rebellion of the half-illiterate rural Jew against the supremacy of the learned urban Jew.... Hasidism, the revolt of the rural simpleton long familiar with hunger and destitution, sounded the keynote of joy and exaltation.... White costumes during divine services, reckless ecstatic gestures of forgetfulness and surrender, transformed the simple and somewhat colorless worship of the synagogue into a frenzied communion with God.[23]

The abolition of serfdom and the development of capitalist land relations produced wealthy landowners looking for investment opportunities and impoverished the Jewish traders and middlemen. Jews became increasingly *luftmenschen*, people who lived off the air, making shift to gain a pittance through chance opportunities for engaging in trade. They also became handicraft workers associated with trade rather than with industry— cobblers, tailors, locksmiths. With the proletarianization of the Jews came the penetration of socialist ideas among them.

This penetration was all the greater because those who are not integrated into a society are less disposed to accept unthinkingly that society as it is. The peasant from southern Italy who spends some years as unskilled and highly exploited labor in Switzerland or France acquires and brings back to his peasant society a radicalism that, poverty-stricken as he was, he did not originally have. So the Jew, who was a half-stranger in the country in which he lived, gained without traveling the radicalism that the Italian "guest worker" acquires.

The Jewish worker in Eastern Europe followed in this the lead of the Europeanized Jewish intellectual, who had the merchant's ability, stimulated by his knowledge of the modes of production and the cultures of different countries, to compare, abstract, and generalize but had been able to free himself from the merchant's unremitting bent for applying these abilities to the making of money. But in freeing himself from the marketplace he also freed himself from the synagogue, not only in his social thinking but in other realms of thought. Thus there arose the tradition of what Isaac Deutscher has called the non-Jewish Jew. This tradition began with Spinoza, who was excommunicated and banished by the rabbis of Amsterdam, following the example of the Spanish Inquisition, of which the Amsterdam Jews had themselves recently been victims. "Spinoza, Heine, Marx, Rosa Luxemburg, Trotsky, and Freud," comments Deutscher,

> all found Jewry too narrow, too archaic, and too constricting.... As Jews they dwelt on the borderlines of various civilizations, religions, and national cultures.... Their minds matured where the most diverse cultural influences crossed and fertilized each other.... Each of them was in society and yet not in it, of it and yet not of it. It was this that enabled them to rise in thought above their societies, above their nations, above their times and generations, and to strike out mentally into wide new horizons and far into the future.[24]

The crisis of capitalism that the Jewish Marxists foresaw brought with it a revival of anti-Semitism, which had seemed to be eliminated with the French Revolution. Following the great stock market crash of 1873, mass discontent, diverted to anti-Semitism, gathered strength in Germany, Austria, and France.[25] In Russia, where there had long been hostility towards the Jews but no widespread violence, there was first the Odessa pogrom of 1871 and then the wave of pogroms in 1881, which ushered in a period of ever-recurring pogroms until the Revolution.

Hostility toward the Jews, as in earlier times, took on a religious guise, consciously adopted by the most reactionary element of the ruling class in central Europe, the Catholic aristocracy, which wished to use the Jews as scapegoats and to draw upon the petty bourgeoisie as a mass base. "Primarily disturbed by the growth of the Socialist parties, [the German Catholic Socialist] Stoecker and [the Austrian Catholic socialist] Lueger organized what [the German Social-Democrat] Wilhelm Liebknecht characterized as 'a bastard edition of socialism for the use of stupid people,' using the 'Christian' slogans to attract a large petty bourgeois following."[26] So too French Royalist and clerical agitation attributed the corruption of the bourgeois republic to the Jews, culminating in the charge of treason against Dreyfus. But not only was the tradition of the Counter-Reformation called on. In Protestant Prussia, Luther's fulminations against the Jews were often invoked. Backward Russia drew from the Middle Ages the accusation of ritual murder.

On the whole, however, the pseudo-science of racism has been more important for the ideology of modern anti-Semitism than Jew-baiting on religious grounds. With the retreat of religion before science as a force dominating people's thinking, what passed for science (that is, pseudo-science) became the chief means of justifying the interests of reaction. In fact, the very term "anti-Semitism," a coinage of the late nineteenth century, is derived from a spurious concept of race.

Pseudo-science flourishes, however, because, combined with a confused perception of the conquests of science, there continues to exist the mode of thinking of medieval religion. As Trotsky put it in speaking of the mass base of Hitler's National Socialism, the twentieth century version of "a bastard edition of socialism for stupid people": "A hundred million people use electricity and still believe in the magic power of signs and exorcisms. What inexhaustible reserves they possess of darkness, ignorance, and savagery!" Progress brought the pauperized petty bourgeoisie nothing but debts. It therefore turned to "the religion of the genuine German blood," a religion which enabled it to escape from history by spinning "fairy tales concerning the special superiorities of its race," whose qualities were said to be eternal despite changing social conditions.[27]

Judaism in Israel

Late nineteenth century anti-Semitism provided the auspices for the birth of Zionism. Zionism, however, claims to be the expression of a two-thousand-year-old yearning for a return to Palestine. That the Jews made no effort during all this time to go there is glossed over or given a religious explanation: the Jews were waiting for the promised messiah to lead them back. A genuine, deep-sustained desire would, however, have produced such a messiah, just as the yearnings of the impoverished Jewish masses under the decaying Roman Empire produced Jesus Christ. In reality, the traditional greeting "Next year in Jerusalem" meant as much to Jews in past ages, before the worsening of the Jewish situation as a result of the decline of capitalism, as it does today to American Jewish millionaires. Jerusalem was a place for pilgrimages, not for settling.

In the West, Zionism was promoted by literary intellectuals such as Theodor Herzl, Max Nordau, and Israel Zangwill, and was financed by magnates such as Baron Rothschild, who were only too glad to send their "unfortunate brothers," the poverty-stricken Jews of the East, to the "land of our ancestors," that is, to the other end of the world, where their presence would not minister to European anti-Semitism. It was only among Eastern European Jews that it had a mass support. But even there the great majority of Jews up to World War II were against Zionism. For the great masses of Jews, Zionism was a capitulation to the anti-Semitic slogan "Jews, get out!"[28] It is therefore more than a little ironic that today Jews in the West often regard anti-Zionism as synonymous with anti-Semitism.

Marxists attacked Zionism because it deflected Jews from the struggle to overthrow capitalism and establish a new social order, which alone could truly emancipate them, and because they believed that a Jewish state in Palestine, even if it came into being—which they regarded as doubtful—would provide not a haven for Jews, but a death trap. Karl Kautsky, whose writings on the Jewish question were accepted by the Bolsheviks and other socialists, stated:

> Every attempt made by the advancing Jewry in that country [Palestine] to displace the Arabs cannot fail to arouse the fighting spirit of the latter, in which opposition to the Jews the Arabs of Palestine will be more and more assured of the support of the entire Arab population of Asia Minor, in whose eyes the Jews appear as foreign rulers or as allies of the English oppressor.[29]

This prediction has of course proven true—except that American imperialism has replaced British imperialism as the power on whom Israel is dependent.

Israel came into being when the capitalist government of the United States, which had kept its gates shut to Hitler's victims, and the Stalinist government of the Soviet Union, which was shortly to engage in an unavowed anti-Semitic campaign, wishing to get British military power out of the Middle East, voted in the United Nations in 1947 for its establishment. Its existence was made possible because the refugees from Hitlerism had no place else to go, because one-and-a-quarter million Palestinians were driven out, and because Jews from the Middle East, who had lived in their native countries for centuries, came as immigrants to it when the antagonism between Israel and the Arab countries escalated.

Making use of a mystique that was in part religious and needing the support of Orthodox Jews in Israel and abroad, Zionism failed to carry out the separation of religion from the state that the American and French revolutions had brought. A small ultra-Orthodox sect, the Natore Karta, which was still waiting for the Messiah and refused to recognize Israel until he came, was permitted to defy the laws on defense service and school attendance. The rest of the Orthodox rabbinate was integrated into the state.

> The Orthodox rabbinate in Israel has been established as a monopoly—neither Reform nor Conservative ordinations are recognized—and it is, in part, supported by the state. This monopoly and state support, in conjunction with the coercive tactics of the religious parties in the Knesset, has given the Orthodox rabbinate a good deal of power. It uses this power to further the observance of Orthodox norms, often violating the civil rights of the nonobservant Israeli.[30]

The influence of American Jewish investors, far from being exerted in the direction of the separation of synagogue and state, has worked the other way. Adherents of "free enterprise," they have supported religious reaction against the trade unions and the "socialistic" kibbutzim.[31]

Racial-talmudic exclusiveness is maintained by the Law of Return, which gives any Jew from any other country the automatic right to settle in Israel and receive immediate citizenship, no other nationality of course having this right. The Law of Return thus outdoes the racist immigration quotas of the United States, which restricted the number of immigrants from Eastern and Southern Europe, including Eastern European Jews, as against the number from Western Europe.

A Jew is defined in the Law of Return as "a person born of a Jewish mother or having converted to Judaism, not being a person affiliated to some other religion." A person born of a Gentile mother and a Jewish father may not, therefore, be admitted unless that person was converted abroad to Judaism. It is a moot point in the law whether such conversions include those made by Reform and Conservative rabbis, but the Orthodox rabbinate has strongly indicated that its religious courts will not accept non-Orthodox conversions.[32]

It is a tragic irony that, as the French Jewish scholar

Maxime Rodinson, a leader in the field of Middle Eastern studies, has pointed out, "it is very probable—and physical anthropology tends to show that it is true—that the so-called Arab
inhabitants of Palestine...have much more of the ancient Hebrews' 'blood' than most of the Jews of the Diaspora, whose religious exclusiveness in no way prevented them from absorbing
converts of various origins."[33] Yet, the Palestinians, dispossessed of their ancient homeland and scattered abroad as the
Jews were, are not permitted to return. They might well be
called the new Jews of the Middle East.

Racial-talmudic exclusiveness is also maintained by the
marriage and divorce laws of Israel: there is no civil marriage
and divorce, and the Orthodox rabbis, the ones empowered to
perform marriages and divorces, do not marry Jews to Gentiles
unless the Gentiles are converted to Orthodox Judaism. Thus a
Jew, even if he is a non-believer, cannot marry a Gentile who
does not wish to convert. This is comparable to the laws in
many states of the United States that, before the civil rights
movement, made miscegenation illegal. That intermarriage may
occur if the Gentile partner is converted to Judaism is reminis-
cent of the conversion of Jews under duress in the past.

One of the bizarre features of the Orthodox monopoly over
marriage is that religious law provides that a descendant of a
priestly family, whose descent is indicated by the common Jewish name Cohen ("cohen" is Hebrew for priest) or one of its numerous variations, may not marry a divorcee. This ancient law
is observed in twentieth century Israel.

The Orthodox rabbinate has the power in education which
the "right to pray" zealots in the United States yearn for. There
are state religious schools that are controlled by the National
Religious party, and in the non-religious primary schools pupils
are taught religion, with classroom discussion being required
each week of the portion of the Bible read that week in the synagogue on Saturday.[34]

To reinforce their institutional power, the Orthodox rabbis
make use of pressure tactics that cause their bourgeois secular opponents all too readily to retreat or to make weak compromises.
Thus when the international convention of the World Union of
Progressive Judaism, meeting in Jerusalem in 1968, proposed to

hold services at the sacred wall, with men and women praying together in accordance with Reform Judaism custom, the minister
of religious affairs and the Chief Rabbi denounced the "desecra-
tion" of the holy place that would be entailed in the two sexes
praying side by side in violation of Orthodox law.

> The religious press...called the Reform Jews "traitors to their peo-
> ple, their land, and their God" and suggested vituperatively that
> they "build a wall near one of their temples and go there to pray
> with their wives and their mistresses."... The Orthodox threatened
> to block the alleged desecrators' access to the wall.

The upshot was that, as the *Jerusalem Post* phrased it, "as the
black-garbed yeshiva students thronged the Western Wall plaza
thirsting for martyrdom, the Premier persuaded the Reform
leaders to yield, postpone their mixed prayer and win kudos for
tolerance."[35] At the sacred wall of Jerusalem "liberated" from
the Arabs, Reform Jews are not permitted to pray.

So too when an amendment to the Compulsory Military
Service was proposed that provided for Orthodox young
women—exempted from the army—serving in social welfare
positions such as hospitals, bedlam broke loose. For the Orthodox rabbinate, taking women out of the house was equivalent
to putting them in brothels. The Chief Rabbi threatened that

> the rabbinical court would ban the military amendment, a world
> wide day of fast would be proclaimed in protest, and Orthodox
> Jewry would "fill the prisons in Israel with their daughters rather
> than comply with the Law.... Rabbi Amram Blau, leader of the
> ultra-Orthodox Natore Karta, urged Orthodox females to commit
> suicide rather than accept conscription.... The police foiled a group
> of fanatics who had plotted to blow up the Knesset and seized a
> small arsenal of weapons that were to be used by a minute band of
> zealots planning a "holy war."

The result was that, although the amendment was passed, it was
never enforced, exemptions being administratively granted from
any kind of service because of "a family's special way of life."[36]

Yet the religious political parties dominated by the Orthodox rabbis are of course the most aggressively expansionist of
the Zionist parties. Their directives come straight from the
Word of God, which commanded the Israelites to wipe out the
inhabitants of the Promised Land and to take it for themselves.

The reactionary influence of the rabbinate is in accord with the reactionary role played by Zionism. Only when Jews and Arabs live in peace as equals in a truly democratic, secular country that is part of a confederation of socialist Middle Eastern states will the Jewish masses have escaped from the death trap into which they have been led by Zionism. So too the victory of socialism in the Western countries is the only assurance for the Jews living there, whose number is far greater than those in Israel, that latent anti-Semitism will not flare up again as the decay of capitalism deepens.

CHAPTER FIVE

Catholicism: Its Origin and Development in Europe

Early Christianity: A Movement of the Ancient Proletariat

The early Christians were mainly members of the ancient proletariat in the cities, the Church getting its first trickle of upper-class members only in the second century.[1] The proletariat of the Roman Empire was not the same as the modern industrial proletariat: it consisted of dispossessed small farmers—driven off the soil by the competition from huge estates ("latifundia") run by slave labor—impoverished and uprooted tenant farmers ("coloni"), poor artisans, unemployed former slaves, peddlers and beggars. These congregated in the large cities in much the same manner as those living in the shanty-towns of the cities in the neo-colonial countries today. This restive, largely unproductive population was maintained by the state as a matter of policy by a program of handouts and spectacles—"bread and circuses."

The teachings of the early adherents of Christianity, who were generally illiterate, were passed on through word of mouth. The Gospels, based on an oral tradition, which had grown in the telling and written by zealots contending for their sectarian concerns, are quite unreliable as records of events. They were, moreover, edited again and again—"three times, four times and many times," says the second century Celsus.[2] It was only after such successive changes that they were accepted as the Word of God by a majority vote of the fourth century Nicene Council, which rejected other writings claiming that title.

Bible criticism has, however, uncovered with some success the different layers of writing in the New Testament that cause it to contradict itself in many places, revealing the evolution of early Christianity. If the New Testament is of little value as historical record, it and other sources of the time do give us a picture of the social conditions from which Christianity grew, just as the *Iliad* and the *Odyssey* tell a story whose historical validity is uncertain but which is useful as a source of knowledge for the society of the time. Thus the observation of Paul to the Christians in the great cosmopolitan Greek city of Corinth, "Few of you were wise or powerful or of high social standing" when they adopted their religion (1 Corinthians 1:26), is one of the sources of our knowledge of the proletarian character of early Christianity.

Christianity's Inception Among the Jews

It was among the Jewish proletarians that Christianity had its inception. Jesus is often spoken of as the messiah whom the Jews looked for to free them from the Roman yoke. This is the significance of the references to him as being of the line of David, from whom the messiah was supposed to come. According to an old Semitic idea, a king becomes adopted by God as his son when he assumes the kingship. So God sends a message to David concerning David's successor: "I will be his father, and he will be my son" (2 Samuel 7:14). So too the king crowned at Zion, "David's city," announces that the Lord has told him, "You are my son; today I have become your father" (Psalms 2:7). Joseph, therefore, is said to be "a descendant of King David" (Luke 1:27), and an angel tells Mary that Jesus "will be great and will be called the Son of the Most High God. The Lord God will make him a king, as his ancestor David was, and he will be the king of the descendants of Jacob forever" (Luke 1:32).

Jesus here is obviously the Jewish Messiah, descended from David through his father Joseph. He is the son of God, like other Jewish kings, only by adoption. This adoption occurred when Jesus was raised to life from the dead:

> It was Jesus, a descendant of David, whom God made the Savior of the people of Israel, as he had promised.... What God promised our ancestors he would do, he has now done for us, who are their descendants, by raising Jesus to life. As it is written in the

second Psalm, "Ye are my Son: today I have become your father."
(Acts 13:23–33)

It is, in fact, only in the Gospel of John, which was rejected
by some Christians even in the third century, that Jesus is represented as a deity existing before time. Since Luke tells of the virgin birth only in the annunciation passage—the virgin birth,
incidentally, is not mentioned at all in Mark and John—and
since he repeatedly calls Joseph Jesus's father after that, the annunciation passage must be a later insertion.

It was the urban poor who longed most fervently for the
messiah. The puppet kings, the priestly aristocracy, and the very
rich collaborated with the Roman occupiers in the same way
that the French ruling class under Petain collaborated with the
Nazis. The religious party of the collaborators, which was called
the Sadducees, was opposed by the Pharisees, the mass of the
population led by the "scribes," rabbis who had risen alongside
the old priesthood. But the most radical of the patriots were the
Zealots, who were composed of the poorest of the poor.

The conservative Pharisee, Josephus, in his *The Wars of the
Jews,* says that the Zealots "persuaded the Jews to revolt...in-
flicting death on those who continued in obedience to the
Roman government...and plundered the houses of the great
men." A series of self-proclaimed messiahs, he continues,
"under the pretense of divine inspiration...prevailed with the
multitude to act like madmen, and went before them into the
wilderness, as pretending that God would there show them the
signals of liberty, but in each case the Roman forces attacked
and killed or dispersed them."[3]

There is evidence that Jesus was such a messiah.

Celsus, a Platonic philospher who about 178 wrote against the
Christians a work known only from Origen's reply [the Christians
suppressed the writings of their opponents], calls Jesus a "ring-
leader of sedition." Hierocles, an imperial governor who attacked
Christianity at the end of the third century in a work quoted by
Lactantius, describes Jesus as a bandit leader [the word "bandit,"
then as now, was commonly applied to rebels] with nine hundred
followers.[4]

It is significant that the Sadducees and the Pharisees are attacked
in the gospels again and again but not so the Zealots, and that

one of the twelve apostles, Simon, is referred to as a Zealot.

Indeed, Mary's song of praise on receiving "the Lord's message" is couched in the radical language of the Zealots: "He has brought down mighty kings from their thrones, and lifted up the lowly. He has filled the hungry with good things, and sent the rich away with empty hands. He has kept the promise he made to our ancestors, and has come to the help of his servant Israel" (Luke 1:52–54). So too Jesus is represented as saying things which seem to be the persisting recollection of a radical leader: "Do not think that I have come to bring peace to the world. No, I did not come to bring peace, but a sword" (Matthew 10:34); "It is much harder for a rich person to enter the Kingdom of God than for a camel to go through the eye of a needle (Mark 10:25); "I come to set the earth on fire, and how I wish it were already kindled" (Luke 12:49); "Whoever does not have a sword must sell his coat and buy one" (Luke 22:36).

The Kingdom of God is repeatedly said to be at hand in the lifetime of those Jesus is addressing (Luke 21:32; Mark 13:30; Matthew 10:23), and in one passage it is represented in materialistic terms: "I tell you that anyone who leaves home...or fields for me...will receive much more in this present age. He will receive a hundred times more houses...and fields.... But many who are now first will be last, and many who are now last will be first" (Mark 10:29–31). The promise of houses and lands clearly seems to be one that survived the numerous editings that made the Gospels less this-worldly than they were originally.[5]

Another sect to which Christianity is undoubtedly indebted is the Essenes.

> A small minority of the revolutionary party, disappointed with the results of the Maccabean revolt, tried to set up a Utopian community of their own. These were the Essenes...of whom we read in Philo, Pliny and Josephus. They practiced strict community of goods.... Some of the sect renounced marriage; others allowed it for the propagation of the race. Travelling Essenes carried no provisions, but relied on the hospitality of local brotherhoods. They took no oaths.... Persian influence shows itself...in their doctrine of eternal reward and punishment.... It appears from recently discovered Essene documents [the Dead Sea Scrolls] that Aristobulus [a Jewish high priest] found the sect dangerous enough to be worth persecuting, and that he tortured and executed a leader

whom they called "the master of justice and the elect of God."
Josephus records their part in the later revolutionary war against
Rome and their bravery under torture when taken by the enemy.[6]

The document also states that "soon the 'master of justice' will
reappear to judge Israel and all nations, and only those who believe in him will be saved."[7]

The Christians also advocated remaining unmarried but
permitted marriage (1 Corinthians 7:8–9), relied on aid from
fellow religionists in traveling to proselytize (1 Corinthians
9:3–7), were against any kind of oath (Matthew 5:33–37), and
believed in eternal reward and punishment. Like the Essenes,
too, they formed closely knit communes, as the Acts of the
Apostles testifies.

> The group of believers was one in mind and heart. No one said
> that any of his belongings was his own, but they shared with one
> another everything they had.... Those who owned fields or houses
> would sell them, bring the money received from the sale, and turn
> it over to the apostles; and the money was distributed to each one
> according to his need. (Acts 4:32–35)

The Christian communes were, in fact, like the Utopian communist colonies of the nineteenth century, most of which were religiously inspired and led. Family, which the modern Christian
extols and claims is best cemented by religion ("the family that
prays together stays together"), was renounced for the commune.
"I came to bring...not peace, but division.... Fathers will be
against their sons, and sons against their fathers.... Whoever comes
to me cannot be my disciple unless he loves me more than he loves
his father and his mother, his wife and his children" (Luke
12:51–53; 14:26). The comradeship of the commune will replace
the loss of family: "Anyone who leaves home or brothers or sisters
or mother or father or children" will receive "a hundred times
more...brothers, sisters, mothers, children" (Mark 10:29–30).

This was a communism of housekeeping, not of production.
Like the "flower children" of the 1960s, the early Christians
made a virtue of poverty and did not believe in working for the
morrow. "Look how the wild flowers grow: they don't work or
make clothes for themselves. But I tell you that not even King
Solomon with all his wealth had clothes as beautiful as one of
these flowers" (Luke 12:27).

Rebels and violators of conventional values as the Christians were, it is little wonder that they were persecuted.

The Effects of the Spread of Christianity to the Gentiles

Numerous roving "apostles" (from the Greek word meaning messenger or traveler), agitators who traveled without money or even "a beggar's bag or shoes" (Luke 10:4), brought the "good news" of the coming messiah to the communities of Palestine. At first Christianity was confined to the Jews and did not break with Judaism. Jesus is represented as having said to his twelve disciples, the earliest apostles: "Do not go to any Gentile territory or any Samaritan towns. Instead, you are to go to those lost sheep, the people of Israel. Go and preach, 'The Kingdom of heaven is near!'" (Matthew 10:5–6). He is, moreover, represented as stating most positively that every jot and tittle of Jewish law is to be obeyed: "Do not think that I have come to do away with the Law of Moses.... Remember that as long as heaven and earth last, not the least point nor the smallest detail of the Law will be done away with—not until the end of all things" (Matthew 5:17–18).

Soon the apostles brought Christianity to the Greek-speaking Jewish proletariat of the cities of the Greco-Roman world. The religion then made its way to the Gentile proletariat of these cities. The second destruction of Jerusalem in AD 70 did away with the base of Jewish revolt. With the defeat of the national hopes of the Jews, Christianity became more and more a religion not of a revolutionary Jewish messiah who was to bring the Kingdom of God to earth but of a universal messiah ("Christ" is the Greek word for messiah) whose kingdom was not of this earth. It more and more dissociated itself from Judaism and made its peace with Rome, becoming a religion that provided solace for the disheartened proletarian masses. In his letter to the Christians in Rome, Paul speaks of personal salvation, not of bringing down kings from their thrones and filling the hungry with good things to eat. The message now is that everyone must obey state authorities, because no authority exists without God's permission, and the existing authorities have been put there by

God (Romans 13:1). With the acceptance of Rome came the rejection of the Jewish revolt against Rome. This is the basis of the anti-Semitic passages of the New Testament.

The development of Christianity was influenced by the cults called "mystery religions" that were practiced by the Eastern masses in such cities as Alexandria, Antioch, Ephesus, and Rome itself. These "mystery religions" were continuations of ancient myths and rituals in which a king with divine powers was presented as dying and being reborn in order that the earth might revive in the spring after the death of winter. For the uprooted and despairing masses in the cities of the Roman Empire, these myths did not have the magical significance for agriculture they had had for their peasant forebears but expressed the hope of continued life in a better existence after death.

How much Christianity is indebted to these cults can be judged from this passage in Robertson:

> Osiris, whose cult had spread from Egypt to Greece and Rome before the Christian era, was believed by his worshippers to ensure to them by his resurrection eternal life in a better world. Even before the age of Alexander this significance had been read into his rites. "As surely as Osiris lives," ran the incantation pronounced over the dead in Egypt, "he shall live...." [Cf. "Just as Christ was raised from death...so also...we shall be one with him by being raised to life as he was"—Romans 6:4–5] Attis, whose rites spread from Asia Minor to the West during the same period, was each year at the vernal equinox bound in effigy to a pine tree, wildly lamented, and buried until the third day, when his joyful resurrection was hailed as a promise that his devotees too would rise triumphant over death [cf. 1 Corinthians 15:3–4, 12]. In token of this they were baptized in the blood of a bull [cf. the hymn "Are You Washed in the Blood of the Lamb?"] and "born again to eternal life.".... [Cf. "Jesus Christ is the one who came with the water of baptism and the blood of his death.... The water and the blood...give the same testimony.... The testimony is this: God has given us eternal life"—1 John 5:6–11. Dionysius...rose from the dead and ascended into heaven; and those initiated into his mysteries, in which his death and resurrection were enacted, were made partakers of his immortality.[8]

From the Persian cult of the worship of Mithra, which, though very ancient, became widely popular in the Roman Empire during the same time, Christianity got a number of its rites and observances.

> The Mithraic priests baptized that god's devotees with holy water, signed them on their foreheads, transferred the holy spirit to them by the "laying on of hands" and exorcised devils by holding two or more fingers directed toward the suppliant.... The abstinence of Lent was paralleled by periods of forbearance in all the purifactory cults. The candle, the smoke of incense, the amulet and the chanted incantation served to purify and protect the Christians as effectively as they served the Mithraists.[9]

The Mithraists also made sacramental use of bread and wine, celebrated December 25 as marking the rebirth of the sun after its seeming death on December 21, the shortest day of the year, and held services on Sunday, the day sacred to their sun-god, from whom the very word "sunday" is derived.[10]

The assimilation of the "mystery religion" doctrines and rituals was so great that it could not pass unnoticed. It was, however, given a characteristic explanation. "These similarities, according to Justin Martyr and Tertullian, were due to the wicked devil anticipating and imitating Christianity, and the same argument was used by Fermicus to explain the parallel between the crucified Jesus and the Attisian image of a young man fastened to a tree."[11]

The Catholic Church and Feudalism

The decrease in the number of independent farmers—who furnished the manpower of the Roman army—meant a cessation of the expansion of the Roman Empire and a cutting down of the supply of slaves drawn from conquered peoples. In time the Roman Empire was faced with the challenge of the barbarians pounding at its gates. In this atmosphere the ruling class lost faith in itself. It turned to philosophies such as Stoicism, which preached the nullity of life and its goods and the need for the individual to rise superior to the vicissitudes of existence. Christianity, no longer a threatening force, became congenial to it, and the Stoical philosophy interacted with the new religion. The most important point Christianity took from Stoicism was the concept of the Law of Nature, which establishes a hierarchical order in the universe and in society.[12] The concept of the Law of Nature was to be used by the Catholic Church through the centuries to support the social order.

As the Church grew in wealth and influence, it ceased to be democratic in its internal structure. The power of the bishops increased, and the Bishop of Rome became pre-eminent over the other bishops. Church property was no longer the common property of the Christian community but of the priesthood as a closed corporation. It was administered by the Church bureaucracy, which became quite separated from the masses it nominally served. The conversion of Constantine was not a happy accident but a coming to terms of the Empire with a mighty force that was needful to it.

The change in Christianity did not occur without a struggle. Before the Catholic Church grew strong enough to suppress all opinions of which it did not approve, Christianity was marked by a multiplicity of sects.

> Celsus...speaks with just indignation of the fury with which a heretic—that is, a man whose opinions differed from those of the majority—was pursued by those who professed a religion of love. "They slander one another with all sorts of charges mentionable and unmentionable, refusing to yield the smallest point for the sake of concord, and hating one another with a perfect hatred."[13]

Even after Christianity became the state religion, heretical popular sects kept rising up.

> Some heresies...were, economically speaking, revolts against the corrupting influence of riches in the Church and the luxury of the Bishops, and advocated a puritan simplicity and austerity of ecclesiastical life. Another type were those heresies which harked back to the apostolic days of the Church when a brotherly communism obtained in some congregations.... Arianism, Monophysitism, Donatism became vehicles of popular expression of nationalism in the countries concerned [Egypt, Syria, northern Africa, respectively], popular protests against...the Latin masters...the privileged orthodox and ruling class.... The clergy, more than the aristocracy, were hated by the masses in these countries.[14]

Thus Christianity, originally a proletarian threat to Rome, became transformed into its opposite, a bulwark of the social system. The Church opposed the abolition of slavery: every parish priest had the legal right to have one male and one female slave. Monasteries had great numbers of slaves and Church slaves were held right on into the Middle Ages.[15] Slavery ceased to exist not by any effort of the Church but as a result of a social evolution by which slavery gradually gave way to serfdom.[16] The decline of the slave economy forced the owners of the large estates to let parts of their land to coloni or tenants. The power of the great landowners, the supersession of the local administrations of the Empire by these magnates, the need of the coloni for protection against military attack, the development of a hereditary aristocracy among the Germanic invading warriors as a result of their contact with the Roman system, the interaction and fusion of the two systems—these are the origins of feudalism, which became the dominant social system in the course of the decline of the Roman Empire.

For the serf, as for the slave, the words of Paul applied: "Slaves, obey your human masters...with a sincere heart because of your reverence for the Lord.... For Christ is the real Master you serve" (Colossians 3:22–24). Poverty continued to be glorified, but now it was hard working, uncomplaining poverty. The Plowman in Chaucer's Prologue to *The Canterbury Tales* is represented as an ideal Christian, just as Piers Plowman in the poem of that title is represented as Christ-like. He is a good, honest worker who loves his neighbor as himself whether things are going well with him or not. On the other hand, "impatient poverty," as it was called, was frequently declaimed against. In the Prologue to the Man of Law's Tale, Impatient Poverty is said to blame Christ and to complain bitterly that he has distributed wealth unequally so that his neighbor has everything and he has nothing. Chaucer in this was following the Church's teaching that social inequality must be accepted as the effect of the fall of Adam.[17]

The idea of charity, derived from the sense of comradeship among the members of the Christian communes and from the mutual aid of their benefit and burial societies, also changed. It ceased to be concerned primarily with helping others and became concerned primarily with buying penance for one's sins and with exalting ascetic self-denial.[18] Self-denial, however, while it reached extreme forms in such as Saint Simeon Stylites, who lived for thirty years on a pillar sixty feet high without descending, being brought the necessities of life by his disciples, was the exception rather than the rule. For most, charity was what Lenin, speaking of the members of the ruling class of his own day, said it was: "Religion teaches them to be charitable in earthly life, thus providing a cheap justification for their whole exploiting existence and selling them at a reasonable price tickets to heavenly bliss."[19]

The Catholic Church, through which alms were distributed, became unaccountable to those on whose behalf it received donations and bequests, its budget remaining a secret even today. Tithes were instituted in the sixth century upon every bit of land. Their cost was paid for in the last analysis by the peasants, upon whom they were a crushing burden. High posts in the Church, the source of great riches and power, became obtainable only by those of noble families. Celibacy was decreed in the eleventh century by the Pope in order to keep the wealth of the priesthood within the church, although it was not instituted until the thirteenth century owing to the opposition of the priests. Thus the Church became the greatest landowner of all, holding, it has been estimated, one-third of the land of feudal Europe. It was firmly integrated into the feudal structure, with its own hierarchy organized on the feudal model (as was, incidentally, the hierarchy of angels in heaven—thrones, dominions, powers, princedoms, archangels, and the rest).

In its own holdings the Church was even more demanding that its serfs fulfill their feudal obligations than the other landowners. James Westfall Thompson cites scholars in French, English, and Belgian medieval history who state that this was so in each of these countries. The explanation is given by Pollack and Maitland: "The immortal, but soulless corporation with her wealth of accurate records would yield no inch, would enfranchise no serf, would enfranchise no tenement. In practice, the secular lord was more humane, because he was more human, because he was careless, because he wanted ready money, because he would die."[20] The Church was in this not so far different from the modern corporation.

A portion of the land of the Church was held by monasteries. Monasticism had come into existence at the beginning of the fourth century, when Christianity spread from the cities to the rural areas and when it was still somewhat subject to communistic impulses.

> But as soon as a monastery had become rich and powerful, it went through the same process that has been repeated since by many a communistic association that covers only a small part of

society, as we see today in successful productive cooperatives. The owners of the means of production find it more comfortable to have others work for them instead of working themselves, as soon as they find the necessary labor power: propertyless wage-workers, slaves or serfs.[21]

So, we may add, have the members of the kibbutzim in Israel learned to use Arab labor.

Monasteries too, therefore, were transformed into their opposites, becoming as exploitative as—and often even more exploitative—than the feudal lords. "So great was the oppression of its serfs by the Chapter of Notre Dame de Paris in the reign of St. Louis," states the historian G.G. Coulton, "that Queen Blanche remonstrated 'in all humility' whereto the monks replied that 'they might starve their serfs as they pleased.'"[22] The words attributed to the Mary who gave her name to their chapter, "He has filled the hungry with good things, and sent the rich away with empty hands," do not seem to have influenced them.

The monasteries were a countervailing power to the power of the bishops. As rich as the bishops, from whom they were economically independent, the heads of the monastic latifundia refused to kowtow to them. In the struggle in which the Bishop of Rome advanced from pre-eminence over the other bishops to absolute domination over them, he made use of the monastic orders, balancing himself between them and the Episcopal aristocracy, as the Renaissance absolute monarch balanced himself between the nobility—from which he himself had risen—and the bourgeoisie.[23]

The Renaissance Papacy

The eleventh, twelfth, and thirteenth centuries saw the development of a money economy in Europe, as agriculture built up a surplus. The process was given a great impetus by the Crusades, which were plundering expeditions to the rich East. The basic structure of feudalism, however, remained intact and the period marked the flowering of medieval culture.

Money became increasingly important, and by the end of the thirteenth century the Church set up a centralized fiscal system.

So long as the wealth of the Church remained decentralized...its central government had remained relatively uncontaminated.

Under the new conditions not only the wealth but the materialism
that went with it seemed to be concentrated in an unprecedented
degree in the papal curia. Contemporary wits noticed that the word
Roma furnished an acrostic base for the apothegm *radix omnium
malorum avaritia* [the love of money is the root of all evil].... The
increasing demands of the papal curia forced preoccupation with finance upon all the officers of the Church down to the parish
level.[24]

The pressure from Rome resulted in the sales of ecclesiastical offices, of pardons for sin, and of supposed saints' relics becoming a shocking scandal. In fact, the competition of churches
and monasteries in the selling of relics as objects with miraculous powers may be said to be one of the earliest expressions of
free competition. The Pardoner in *The Canterbury Tales*, whom
the Host charges with selling his filthy underclothes as saints'
relics, is a kind of travelling salesman of "spiritual goods."

On the highest level, the papacy itself was openly bought at
papal elections. The culmination was reached during the Renaissance. Of the election of Alexander VI, the Holy Father
who sired the notorious Cesare and Lucrezia Borgia, it has been
said that at "no previous or subsequent election were such immense sums of money spent on bribery."[25]

The Counter-Reformation

With the exception of sixteenth century England, where it was
not very deep going, the Reformation occurred in the poorest
countries of Europe. This was no accident:

> Not only had the kings and the clergy of France and Spain, in con-
> sequence of the higher economic development of their countries,
> practically obtained before the Reformation what the princes and
> clergy in Germany had to wrest in a severe struggle, but they had
> become strong enough to try and make the Pope himself their tool
> and exploit his influence and power for themselves. Thus it was in
> their interest to maintain his rule over Christendom, which was in
> truth their rule.... That Italy, France, and Spain remained Catholic
> is not to be ascribed to their spiritual backwardness, but rather to
> their higher economic development.[26]

The Reformation deprived the papacy and the Catholic
countries of a great deal of wealth. With the new discoveries,

moreover, commerce passed from Italy to the Atlantic seaboard countries. Catholicism was forced to respond to the new conditions by a process of retrenchment, reaction, readjustment, and reform. This was the Counter-Reformation, the means by which the Church retained its rule over what was left to it after the Reformation.

In the realm of dogma, the Protestants had acknowledged the authority of the Bible only, thereby challenging the authority of the Church; the Council of Trent declared that authority consisted of both the Bible and the tradition of the Church. To justify practices of recent date, the Church discovered nonexistent ancient roots. As Francis Bacon said of this churchly device, "By show of antiquity they introduce novelty."[27] Luther had insisted that justification, the act of God absolving the sinner from sin, was achieved by faith, not by works, the deeds of charity determined and administered by the Church; the Council of Trent declared that both faith and works were necessary for justification, a compromise which upheld the notion of the Church as an essential mediator between God and humanity.

An index of forbidden books was set up: this was the Church's method of grappling with the dissemination of knowledge through the invention of printing. One work included on the index was a report from a commission of the Church that recommended certain reforms, some of which were later enacted, but which drew the line at forbidding the sale of dispensations, benefices, and other privileges, finding that half of the papal revenue came from them. The Bible and works of theology were declared mysteries too great to be conveyed through vulgar languages, thus reinforcing the monopoly of the Church in these matters.

The Inquisition, a revival of Church practices of the Middle Ages, was licensed by a papal bull. The dungeon and the torture chamber became the means of combating heresy. In Spain the *auto da fé* became the favorite holiday entertainment. Just as the Roman Empire had thrown early Christians to the lions before delighted multitudes of spectators, so did the Spanish Inquisition burn heretics alive before equally delighted multitudes. To be sure, those heretics who recanted before execution were strangled before being cast into the flames.

A new religious order, the Company of Jesus, was instituted. Its members, the Jesuits, imbued with a militant spirit—"company" is a military term meaning the followers of a warrior chieftain—used humanistic learning as a weapon against the humanists and the Protestants on behalf of the Church. But if Jesuitism was a kind of humanism, it was humanism deprived of its independence in order to serve the Church. "To make sure of being right in all things," said its founder, Ignatius Loyola, "we ought always to hold to the principle that the white I see I should believe to be black if the hierarchical church were so to rule."[28]

Like Jesuitism, the Counter-Reformation, of which Jesuitism was a part, was partially an adjustment to the conditions of the modern world, partially a return to the past. But, halting though it was, it was enough of an adjustment to enable the Catholic Church to continue into modern capitalist society.

The Effects of the French Revolution

The absolute monarchy of the Renaissance used the ascending bourgeoisie as a balance against the old nobility. With the further development of commerce and industry, the bourgeoisie became too heavy on the political scale for it to be used by the monarchy as a counterweight to the nobility. The absolute monarchy, which was itself the product of the diminished power of feudalism, turned to the nobility against the threat of the bourgeoisie and now became intent on preserving the remnants of feudal privileges and distinctions. The bourgeoisie, on the other hand, wanted not merely equality with the aristocracy, but freedom from feudal restrictions.

Aristocracy and bourgeoisie had evolved and changed in character through the centuries: each of the two classes had social divisions within them; each had strata that had points of interest with strata in the other class; yet the basic opposition between the two classes had to be resolved. The French Revolution, which came after the English Revolution of the seventeeth century, was all the more thoroughgoing, relying strongly on the plebeian masses; it affected all of Europe.

The Church had been very much an integral part of the old order. "In one way or another," wrote Sieyes, a contemporary spokesman for the bourgeoisie, "all the branches of the executive have been taken over by the caste that monopolizes the Church, the judiciary, and the army. A spirit of fellowship leads the nobles to favor one another in everything over the rest of the nation. The usurpation is complete; they truly reign."[29] The higher offices of the Church were indeed very much restricted to members of the aristocracy, who were often worldly persons more concerned with shining at salons or with practicing intrigue at court than with taking care of their administrative duties in the Church.

The French Church, which had immense wealth and which through its alliance with the crown had loosened its ties with the papacy, was pre-eminent among the churches of Europe. It was exempt from taxation, and its members could not be tried in civil courts, only in ecclesiastical courts. It had nearly absolute control over education, and one could not get married— or, for that matter, be born or die—outside its jurisdiction.

The wealth of the Church was, however, very unevenly distributed. The higher clergy had incomes of 100,000 livres or even in some cases as much as 400,000 livres while country priests might have an income of as little as 300 livres. Because these priests were close to the people in their parishes, democratic sentiments—which often took the form of extolling the egalitarianism of the early Christians—spread among them.[30]

The Revolution confiscated the land and other property of the Church and sold it to bourgeois property-owners. Churchmen had to take an oath of loyalty to the new constitution to keep their positions. About half of the parish priests but very few of the higher clergy did so; the rest joined the counter-revolution.

The Napoleonic army overthrew the old regime in the conquered countries, abolishing serfdom and freeing the peasants from feudal obligations and church tithes. Napoleon was the heir of a revolution and, basing himself on it, had to carry through these progressive measures, but, like Stalin was to do, he was an heir who misappropriated his legacy. He made an agreement with the Pope through which he appeared as the Church's savior while seeking to exploit it for his own purposes. But by making the clergy dependent on him, he created among them a trend that was to make itself more and more manifest to look to the papacy to escape the domination of the national state.

With the cynical realism of an ex-Jacobin, Napoleon understood the usefulness of the Church in stabilizing French society. "What is it," he asked, "that makes the poor man take it for granted that...on my table at each meal there is enough to sustain a family for a week? It is religion which says to him that in another life I shall be his equal, indeed that he has a better chance of being happy there than I have."[31] Bourgeois society itself needed religion now.

The European Counter-Revolution and the Church

The defeat of Napoleon meant the triumph of counter-revolution. The restored monarchies and aristocracies could not wipe out the social gains of the Revolution, but they did mitigate them. In doing so, they aligned themselves with the Church, which, widely believed at the end of the eighteenth century to be at the point of death, gained a new lease on life. The former differences between the French and German monarchies and the Church concerning the degree of independence of the churches from the papacy were forgotten in the alliance between "throne and altar."

Even in Protestant countries the Catholic Church was looked upon by conservatives with new sympathy as a time-tested bulwark against the revolution which the French experience had taught them to fear. The papacy, the oldest monarchy in Europe, was regarded as essential for the existence of the other monarchies, and consequently the three non-Catholic monarchies, England, Russia, and Prussia, sought to strengthen its political influence.[32]

But as industrialism advanced during the century the Pope found himself isolated, as his aristocratic allies lost out to the bourgeoisie. He even lost his own princedom when Italian liberals, intent on unifying Italy, captured Rome. If the national states were no longer disposed to ally themselves with the Church, there was the danger that it would become fragmented. Pius IX therefore sought to withdraw into an intellectual fortress guarded against the outside world, which had produced Mazzini and Garibaldi. His Syllabus of Errors was

an over-all condemnation in the most unqualified terms of rationalism, indifferentism, socialism, communism, naturalism, freema-sonry, separation of Church and State, liberty of the press, liberty of religion, culminating in the famous denial that "the Roman pontiff can and ought to reconcile himself and reach agreement with progress, liberalism and modern civilization."[33]

The Vatican Council he summoned did his bidding in de-claring that when the Pope spoke with the authority of his of-fice on matters of faith and morals he was infallible and therefore could not be challenged. Pius IX promoted adulation for the Vicar of Christ, a Catholic "cult of the personality."

> The pope was spoken of as "the vice-god of humanity." Hymns, which in the breviary were addressed to God, were addressed to Pius IX. A Jesuit review, which he patronized, explained that when the pope meditated God was thinking in him, and a leading French ultramontane [Catholic party for increasing the power and authority of the pope] bishop spoke of him as the continuation of the Incarnate Word.[34]

Social Catholicism

Shortly before his death, Pius IX was reported to have said, "My system and my policies have had their day, but I am too old to change my course; that will be the task of my successor."[35] The fortress could not keep out the forces of the modern world. Leo XIII, Pius IX's successor, urged European Catholics to abandon royalism and come to terms with bourgeois democracy. At the same time that he was extending a hand to the bourgeois demo-crats, he sought to press to his bosom the proletariat, which had become increasingly alienated from the Church, or at least those members of it which followed a reformist leadership.

Earlier in the century, members of the Catholic aristocracy in Germany, France, Austria, and Switzerland had sought to gain the allegiance of workers to aid them in their losing contest with the bourgeoisie. "That a group of feudal aristocrats should become radicals, almost socialists, in economic doctrine," says a historian of French Social Catholicism, "is no paradox; to any-one familiar with the early history of social legislation it appears almost as a commonplace."[36] Often this "feudal socialism," as Marx and Engels called it, which went "hand in hand" with "clerical socialism,"[37] was associated, especially in Austria and

France, with anti-Semitism, with aristocratic contempt and hatred of the newly rich Jewish members of the bourgeoisie.

But, as Marx and Engels said, while the aristocracy, seeking
"to rally the people to them, waved the proletarian alms bag in
front for a banner," "the people, as often as it joined them, saw
on their hindquarters the old feudal coats of arms, and deserted
them with loud and irreverent laughter."[38] Leo XIII took the
economic doctrine of "feudal socialism," which had supported
state and Church intervention to ameliorate the condition of the
working class in what Baron von Ketteler, the Bishop of Mains,
called "the slave-market of our liberal Europe,"[38] and separated it from royalism.

Eugene Spuller, a prominent French anti-clerical liberal of
the time, indignantly exclaimed, "The Church is taking a step in
the direction of the masses, now that she is detached from the
princes and the monarchies and needs another support." He expressed alarm as to what might happen if the Church "starts to
excite the masses in what they call their social claims." Later,
however, Spuller changed his mind and "offered a truce in the
battle against clericalism if the clericals would join in a crusade
'against all fanaticisms, whatever they be, against all sectaries,
to whatever sect they belong,' i.e., chiefly against Revolutionary
Socialism and Anarchism."[40]

The averting of socialism was from the first Leo's avowed
objective. *Laissez-faire* capitalism had produced a working class
that listened all too readily to the siren voice of revolutionary socialism; adherence to the ancient principles of Catholicism—the
obligation of charity, the sinfulness of the greed for money, the
dignity of labor, and the responsibility to God owed by property-owners—would alter this sad state of affairs. "The Church
of Christ," he said, "is possessed of power to stave off the pest
of socialism,"[41] which violates the right to property decreed by
the law of nature and which falsely preaches that "rich and poor
are intended by nature to live at war with one another."[42]

In addition to advocating social welfare measures and urging
employers to be just and workers "never to employ violence,"
Leo called for the formation of joint associations of employers
and workers in which both would work together to "infuse the
spirit of justice into the mutual relations of employer and employ-

ees."[43] Where either a capitalist or a worker felt that his rights had been infringed upon, a committee composed of members of the association would decide the dispute. He also accepted workers' trade unions but counseled that they should be formed by Christians so that they would be free of irreligious influences.

Thus Leo sought to split the workers on the basis of religion and to promote class collaboration. He anticipated the Christian Democratic parties, the compulsory arbitration that the bourgeois state has sought to make use of, and the corporate unions of capital and labor of fascism.

The Catholic Church's Collaboration With Fascism

Although Saint Thomas Aquinas, the precapitalist thinker to whom Leo XIII looked for guidance concerning social relations under capitalism, had called monarchy the best form of government, Leo, reaching out to the bourgeois democrats, proclaimed that the Church was indifferent concerning the form of government "provided the respect due to religion and the observance of good morals be upheld."[44] The Church, abiding by this principle, found it easy enough to enter into agreements with the governments of fascist Italy and fascist Germany, to say nothing of fascist Spain. Since subsidies to the Church and Catholic education of school children were provided for in these agreements, it found that they observed "good morals."

After the Second World War, the Vatican sought to mend its damaged prestige by establishing anti-fascist credentials. It pointed to members of the lower clergy who had participated in the Italian Resistance in the latter stages of the war and to Catholic priests who had been the victims of the Nazi regime. It also published documents showing frictions between the Holy See and Hitler's government. But these frictions arose from conflicts over the institutional power of the Church, not any concern for human rights on the part of the Holy Father, and the priests who bravely resisted the Nazis did so against the adjurations of their bishops. The record of collaboration between the Church and both Italian and German fascism cannot be expunged. It is amply documented in, among other places, Richard A. Webster's *The Cross and the Fasces*, although Webster is all too charitable toward the Vatican, and Guenter Lewy's *The Catholic Church and Nazi Germany*, which, although Lewy does not pretend to be impartial ("I am not neutral on issues such as dictatorship, genocide or moral hypocrisy"),[45] is utterly damning.

One quotation from Lewy will suffice to show how the governing authorities of the German Catholic Church supported the Nazi regime:

> From the beginning until the end of Hitler's rule the bishops never tired of admonishing the faithful to accept his government as the legitimate authority to whom obedience had to be rendered.... After the unsuccessful assassination attempt upon Hitler in Munich on November 8, 1939, Cardinal Bertram, in the name of the German episcopate, and Cardinal Faulhaber for the Bavarian bishops sent telegrams of congratulations to Hitler. The Catholic press all over Germany, in response to instructions of the *Reichspressekammer*, spoke of the miraculous working of providence that had protected the Fuhrer.[46]

The rationale for this support was the need for obedience to duly constituted authority. However, this need had not prevented the Church from giving its blessing to insurrection by counter-revolutionists in Mexico or by Franco in Spain.

The bishops found that Hitler was waging a just war in the eyes of God, declaring in a joint pastoral letter a few days after the invasion of Catholic Poland:

> In this decisive hour we encourage and admonish our Catholic soldiers, in obedience to the Fuhrer, to do their duty and to be ready to sacrifice their whole person. We appeal to the faithful to join in ardent prayers that God's providence may lead this war to blessed success and peace for fatherland and people.[47]

The governing authorities of the Catholic church in the allied countries found that the war being waged by Hitler's opponents was also a just war. God, it seems, was rooting for both sides.

The Holy See was officially neutral, but, as German documents show, it repeatedly assured Nazi diplomats that, in the words of one memorandum, "in his heart...Pius XII stands on the side of the Axis powers."[48]

> On two important points the German documents show impressive agreement: on the one hand, the Sovereign Pontiff seems to have

had a predilection for Germany which does not appear to have been diminished by the nature of the Nazi regime and which was not disavowed up to 1944; on the other hand, Pius XII feared a Bolshevization of Europe more than anything else and hoped, it seems, that Hitler's Germany, if it were eventually reconciled with the Western Allies, would become the essential rampart against any advance by the Soviet Union toward the West.[49]

About the millions exterminated in the Nazi concentration camps, the Holy Father kept silent. Condemnation, public or private, would not have advanced Vatican interests or its diplomatic strategy.

The Catholic Church Today

Early in the nineteeth century the conservative French Catholic, the Count de Maistre, upholding the Latin liturgy, declared, "If they do not understand the words, so much the better. Respect increases.... He who understands nothing understands better than he who understands badly."[50] This was the policy of the Church in the nineteenth century in standing firm against all who would introduce to its flock modernist Bible criticism and modernist attempts to cope with science. The Anglican clergyman Vidler comments sympathetically:

> On behalf of the Roman authorities it may be said that they were responsible for the government of a Church the vast majority of whose members were peasants, so that pastoral solicitude inclined them to protect the faith of simple believers, however much they might scandalize the educated in the process.[51]

From this point of view pastoral solicitude consists in keeping church members sheep-like.

This policy, however, is not practicable in the twentieth century, when important sections of the Church membership are no longer peasants. The changes made by Vatican II, the council called by John XXIII in 1962, were designed to meet a situation in which the world-wide drift, except for a few countries such as the United States, was away from Catholicism. The number of Frenchmen choosing the priesthood, for instance, dropped more than 50 percent in the ten years before the council, and less than 25 percent of the population received Easter communion, the most obligatory attendance requirement, in a country where 83 percent were baptized Catholics. Although the population of Italy had increased almost 100 percent in the period between Vatican I and Vatican II, the number of priests had dropped by 70 percent, and the number of men who received Easter communion was only 12 percent, regular church-going being almost entirely confined to women. And, as the Superior General of the Jesuits informed the Council, apparently referring to the number of baptisms and including as Catholics the number of nominal Catholics who never went to church, "In 1961 Catholics formed 18 percent of the [world's] population; today [1965] they form 16 percent."[52]

Under these circumstances the Church sought to replace its image of a rigid, authoritarian, hidebound institution with an image of a church close to the people it serves. It permitted the mass to be given in the vernacular despite the 150-year-old pronouncement of the Count de Maistre. It permitted nuns to wear lay clothes so that they would not be seen as forbidding figures in black garb. It permitted the eating of meat on Friday 450 years after Erasmus made fun of this prohibition, the Church apparently now feeling that Catholics had grieved sufficiently for the crucifixion of Christ, supposedly on this day of the week. Without acknowledging its collaboration with the Nazis, it removed centuries-old anti-Semitic references in its texts. It took some steps in the direction of de-centralization and internal freedom.

Nevertheless, the power of the conservative bureaucracy of the papal Curia was left basically unimpaired, and the doctrine of papal infallibility remained. To be sure, popes nowadays rarely speak *ex cathedra*—that is, proclaim to the world that what they are saying at that moment is the indisputable truth because it is they who are saying it—but the claim to absolute authority has not been disavowed, and papal autocracy is still supreme. In the first flush of enthusiasm after Vatican II, the Reverend Alec Vidler stated:

> Roman Catholic theologians ["e.g., Hans Kung, Karl Rahner, S.J., Edward Schillebeeckx, O.P., etc."] can now with impunity publish work on doctrinal and other subjects, and indeed on the foundations of belief, that would make Pius XII, let alone Pius X and Pius XI, turn in their tombs.[53]

The various Piuses may rest easy: Kung has been forbidden by

John Paul II to teach as a Catholic theologian, and Schillebeeckx has been censured.

The need to attempt to satisfy different kinds of constituencies has meant continued trouble for the Church. In Europe these differing demands are illustrated by the speeches of John Paul on visiting different countries. In Poland, where the bureaucracy is linked to the Soviet bureaucracy and where there is the tradition of the Church as a vehicle for national feeling against the Tsarist empire and the Russian Orthodox church, he made some allusions to the necessity for freedom of thought that aroused the enthusiasm of the masses. In Ireland, however, unlike in Poland, the Pope said nothing of freedom of thought. But in Ireland it is an oppressively authoritarian clerical power, which has long deprived the people of such freedom. The changes wrought by industry have, however, been sufficient for the Pope to warn the Church not to become too westernized.

In France, the home of the Enlightenment, the Revolution, anti-clerical republicanism, and Marxist socialism, preparations for 1,200,000 people to greet the Pope were made. Only 200,000 showed up, with the only sizable contingent from outside the immediate region of the reception being Polish immigrants. In a nation that is nominally Catholic the media were far less effusive than the American media when John Paul visited the United States. Although the Pope referred to France as "the eldest daughter of the Church," she seems to be a daughter who doesn't pay too much attention to Papa.

The delicate balancing to which the Church must sometimes resort in order to maintain its position is illustrated by its conduct in Poland. Despite the Pope's verbal thrusts, the Church has a working relationship with the Polish state by which it has chaplains in the "Red" Army and teaches religion in the public schools. In this relationship, as the October 31, 1979, *New York Times* stated, "the church functions as something of a loyal opposition, pressing its demands but cooperating in times of crisis. In 1970 and 1976, when the workers rioted against price increases and over economic problems, Cardinal Wyszynski urged restraint and was heeded." In the midst of the great strike wave of 1980, Cardinal Wyszynski appeared on government television to deliver a sermon in which he urged the need of fulfilling "our everyday duties" and strengthening "the feeling of vocational responsibility so as to have proper order."[54]

For such services, the Church gets concessions from the regime. A government official told the *Times* reporter *(New York Times*, September 3, 1980) that "it was undeniable" that the Church "had attempted to help the government in resolving the crisis and that as a result, there would be 'a bill coming due soon.'" If neither the bureaucracy nor the Church is entirely happy with the other, the bureaucracy is glad to make use of the authority of the Church among the workers and the Church desires the security afforded by its relationship with the state.

This relationship was tested during the imposition of martial law in 1981. The first message of the Primate, Archbishop Josef Glemp, after martial law was declared was issued on December 13; "The net effect of the message was that resistance to the authorities...would be both futile and dangerous for the country" (*New York Times*, January 6, 1982). The government broadcast it repeatedly over the radio.

The Church was, however, under great pressure from the Polish masses. On December 16, the General Council of the Episcopate, headed by the Primate, drew up a strong statement which proclaimed that the nation was "terrorized by military force" and was filled with "bitterness, disgust and extreme hate," but this statement was held back at the last moment, being read by only a few priests from their pulpits either because of a failure of communications or as an expression of dissent. A "well-informed Communist Party source" told the *New York Times* (January 6, 1982) that there had been "intense contacts" between the government and the Church. "The church's 'moderate role,' he added, had been 'extremely helpful' to the government, although 'not everything the church does has met with satisfaction.'" A Western diplomat said, "The church still sees itself in a mediating role, although that's a difficult role to play."

Two days before the general strike called by Solidarity for November 10, 1982, Archbishop Glemp met General Jaruzelksi, the head of the government. Following the meeting the government announced that the Pope would be coming to visit in June, and the Primate and the General issued a joint statement expressing "mutual concern" about the course of events. This was a reiteration by Glemp of his previous statement that he was "completely opposed" to the strike call, from which he had partly backed away. The promise of the Pope's visit was a concession by the state that could be revoked, as it had been before, if there was a massive display of unrest. The Church is still attempting to act as a mediating force and to preserve "its unique tolerated position in the Soviet bloc" (*New York Times*, November 14, 1982).

But the balancing act of Glemp is becoming more and more difficult to maintain. In February 1984 two thousand Poles packed into a protest mass directed at Glemp when he transferred a highly popular priest, an outstanding supporter of Solidarity, from his parish in a Solidarity stronghold in response to government pressure. "The protest mass," said the *New York Times* reporter (February 20, 1984), "appeared to reflect a growing division between Cardinal Glemp and many of the younger priests and laity."

CHAPTER SIX

Protestantism: Its Origin and Development in Europe

The Lutheran Revolt Against Catholicism

The doctrine of the justification by faith is the central tenet of Luther's theology. Man is normally a sinful creature, but by having faith in God and giving himself entirely up to Him, man's heart is cleansed. It is only in this way that one is saved, not through the good works dictated by the Catholic Church. "Fixed holidays and fasts, fraternities, pilgrimages, worship of saints, rosaries, monasticism and such-like" are, says *The Confession of Augsburg*, "childish and unnecessary works."[1] They are purely mechanical actions like the paternosters, prayers which, raced through as a meaningless gabble, contributed the word "patter" to the English language.

Thus Luther broke the Church's monopoly on God. The Church had held that, thanks to Christ, to its saints and martyrs, and to the monks and chantry priests who devoted their lives to the performance of religious observances, there was built up from these good works a store of grace that was under its keeping. "This treasure," said a papal bull, "is entrusted to be healthfully dispersed through blessed Peter, bearer of heaven's keys, and his successors as vicars on earth...to them that are truly penitent and have confessed."[2] An essential part of being "truly penitent" was confessing to the priest and "doing" such "penance" as he, who got his authority from the "bearer of heaven's keys," prescribed. But Lutheranism did away with the Church as an intermediary between the individual and his God.

The artisans and small merchants of the towns, who desired a cheap church, just as the petty bourgeoisie today desires lower taxes, were attracted to Lutheranism. Earlier heresies of the Middle Ages such as the Albigenses of France, the Wycliffites of England, and the Hussites of Bohemia, had likewise had their centers in the towns. Luther, in casting opprobrium on monasticism, opposed it to the market where the merchant did his business:

> Hitherto it hath been the chief holiness and righteousness... [for a man] to run into monasteries...and thus, resting in a show of good works, we knew not but we were holy from top to toe, having regard only to works and the body and not to the heart.... When the heart is pure...the market is as much esteemed as the monastery.[3]

However, although Lutheranism and other forms of Protestantism had their initial base in the towns, their doctrines were seized upon by other classes in countries—Scandinavia, Hungary, Scotland—in revolt against the Catholic Church.

The peasant leaders of Germany itself read the Bible, communed with God, and did what their hearts told them to do. They found that the peasants, oppressed more heavily than ever by princes, knights, burghers, and the Church, were justified in rising up against their oppression. They demanded the abolition of serfdom "unless it be shown from the Gospel that we are serfs" and cited the New Testament on the community of goods.[4]

Luther, however, declared that the true promptings of God are revealed by men's actions. These actions are a sign of God's grace, not a way of earning it. They spring from faith, which is "nothing else but truth of the heart,"[5] but that "truth" turns out to be what the conscience of a good burgher tells him is right. Foremost among the principles God has written in the hearts of men, to be perceived when these hearts are pure, is the sacredness of private property. Private property is what raises man above the animals.[6] It is the basis of the social order within which those who have received God's grace perform good works by laboring in their callings in the spirit of serving God.

So carried away was Luther by his zeal against the rebellious peasants that he proclaimed that those who died fighting against them were "true martyrs for God"[7] who were assured of salvation. Apparently, killing peasants was a "good work" so extraordinary that it guaranteed salvation regardless of whether or not it was performed with a pure heart. Moreover, Luther was so fearful of the threat to the social order that he, the upholder of the individual conscience against the Catholic Church, gave the absolutist princes, who had the support of the middle class, power over the religion of their subjects.

Calvinism and Revolution

If Lutheranism thus went back on its original premises, Calvinism followed its own revolutionary logic. "Calvin's creed," as Engels said, "was one fit for the boldest of the bourgeoisie of his day."[7]

The heart of Calvinism is its doctrine of predestination. A chosen few, the elect, have been predestined by God to salvation by "his gratuitous mercy, totally irrespective of human merit." The rest of mankind has been predestined to damnation "by a just and irreprehensible, but incomprehensible, judgment."[8] The aim of existence, therefore, is not salvation, which is not affected by human actions, but the glorification of God by doing his work on earth. As with Lutheranism, the moral life is the sign of salvation, not its cause. But stronger even than the assurance that came from the faith which enabled one to enter intermittently into direct communion with God was the assurance that came from the knowledge that one was of the elect, attested to by good people like one's self recognizing one's godliness. To its bourgeois adherents in Geneva and the great business centers of Antwerp, London, and Amsterdam, which were far more advanced than the towns of Germany, Calvinism gave the unity and strength that enabled them to transform society.

The concept of the calling developed by the later Calvinists was a powerful tool in that transformation. For Luther the calling meant that occupation in life to which one has been appointed by God, against which it would be impious to rebel. For the Calvinists the calling was an enterprise to be chosen by the individual with a sense of his responsibility to God. "It is a preposterous and brutish thing," says Richard Steele in *The Tradesman's Calling* (1684), "to fix or fall upon...a calling or condition of life, without a careful pondering it in the balance of sound reason."[9]

Far from poverty having some special merit in the eyes of God, the good Christian must regard it as his religious duty to make as much money as he can.

> If God shows you a way in which you may lawfully get more than
> in another way (without wrong to your soul or to any other), if
> you refuse this, and choose the less gainful way, you cross one of
> the ends of your Calling, and you refuse to be God's steward.

And what is lawful and right is not to be determined by previous doctrines, which no longer suit contemporary conditions, but by the individual conscience: "An upright conscience must be the clerk of the market."[10]

In his calling, the Calvinist labored unremittingly for the glory of God. It was the organization of his life for this purpose that set him apart from what the Puritan William Perkins spoke of as the unproductive classes—beggars, monks, unenterprising gentry and aristocracy with renter mentalities and feudalistic traditions, and their dependent servants—"such as live in no calling, but spend their time in eating, drinking, sleeping, and sporting."[11] During the period of capital accumulation, what Weber called "worldy asceticism" was appropriate; later, luxury was an "unfortunate" necessity as a means of displaying wealth and hence gaining credit.

"Discipline" was another key word in the Calvinist lexicon. As Adam Smith noted, there is a connection between church discipline, Puritan self-discipline, and labor discipline.[12] Each was an integral part of the strategy in the war against all evil in which the Puritan was a soldier. The laxness of the Catholic Church, the debauchery of the courtier and the carousing of the country squire, the frequent and irregular festivities during the course of the seasons of an agricultural economy—all of these were not to the Puritan way of thinking. To them the Puritan opposed the discipline of the reformed church, of his sober and methodical life, and of the regular and continuous work rhythms of an emerging urban society that eliminated the Catholic holidays and substituted the strict observance of Sundays, during which one rededicated one's self (and one's workers) to the service of the great Taskmaster.

The wealth which one gained in laboring for the Lord was an indication of his favor, as had been the prospering of the patriarchs in the Old Testament. Wealth, to be sure, should be pursued in the proper spirit. "Seek riches not for themselves but for God" was the way one English Puritan formulated it.[13] Contemporaries hostile to the Puritans accused them, however, of hypocrisy and covetousness, using such epithets as "Presbyterian old usurer" and "devout misers."[14] We may assume that many Puritans adored gold more than God or confused one with another, finding less than an ell of difference between the two. Yet the statement of the Earl of Clarendon, Charles I's adviser and the historian of the Civil War, that "religion was made a cloak to cover the most impious designs"[15] of the members of the Long Parliament no doubt exaggerates the consciousness with which they used religion to advance the interests of their class: ideology acts as a rationalization of a class to itself as well as to other classes. Basically, however, their religion was an expression—a "religious disguise," as Engels phrased it,[16] in an interesting repetition of Clarendon's clothing metaphor—of the interests of those whom Clarendon identified as "people of an inferior degree who, by good husbandry, clothing, and other thriving arts, had gotten very great fortunes," which they developed "with more industry" than "the gentlemen of ancient families and estates" who "were for the most part well affected to the king."[17]

This religion put iron in the souls of the bourgeoisie and of the enterprising gentry engaged in commercial agriculture and gave them the strength of spirit to make a revolution. Calvin had defended absolute monarchy, but when absolute monarchy outlived its value to the bourgeoisie his adherents discovered that it was the work of God to rebel against the ruler who had previously been declared the viceregent of God. The Calvinist leaders in the Netherlands had shown the way in 1581 by deposing the Spanish monarch; the English "root-and-branch" Puritans beheaded Charles and brought down the monarchy and the House of Lords.

The English Revolution and the Radical Dissenting Sects

The English Revolution of the seventeenth century went much further than the few steps taken by Henry VIII, who severed the English Church from Catholicism without radically transforming it, and dissolved the monasteries—most of whose land (one-fifth of that of England) went directly to members of the gentry, merchants, and wealthy yeomen or eventually ended up in their hands. The Revolution of the seventeenth century confiscated crown and Church land and that of many leading royalists, using the money to finance a commercial policy that won the shipping trade of Europe from the Dutch, and removed many restrictions on trade and industry. It gave the English bourgeoisie a tremendous head start over the bourgeoisie of the European countries. Like the French Revolution, it gained a good deal of its impetus from the pressure of the plebeian masses.

This pressure was exerted through numerous religious sects—hostile contemporary observers, no doubt exaggerating, counted twenty-nine in London and 199 in England—that were strong in Cromwell's New Model Army, in London, and in other parts of the country. Wandering "mechanick" preachers spread the word like the early Christian apostles. The title of one contemporary pamphlet sums up how their opponents regarded them: *A Swarm of Sectaries and Schismatics; wherein is discovered the strange preaching (or prating) of such as are by their trades Cobblers, Tinkers, Pedlars, Weavers, Sow-gelders and Chimney-Sweepers.*

Calvinism had declared that worldly success was a sign of membership in the elect arbitrarily chosen by God. The sects denied that the poor were damned and asserted that salvation came through an intense religious experience, which was more likely to come to those not corrupted by wealth. Calvinism had substituted the authority of the Bible for the authority of the Catholic Church, making God the monopoly of the educated. The sects denied the need for formal learning to know the ways of God. It was not through burning the midnight oil that one attained a knowledge of divinity but through the "Inner Light," the spiritual spark capable of bursting into flame and revealing God, that was the possession of every human being. As one contemporary pamphlet exclaimed indignantly about the claims of revelation, "Many of them from mechanic trades...take upon them to reveal the secrets of almighty God, to open and shut heaven, to save souls."[18]

Yet, if the sects spoke in terms of mystical revelations of God, they sought to reform the educational system to make learning accessible to all, and there is discernible in some of the writing produced by them the beginning of scientific material-ism. For the Digger leader Winstanley the "Inner Light" came to be pretty close to the light of reason through which man was able to perceive the workings of nature. "This spirit of reason (the creative reason which is the divine Logos)," he said, "is...within every man."[19] So too Richard Overton's pamphlet *Man's Mortality*, which affirms that man is "a compound wholly mortal contrary to the common distinction of soul and body" and that heaven and hell are "a mere fiction," is, while using theological phraseology, basically materialist in its philos-ophy.[20] In this Winstanley and Overton are like the sixteenth century German Anabaptist Münzer, of whom Engels wrote:

> Under the cloak of Christian forms he preached a kind of panthe-ism, which...at times even approaches atheism.... The real and liv-ing revelation, he said, was reason.... Heaven is...not a thing of another world...and it is the task of believers to establish this Heaven, the kingdom of God, here on earth. (*On Religion*, 111)

Where the "Inner Light" could lead is indicated by a con-temporary work detailing "the barbarous outrages committed by the sectaries" that tells of how they preach that "the com-mon people" had been "kept under blindness and ignorance" but that "God hath now opened their eyes and discovered unto them their Christian liberty; and therefore it is now fit that the nobility and gentry should serve their servants or at least work for their own maintenance."[21] The reversal of the servants being served recalls Jesus's words about the first becoming last and the last becoming first at the millennium, which was confi-dently expected by the various sects. "I tell you," said Winstan-ley, "the scripture is to be really and materially fulfilled.... You jeer at the name of Leveller [one of the sects]. I tell you, Jesus Christ is the head Leveller."[22] The idea of bringing the mighty down from their seats and raising those of low degree was ex-pressed in a frequently used phrase of the time, "the world turned upside down." Today we have the word "revolution."

"The revolutionary decades," says Christopher Hill in *The World Turned Upside Down*, the definitive study of radical ideas during the English Revolution, "produced a fantastic outburst of energy, both physical and intellectual.... For a short time, ordinary people were freer from the authority of church and social superiors than they had ever been before."[23] Fearing that freedom, the bourgeoisie turned to Charles II. The Restoration, however, could not change things back to what they were before. Society had been too profoundly altered, and too many of the changes were to the advantage of the bourgeoisie. In religion, the Restoration was expressed by the two wings of the Anglican Church, the upper-middle-class Low Church and the aristocratic High Church, with the Broad Church functioning as a centrist group.

Quakerism: From Radicalism to Respectability

The radical sects of the seventeenth century, whose members were the poorer artisans, journeymen, and apprentices, the nascent proletariat of a nascent capitalism, died out with the advance of capitalism or became absorbed by the Quakers. The Quakers—whose name, alluding to their trembling with excitement during their religious meetings, was a term of opprobrium fastened upon them by their opponents like that of the Ranter sect—started out in the seventeenth century with the radical doctrines of the other sects. They refused to take their hats off before the richest of the kingdom, and the Quaker leader George Fox, a cobbler and the son of a weaver, warned the rich in the vein of the Old Testament prophets and of Jesus that misery was coming upon them. Although Fox was later a preacher of nonviolence, as were the German Anabaptists after the failure of their uprising, he charged the generals of Cromwell's army with having betrayed the Revolution in not having gone "into the midst of Spain...and knocked at Rome's gates...and trampled deceit and tyrants under."[24]

After the Restoration, however, Fox concluded that the Kingdom of God was not of this world. With the abandonment of its millennial expectations, Quakerism, whose early enthusiasts had appeared in public in the nude to demonstrate their adherence to the "plain truth," became respectable. It became the religion of those artisans and petty tradesmen who under the conditions of the expansion of capitalism became well-to-do businessmen. Quakers became known for their sobriety, industry, orderliness, and (in the tradition of their earlier civil disobedience) their dislike of legal proceedings. They flourished as dependable businessmen who demanded prompt payment and themselves paid promptly. But Quakerism remained a religion of the middle class. Those Quaker families which became more than well-to-do generally gave up their religion in the course of time.[25]

Methodism: From Working Class to Middle Class

The Quakers set the pattern for the Methodists of the 18th century. Methodism stressed man's corruption but stated that by relying on the divine power he can change his nature. It found its original audience among artisans and a portion of the new industrial proletariat.[26] The aristocratic and commercial oligarchy looked upon it with contempt because of the mass hysteria that prevailed at its revival meetings and because of the social composition of its membership. "Their doctrines" wrote the Duchess of Buckingham, "are most repulsive.... It is monstrous to be told that you have a heart as sinful as the common wretches that crawl the earth." Like the aristocratic spinster who discovered sex and pronounced it too good for the lower classes, she regarded a religion which stated that the poor share a common humanity with the rich as "strongly tinctured with impertinence."[27]

Many capitalists, however, soon enough came to a recognition of Methodism's virtues. The Industrial Revolution had destroyed rural domestic industry, and with it the lingering patriarchal relationships, and had congregated large masses of dispossessed peasants and artisans in the cities. Like the Black Muslims of a later date who took lumpenproletarians and instilled them with self-respect, ridding them of their dependence on drugs, the Methodists freed their converts, frequently disoriented by their new lives in the cities, from their addiction to drink, turning them into dependable workers. In the Methodist preaching-houses, said a contemporary, the worker finds "a stimulus...not less powerful than what he formerly sought at the alehouse" but that has "no morning headache and after-reckoning."[28] Methodists were determined, as their originators said, to conduct their lives by "rule and method" (hence, the name "Methodism" given to their religion), and worked zealously with a sober exaltation unmarred by hangovers.

This was naturally to the liking of employers, who often

chose Methodists to impose the "rule and method" of the factory on their workers. "Actuated by interest," stated a contemporary historian of Methodism, "proprietors of factories...chose sober and pious men for their foremen and overlookers."[29]

Nevertheless, the fact that the mass base of early Methodism was working-class made many Methodists become affected by eighteenth century radicalism despite the Toryism of its Oxford founder John Wesley, and made them agitate for greater democracy within their movement.[30] In the next century Engels said of the Salvation Army, which was founded by the Methodist preacher William Booth precisely because Methodism no longer had a grip on unskilled workers or on the lumpenproletariat:

> The English bourgeois...accepted the dangerous aid of the Salvation Army, which...appeals to the poor as the elect...and thus fosters an element of early Christian class antagonism, which one day may become troublesome to the well-to-do people who now find the ready money for it.[31]

So now it seemed as if Methodism, whose founder had often affirmed that "the poor are the Christians," might prove troublesome to its middle-class leaders and to the leaders of capitalist society.

The revolt, however, was suppressed, thanks to the authoritarian organization of each: the generals prevailed against the rank-and-file. The Methodists lost their militancy, just as the Salvation Army has lost its former militancy and become merely a charitable organization for tax-deductible donations. As was true of Quakerism, Methodism became a religion of the middle class, although Methodists, especially the Primitive Methodists, who split off in the early nineteenth century to reach out to the working class, which the Wesleyans were losing,[32] were also represented among the artisans of the industrial towns and villages. The growth of commerce and industry, the social character of the Methodists, who revealed "a singular aptitude" for trade and industry, and the functioning of the Methodist societies as mutual aid groups advancing loans to their members enabled Wesley to say that Methodists who were "in business have increased in substance sevenfold, some of them twenty, yea, an hundredfold."[33]

Wesley's teachings called for the Methodists to "gain all they can, and save all they can" but "likewise give all they can" so that "they will grow in grace."[34] But as the Methodists grew in wealth they forgot about the principle of giving back to the community everything beyond one's necessities.[35] The richest Methodists came to dominate the chapels, the habits of austerity and frugality were in good part lost (Methodists, said the old-timers, were sending their children to fashionable schools where "music, dancing and finery" were prevalent),[36] and Methodism, like Quakerism, became respectable. Nevertheless, despite this transformation, the lure of the Established Church, attended by members of aristocratic society, was great for Methodists who had "made it." "It is an appalling truth," it was stated in 1821, "that very few of the children of rich Methodists ever become members of our Society."[37] Methodism, like Quakerism and indeed like the other middle-class nonconformist sects, was a rung on the social ladder for the upwardly mobile. As the author of a *Serious and Earnest Address to Protestant Dissenters of All Denominations* (1772) said, "The rich and fashionable...are apt to forsake the cause...merely because going to the Established Church is more fashionable."[38]

English Protestantism and the Alienation of the Working Class

The workers in the large cities were attracted neither by the Anglican Church nor the nonconformist chapels.

> From the beginning of the [nineteenth] century, the "spiritual destitution" of the lower orders was a commonplace of religious discussion. Engels was not exaggerating much when he wrote in 1845: "All the writers of the bourgeoisie are unanimous on this point, that the workers are not religious, and do not attend church!"[39]

The official report of the census of 1851, the only one in English history that asked questions about religious worship, stated: "The masses of our working population...are never or but seldom seen in our religious congregations."[40] In the twenty largest cities less than one person in ten went to a place of worship on a given Sunday.

At first it was believed that this deplorable situation existed because there were not enough churches, but the churches were built and stood empty. Various explanations were advanced,

from that which stated the workers did not attend church because they were embarrassed by the contrast between their
rough, shabby clothing and the Sunday best of the middle class,
to that which stated that the evil pleasures of the public house
and the music hall drew them away from the House of God. The
conclusion of serious observers, however, was expressed by an
Anglican bishop heading a committee "to reach classes outside
of religious ministrations," who spoke of "a terribly deep-rooted
notion that the Church was for the rich and comfortable," and
by an eminent Congregationalist minister, who said that the
churches had tended "to grow into societies for the demarcation
and consecration of class. And the more they have done so, the
more distasteful have they become to working men."[41]

The laboring poor of the country were content to go to
church with the local gentry, whom they would greet respectfully;
the workers of the cities, brought together in the factories and
their living-places, were more class conscious and independent. As
a minister concerned with the situation said in 1821, "There is a
mighty unfilled space between the high and the low of every large
manufacturing city" which the church could not bridge.[42]

Workers observing how religious institutions reacted to the
great political and social struggles were confirmed in their feelings. The Anglican bishops vehemently opposed the Reform Bill
of 1832, which enfranchised the middle classes and opened the
door to reform of the scandals of pluralism, non-residence,
sinecures, and nepotism in the Church. Both the Church of England and the dissenting Churches were as vehemently opposed to
the radical Chartist movement, which sought to gain the vote for
workers—which they had not been granted by the 1832 Reform
Bill—and to redress other political and economic grievances.

The churches accepted the dictum of Edmund Burke, "The
laws of commerce are the laws of Nature and consequently the
laws of God."[43] Calvin's Geneva had not been what one would
call a permissive society (the City Fathers, as stern as their God,
beheaded a child for striking its parents),[44] and it regulated business as well as everything else. But as the bourgeoisie grew in
strength and rejected the protections and the restrictions of mer-
cantilism for the doctrine of *laissez-faire*, religious theory followed suit. Since evils like poverty exist as part of the divine

scheme of things, it was held, the Christian "will not presume to believe that he may help in any save a passive way to enforce the constitution of the universe,"[45] the laws of nature which are the laws of God. God here is remarkably like "the unseen hand" which Adam Smith found to control the working of *laissez-faire* capitalism, with which it would be disastrous to interfere.

Many sermons on these lines were preached. One of them, *Chartism Unmasked*, which went through nineteen editions on publication, stated:

> The Chartist leaders preach and teach the doctrine of "equality"; but we have no such doctrine taught in the Book of Nature or the Book of God.... Another Chartist doctrine opposed to the Word of God is that poverty is not the result of the everlasting purpose of a Sovereign God but is only the result of unjust human laws.... This is disproved by the Bible which says "The poor shall never cease out of the land."[46]

It is no wonder that workers found the churches "distasteful"!

Christian Socialism

Christian Socialism was a response to Chartism and the French revolution of 1848. J.M. Ludlow, in Paris during the 1848 revolution, wrote at the time to F.D. Maurice, who became the leading figure of Christian Socialism, that "Socialism...must be Christianized or it would shake Christianity to its foundation, precisely because it appealed to the higher and not to the lower instincts of the [Parisian working] men."[47] Maurice replied that such ideas had long been present in his mind and that he now appreciated more than ever "the necessity of an English theological reformation, as the means of averting an English political revolution and of bringing what is good in foreign revolutions to know itself."[48]

The theological reformation of which Maurice spoke was to be the alteration of the kind of thinking displayed in *Chartism Unmasked*. It was through co-operation, not competition, that human beings, he stated, realize their true natures as brethren in Christ and can best actualize God's inherent social order. The Church, as the finest expression of such a fellowship, should be "the bond of all classes, the instrument for reforming abuses, the admonisher of the rich, the friend of the poor."[49] Maurice was, therefore, opposed to "an attempt to create a new constitution of society, when what we want is that the old constitution should exhibit its true functions and energies." Such an attempt can only hinder "what I regard as a divine purpose."[50]

In the same year that Ludlow was writing to Maurice about the need for socialism to be Christianized if Christianity were not to be shaken to its foundation Marx and Engels published the *Communist Manifesto*. In it they described "conservative, or bourgeois, socialism" as follows:

> A part of the bourgeoisie is desirous of redressing social grievances, in order to secure the continued existence of bourgeois society.... The bourgeoisie naturally conceives the world in which it is supreme to be the best.... In requiring the proletariat to march straightway into the social New Jerusalem, it but requires in reality that the proletariat should remain within the bounds of existing society, but should cast away all its hateful ideas concerning the bourgeoisie.[51]

It will be seen that, although English Christian Socialism was then only in gestation, this is not a bad description of it. Christian Socialism went hand-in-hand with "bourgeois socialism," just as Social Catholicism went hand in hand with "feudal socialism."

Modern English Protestantism

Christian Socialism, despite the stir it created, was not conspicuously successful until the latter part of the nineteenth century when it caught hold but not under that name. The period between 1880 and 1895 shook up English politics and changed the policies of the British political parties and the churches. This was the period of the militant London dock strike, the birth of the Independent Labor Party, and the growth of various socialist organizations. Moreover, the expansion of the British Empire, as Lenin pointed out in *Imperialism*, made it possible for the British ruling class to bribe a labor aristocracy with the superprofits extracted from the Empire. Social action such as the Eight-Hour Act, it was now discovered, could be taken against social ills without violating the decrees of God. As Sir William Harcourt complacently stated, "We are all socialists now."

The Church of England, fearing that its special privileges were threatened by the enfranchisement of the working class, was more concerned than ever with reaching the masses. "We cannot do without 'the masses,'" said the Bishop of Liverpool in 1882. "The Church, whose adherents are a minority in the land, will not be long allowed to retain her endowments and her connection with the State in this age."[52] Toward the latter part of the nineteenth century, therefore, those within the Church anxious about its isolation from the masses urged that it support social reforms and act as a benevolent mediator between capital and labor.[53]

This middle-class reformism was given theological sanction. In place of the old Protestant emphasis on "faith," there was now an emphasis on "good works," "not the old theological ones, to be sure, but those of modern humanitarianism: social uplift, popular education, public health, and crusades against alcoholism, against juvenile delinquency, against cruelty to animals."[54] The belief in continuous progress within the social system, popularized by Herbert Spencer and T.H. Buckle, a progress that would enable humanity, led by the English people, to attain heights greater than any hitherto conceived, had its theological counterpart in the belief in "a steady, ever higher evolution of man's religious experience, from primitive myths to early Christianity and from 'superstitious' Catholicism to 'enlightened' Protestantism."[55] The liberal modernist Protestants, as against the many Protestant evangelicals who opposed social reform as too concerned with this world and the many Protestant literalists who preferred Genesis to Darwin, saw man as growing in his social wisdom and in his understanding of the Bible, which was no longer the unchanging source of pure religion but a progressively evolving revelation of God, attained to the highest degree by the liberal Protestants.

The reformism of the liberal Protestants, however, has not greatly affected the religious indifference of the working class. Although church-going is no longer one of the "traditional properties of the middle class to the same degree as before," says Inglis, "differences of religious behavior between classes" are "still discernible."[56] This is borne out by a 1957 sociological survey comparing church attendance and social class. The survey found that the percentages attending church at least "now and again" were as follows: upper class 73 percent, upper-middle 71 percent, middle 56 percent, lower-middle 52 percent, working class 39 percent.[57]

The value of these figures is somewhat impaired by the fact that class was determined by "subjective identification" (although the high degree of class consciousness in England makes this procedure less questionable than it might be in the United States) and by the lack of data on such matters as the numbers of those of Irish descent (the Irish mostly being traditionally Catholic because of national oppression). Nevertheless the general picture of the differential attitude seems clear.

The comparative lack of church-going among workers does not mean that they are in philosophical opposition to religion. Surveys have found that the percentage of workers expressing belief in various Christian doctrines is much higher than that of those going to church although it is still lower than that of members of other classes expressing such belief.[58] However, while they are generally not conscious adherents of a materialistic philosophy, they are what was called in the nineteenth century "unconscious secularists." Although institutional religion continues to be in good measure related to political conservatism (54 percent of the workers who preferred the Conservative party attended church at least "now and again," but only 33 percent of those who preferred the Labor Party did so),[59] non-institutional religious belief only marginally affects their political and other behavior.

One reason that English workers are not conscious materialists is that their political leadership, far from teaching materialism, is itself tied to religion. Many of the leaders come from the Primitive Methodist communion, which has historically been strong among the aristocracy of labor. In fact, when Winston Churchill taunted the Labor Party leaders with being un-English, getting their ideas from a German, Karl Marx, a leading Laborite replied defensively that the party owed more to Methodism than to Marxism. He might also have stated that ideas know no boundaries and that the British ruling class itself has used the ideas of Calvin, a Frenchman, to say nothing of using—or rather misusing—the ideas of a Middle Eastern Jew of 2,000 years ago.

Continental Protestantism Since the Industrial Revolution

Continental Protestantism since the Industrial Revolution has proceeded along fairly much the same lines as English Protestantism. Just as the Anglican Church attacked the Reform Bill of 1832, so did the state Lutheran Church in Germany attack political and social democracy. So too the same alienation of the working class as in England developed in Scandinavia and Germany, although at a slower pace than in the home of the Industrial Revolution. In Germany the evangelicals, the descendants of the Pietists who had taught John Wesley "the religion of the heart" and had gained adherents among carpenters, weavers, cutters, and shoemakers in patriarchal village industry, were as out of touch with the new urban proletariat as were the other Protestant clergymen. Although Pietism had been scorned by those who did not consider it proper for aristocratic children to be christened with the same water as ordinary children, the Pietist leaders had been proud of the respectability of their movement and the docility of their followers.[60] But the nineteenth century evangelical clergymen did not know how to talk to the workers, let alone convert them to respectability and obedience. Their traditional disdain for the worldliness of politics and their sermons on the "natural social harmony" of *laissez-faire* capitalism did not help them to reach an audience.

As in England, however, a change in religious opinion coincided with a change in the social policy of the ruling class.

> The turbulent seventies left few German employers confident their single-handed measures could stem the radical labor movement. By the late seventies evangelical opinion strongly favored state intervention, a vogue promoted by the "social conservatives" [the aristocracy favoring social legislation] and established as a norm of benevolent Christian statecraft by the "socialists of the chair" [academicians seeking moderate reforms].[61]

One of these "socialists of the chair," Adolf Wagner, in addressing an assembly of Protestant clergymen, appealed to their nationalistic sentiments to combat the doctrine of *laissez-faire*. "The emphasis upon ethics," he said, distinguished 'German economies'...from the classical economy of English origin." But it was not only to morality that he appealed; it was even more to prudence. "Only the timely redressment of lower class grievances by a state-directed social reform could avert the [socialist] revolution."[62] The social legislation of the "Iron Chancellor" Bismarck, by means of which he sought to cut the ground from under the Social Democrats after his stringent anti-socialist laws proved unsuccessful, received, therefore, the support of the Church.

But, again as in England, despite the changes in Protestantism, mass support for it has not advanced in Germany or in other European countries. Unlike in the United States, there has been a marked decline of church-going in the advanced capitalist countries of Europe. This has been particularly true in the predominantly Protestant countries, which are more advanced industrially than the Catholic countries.[63]

With the softening of dogmatic differences between the Protestant churches and the weakening of the positions of the churches themselves, the ecumenical movement seeking to unite fragmented Protestantism—and even looking to join with the Catholic Church in a unified Christendom—gained force after the First World War. There were, as Vidler says,

> strong arguments for union, e.g., the absurd wastage of Christian effort through overlapping and competing organizations at a time when the pinch was beginning to be felt of a shortage of ministers. It was also being perceived that united churches are in a stronger position than divided churches to collaborate with friendly governments and to withstand hostile ones.[64]

It remains to be seen, however, whether hierarchical interests will permit the churches to unite the better to meet their common problems.

CHAPTER SEVEN

Religion in the United States

The Puritans and the Conquest of the Indians

The Puritans who settled in New England were convinced that they were a chosen people with whom God had made a compact. They were to build a "New Israel" in America to glorify Him, and He was to help them to achieve this holy work. Their belief in themselves gave them the strength to build a civilization in the New World. It also gave them a sense of righteousness in slaying the native inhabitants of this New World, as the Israelites had slain the inhabitants of Canaan at the behest of Jehovah. This sense of righteousness is manifest in the account by Mary Rowlandson, a clergyman's wife, of her captivity by the Indians. "Her remarkable narrative of her captivity," says Larzer Ziff, "is most remarkable in the many details of Indian kindness toward her she is able to record without apparently being once shaken in her dominating conviction that she is among satanic people."[1]

The Puritans had begun by trading with the Indians for furs, but with the near-extermination of the beaver population as a consequence of this trade, the seizure of Indian hunting grounds for agriculture became the new determining force in Puritan-Indian relations: the near-extermination of the beavers was the prelude to the near-extermination of the Indians. John Winthrop, the governor of Massachusetts, argued that since the Indians held land in common, its seizure was not a violation of God's prohibition against the stealing of private property. Roger Williams was banished from Massachusetts not only for his views on the separation of church and state but because he held that the "natives

are the true owners" of the land.[2] When the Indians made sporadic strikes against the most vulnerable of the colonists' settlements on their land, the colonists responded with genocidal war.

The war against the Pequot tribe in 1643 set the mode for
eighty years of war by the New England colonists, a mode,
which was repeated in other colonies and continued through
the nineteenth century. Unlike the Pequots, who were not accustomed to thinking in terms of extermination of the foe, the Puritans, convinced that they were doing the Lord's work, emulated
the Israelites in their Old Testament wars.[3] When they made a
surprise attack on the village of the Pequots,

> the Pequots, according to Underhill [one of the two Puritan military
> leaders], "brake forth into a most doleful cry; so as if God had not
> fitted the hearts of men for the service, it would have bred in them a
> commiseration towards them." But God did steel the Puritans'
> hearts.... More than four hundred men, women, and children were
> killed. An entire tribe was obliterated.[4]

This Puritan ruthless self-righteousness was echoed in the nineteenth century proverbial saying "The only good Indian is a
dead Indian."

Secularized Puritanism and the Doctrine of "Manifest Destiny"

The modification of the Calvinism of the heroic period of the
bourgeoisie, which took place in England also, took place in
New England, where in fact it was more complete. Edward
Dowden in his *Anglican and Puritan* described the descent of
the English bourgeoisie from the heights of religious and revolutionary fervor as follows:

> To make the best of both worlds was the part of prudence, and of
> the two worlds that on which our feet are planted is, at least, the
> nearer and the more submissive to our control. Divine providence
> is doubtless to be acknowledged, but it is highly desirable to sup-
> plement Divine providence by self-help.[5]

So De Tocqueville noted in his *Democracy in America* (1835) that

> American preachers are constantly referring to the earth, and it is
> only with great difficulty that they can divert their attention from
> it.... It is often difficult to ascertain from their discourses whether

the principal object of religion is to procure eternal felicity in the other world or prosperity in this.[6]

The Calvinism of the mercantile bourgeoisie of New England became attenuated as this bourgeoisie became a comfortably established class. God became not so much an awesome taskmaster, an adored but sternly rigorous father figure whose ways were ultimately impossible to fathom, as a distant benevolent presence, which could be confidently expected to help those who helped themselves. This secularized Puritanism, which retained the Calvinist self-righteous sense of the Americans being a chosen people but not its overriding concern with the soul's salvation, became the matrix that set its stamp upon the innumerable Christian sects which came from Europe to America or were born in America itself.

The cosmic purpose, it was held, called for the conquest of a continent. This was America's "manifest destiny." When the United States annexed California in 1849 after having seized it from Mexico, a church paper, *The Home Missionary*, stated:

> God kept the Coast for a people of the Pilgrim blood.... The Spaniard came thither a hundred years before our fathers landed in Plymouth; but though he came for treasure, his eyes were holden that he should not find it. But in the fullness of time, when a Protestant people have been brought to this Continent, and are nourished up to a strength by the requisite training, God commits to their possession that Western Shore.[7]

Thus, having undergone the requisite training—no doubt, in the wars against the Indians—the Americans, fulfilling God's purpose, found the California gold that the Spanish had missed. God helps those who help themselves.

The belief that Americans are the chosen people of God is still voiced today. Thus Ronald Reagan has said: "I have always believed that this land was placed here between the two great oceans by some divine plan. It was placed here to be found by a special kind of people...."[8] Obviously, this special kind of people—or, rather, the ruling class falsely claiming to speak for it—has the right to ride roughshod over other nations, as the Puritans did over the Indians.

The American Revolution: A Setback to Religion

Although, from the beginning, religion gave support to American nationalism, religion paradoxically received a severe setback at the time of the American Revolution, the birth of the nation.

One element in the coalition that effected the American Revolution was the Southern plantation-owning aristocracy, which was deeply in debt to English merchants and bankers as a result of being constrained by law to sell only to England, giving English merchants the whip-hand in setting the price for tobacco, rice, and indigo. The other element in the coalition was the Northern mercantile bourgeoisie, which had prospered under the colonial system but had always resented the British officials as leeches, and which joined forces with the planters after the British, seeking to reduce their swollen national debt following the war with the French, imposed taxes and import duties on the colonies. The mercantile bourgeoisie, hoping to return to the day of its prosperity under the old system, was the vacillating partner in the coalition, always eager to accept concessions from the Crown. But the dynamic of the Revolution was toward independence, which at first its leaders had not contemplated.

As in the case of the English and French revolutions, the Revolution was driven forward by the plebeian masses, the artisans and mechanics. These understood that a revolution is not a tea party—unless it is a tea party like the Boston Tea Party, which without regard for bourgeois property notions dumped £18,000 worth of tea of the hated East India Company into the harbor.

> Artisans and laborers...formed themselves into societies known as the "sons of Liberty."... The agitation, contrary to the intent of the merchants and lawyers, got quite beyond the bounds of law and order.... Indeed, the conduct of the mechanics and laborers was so lawless that it is difficult to paint a picture of the scene in tones subdued enough for modern Sons and Daughters of the Revolution.[9]

Samuel Adams, the organizer of the popular masses, backed by "his vulgar men," as they were called, helped to stiffen the resolve of the timid and wavering merchants, who regarded them with mingled admiration and mistrust.

Many of the artisans were highly skilled craftsmen who associated with physicians, scientists, and other intellectuals. David

Rittenhouse, a watchmaker, became the leading scientist of his time after Franklin, and entrée into the scientific world was quite common among members of his craft. Such artisans were touched by the deistic ideas of the Enlightenment.[10] Deism was especially prevalent among printers,[11] among them Franklin.

Allied with these deistic republicans were evangelistic republicans. The revivalist movement that religious historians call the Great Awakening (1735–45) had been basically a revolt by the backwoods farmers, who were to supply most of the manpower of the revolutionary army, against the controls of the Church and the mercantile aristocracy of the coastal towns. "The frontier," says Perry Miller, "conspired with the popular disposition to lessen the prestige of the cultured classes and to enhance the social power of those who wanted their religion in a more simple, downright, and 'democratic' form."[12] So too William G. McLoughlin tells us that "the Evangelicals emphasized the essential equality or 'brotherhood' of all men, especially all regenerate men, and implied that a community of yeoman farmers was preferable to any commercial or entrepreneurial system."[13]

Itinerant preachers—Separates, Baptists, and Methodists—spread the word that the Bible itself said that the poor and the ignorant would confound the wealthy, the learned, and the powerful. The message had its effect not only on the farmers but on the city poor—the laborers, the servants, and some of the artisans.[14]

Both the deistic republicans and the evangelistic republicans were early adherents of independence and looked forward to far-reaching social changes after independence. Evangelistic Presbyterians, characterized by General Charles Lee as "low Scotch-Irish whose names generally begin with 'Mac' and who are either the sons of imported servants or themselves imported servants," harked back to Cromwell and as early as 1765 were saying, "No king but King Jesus." On the other hand, Thomas Young, a self-educated physician closely associated with Samuel Adams, was a deist who was brought to court in his youth for blasphemy. Yet Adams, despite his own religiosity, insisted that Young be judged by his politics, not by his religion.[15]

Both kinds of republicans were for the separation of church and state. In 1770, nine of the colonies had established churches, to which everyone, whether or not a member of the church, had to pay tithes. In six of these—Virginia, Maryland, New York, New Jersey, the Carolinas, and Georgia—the Episcopalian Church was the established church, although in none of them were the Episcopalians in a majority. As the church of the English bureaucracy and of the large landowners, who in the Northeast were Tories, it was loyal to the king. The rector of Trinity Church in New York, like representatives of privileged classes in all revolutions, found that the deprivation of these privileges constituted the most egregious tyranny. "You will find these pretended enemies of oppression the most unrelenting oppressors," he fulminated, "and their little finger heavier than the king's loins."[16]

These churches were disestablished. In Virginia, where the plantation owners supporting the revolution were Anglicans, there was some resistance, but the dissenting churches had the assistance of the freethinking Jefferson and Madison. Foremost among the dissenting churches in fighting for the separation of church and state were the Baptists, whose clergy were not highly educated but were close to the common people. The Baptists wanted religious freedom not only from their Anglican revolutionary associates in Virginia but from their Congregational revolutionary associates in New Hampshire, Massachusetts, and Connecticut, where the Congregational Church was state established. They argued that the revolutionary battle cry "no taxation without representation" applied also to religion, that taxes for a state religion contradicted the principle over which the war was being fought.[17]

The spirit of revolution, which challenged special privileges, asserting that all men are created equal, favored the Baptist Church as against the Congregational Church, where seats for worship were assigned on the basis of status and wealth. However, the Methodist Church, despite its being based on the poor, was almost destroyed because of its ties with English Methodism, whose founder was opposed to American independence.

But if the Baptists gained at the expense of other churches, there was a general decline of religion during and immediately after the Revolutionary War from which the Baptists themselves were not immune. In Richmond, with a population of three or four thousand, the only religious services held for some years after the war were Episcopalian and Presbyterian services on alternating Sundays in a room in the capitol building.

> Nor was this deadness confined to the Episcopal Church.... Travellers as various as the royalist French Duke of La Rochefoucauld, the republican Brissot de Warville, the English manufacturer Henry Wansey all unite in testifying to it as common among the Congregationalists and Presbyterians as well, in Boston, in New York, and in Philadelphia. The old historian of the Virginia Baptists tells us...that "the war, though very propitious to the liberty of the Baptists, had an opposite effect upon the life of religion among them....With some few exceptions, the declension was general throughout the state."[18]

Deism and skepticism had long been widespread among intellectuals and the sophisticated members of the upper classes, particularly the Southern planters, who regarded it as a thing of intellectual distinction to be known within one's social circle as a skeptical freethinker.[19] Locke, the apologist for the so-called Glorious Revolution in England, to whom Jefferson was indebted for the ideas of the Declaration of Independence, was a source of rationalist thinking. His inquiry into the means of human knowledge, said the militant deist Elihu Palmer, did more than anything else to "subvert the credit of divine revelation."[20] Other British rationalists such as Hume and Gibbon and writers of the French Enlightenment such as Holbach and Voltaire were also influential among American freethinkers and deists. But these freethinkers regarded religious skepticism as beyond the capacity of the masses and considered that to be just as well. Many of the Founding Fathers were such "closet" skeptics and deists.[21]

The revolutionary spirit, however, prompted the masses to question all authority, clerical as well as secular. American officers and soldiers were, moreover, affected by their contact with French officers and soldiers. Ethan Allen, excited by his encounter with French anti-religious ideas, exclaimed, "My affections are Frenchified," and in his *Reason the Only Oracle of Man* proclaimed that he was "no Christian."[22] Thomas Pickering told of how religious doubt first came to him when he heard General von Steuben, the Prussian aristocrat who came to aid the Americans because of his revolutionary sympathies, speak about the deist ideas he had learned in France.

Palmer, a fervent republican, founded deistic societies in

New York, Newburgh, Philadelphia, and Baltimore, whose members were mostly artisans. They were inspired by the ideals of the French Revolution and were vehemently opposed to the Federalists, whom they regarded as America's own aristocracy.[23]

Palmer's deistic societies constituted the most militant expression of the anti-religious feeling that was strong in the last three decades of the eighteenth century. This feeling affected the writing of the United States Constitution, in which there is no mention of Christianity and the only two references to religion are negative, forbidding religious tests as a qualification for public office and prohibiting Congress from establishing any religion. In the 1796 treaty with Tripoli the United States government declared: "As the government of the United States of America is not in any sense founded on the Christian religion...no pretext arising from religious opinions shall ever produce an interruption of harmony existing between the two countries."[24] The truth is rather different from the fairy tale of ultra-religious patriots today that the country was founded by pious men who meant Christianity to be part of the American system.

The Religious Reaction

A religious reaction, however, soon set in which gathered force in the 1790s. It was led by men who were the pillars of the Congregational Church and of the Federalist party of the New England bourgeoisie. In the vein of attacks in our own day on "godless communism" it inveighed against the radical republicanism and infidelity that was said to be exported by Jacobin France. Just as the McCarthyism of the 1950s had its *Red Network*, so did this campaign have its book exposing a "deep-laid plot" to subvert the United States. This was John Robison's *Proofs of a Conspiracy Against All the Religions and Governments of Europe, Carried on in the Secret Meetings of Free Masons, Illuminati, and Reading Societies*, which was cited again and again by preachers, pamphleteers, and politicians. The Society of Illuminati, it was said, had "secretly extended its branches through a great part of Europe and even into America." Paine's *Age of Reason* came "from the fountain head of Illumination" and was "written and sent to America expressly in aid of this demoralizing plan." It was a plan, said the Reverend Timothy Dwight, the president of Yale University, which "was formed and to an alarming degree executed for exterminating Christianity...for rooting out of the world civil and domestic government, the right of property, marriage, natural affectation [sic], chastity, and decency."[25]

Just as there were those who believed that, while McCarthy may have been too wild in some of his charges, he performed a salutary service for the country, so

> the Rev. David Tappan, Hollis Professor of Divinity at Harvard...was not prepared to accuse the Illuminati of *all* the wickedness that Robison had attributed to them, but did not doubt that the facts "indicate a real and most alarming plan of hostility against the dearest interests of man."

And just as McCarthy found everywhere persons who were crypto-communists or who were "soft on communism," so did Theodore Dwight, the brother of Yale's president and, like him a staunch Federalist, state: "I know not who belonged to the society [of Illuminati] in this country, but if I were about to make proselytes to illuminatism in the United States, I should in the first place apply to Thomas Jefferson, Albert Gallatin, and their political associates." Jefferson, said a disciple of Dwight more plainly, was "the real Jacobin, the very child of modern illumination, the foe of man, and the enemy of his country."[26]

Religious Revivalism Among the Frontier Farmers and in the Big Cities

Jefferson was elected president two years later, but chaos, contrary to the Federalists, did not ensue. Under his administration and until 1860 the "agricultural interest," as he called it—the planters, using the small farmers as a mass base—was predominant. The opening of the western lands and the addition of agricultural states, made possible by the Revolution's abolition of royal restrictions on the acquisition of land and by its abolition of primogeniture and entail, gave greater weight to the "agricultural interest." The Northern bourgeoisie could not recover its initial dominance until the development of industry strengthened its position.

With the opening of the western lands, which acted as a safety valve, the boiling fervor among the artisans and the budding proletariat of the Northeast gradually subsided. For a while workers organized trade unions and even, in 1829, a political party, the Workingmen's Party, led by the feminist Frances Wright, by Robert Dale Owen, the son of the Utopian socialist, and by other freethinking intellectuals. Frances Wright was denounced by Protestant clergymen as "the High Priestess of Beelzebub," and the Workingmen's Party was denounced as an "infidel trumpet-call to all the envious and vicious poor."[27] But the nascent labor movement allowed itself to be co-opted by the Democratic Party of Andrew Jackson, whose forerunner was the republican anti-Federalist party of Jefferson.

The frontier farmers of the Democratic Party were hostile to the moneyed interests of the East, but French Enlightenment thought was foreign to them. They were opposed to the controls of absentee bankers and merchants, of ecclesiastical hierarchies speaking for a distant God, and of solemnly ritualistic religions that were for them remote and empty. The individualism, anti-rationalism, and democratic structure of the evangelical churches were, therefore, congenial to them. The paradox, then, is that "infidelity" was overcome not by the efforts of the Federalist divines of Yale and Harvard but by those who were republicans.

> "Had those principles of infidelity," says an 1845 history of the Methodist church, "with which the minds of many of the leading men of our nation had been affected and which at one time were descending with fearful rapidity to the lower ranks of society been permitted to operate unchecked by any other barrier than a mere lifeless form of Christianity...is there not reason to apprehend that such streams...of pollution would have poured their poisonous waters over the land?... It must, I think, be admitted by all...that the labors of the itinerating Methodist preachers tended mightily to purify the corrupt mass of mind."[28]

The revivalist Methodist Church itself underwent a revival on the frontier, as did the Baptist Church and the Presbyterian Church, which, however, suffered a split, its more decorous Easterners being unable to countenance the stamping, screaming, moaning, shaking, and stripping off of upper garments at western camp-meetings, which made English Methodist meetings seem positively Episcopalian. The loneliness of frontier life and the sense of being subject to the uncertainties of nature were overcome by the frenzies of the camp-meetings, at which great numbers worked themselves up to a collective pitch of excitement, each one assured of his or her individual salvation. The frontiersmen's individualism was expressed by their splits from older churches and their spawning of new churches such as the Disciples of Christ, but at the camp-meetings they were subject to mass manipulation, just as, politically, the farmers of the Southwest were manipulated by the Democratic Party of the slave-owning aristocracy and those of the Midwest were later manipulated by the Republican Party of the bourgeoisie.

Indeed Charles Grandison Finney, the leading revivalist of the 1820s and 1830s, compared his methods with those of the Jacksonian politicians in advertising and conducting their election rallies, saying that preachers likewise seek to "get all the people to feel that the devil has no right to rule in this world but that they ought all to give themselves to God and vote in the Lord Jesus Christ as the governor of the Universe."[29] A commitment to God was a vote for Jesus against the Devil, the incumbent scoundrel who must be turned out of his place in the hearts of men.

The preachers not only used the methods of the politicians but of the enterprising peddlers. The itinerant preachers of the rival sects would, as De Tocqueville phrased it, "hawk about the word of God from place to place"[30] like competing snake-oil salesmen. Revivalism became a characteristically American phenomenon. In the latter part of the nineteenth century it developed the techniques of modern salesmanship and took its message of a happy life after death to the poor in the cities. Dwight D. Moody, a successful shoe salesman before laboring for the Lord, was the first of the modern evangelists. "Moody combined the showmanship of P.T. Barnum with the calculating financial acumen of Andrew Carnegie. Advance men, publicity agents, advertising campaigns, guaranteed gates, were all a part of the accoutrements of the new big-city revivalism."[31]

Not only did this evangelism use business techniques; it was financed by big business.

> In Chicago, Cyrus McCormick and George Armour pitched in with funds.... In Philadelphia, it was John Wanamaker, the department store king. In New York the welcoming committee was led

by Cornelius Vanderbilt and J.P. Morgan. In Chicago, for example, he said to McCormick and Armour and their friends: "I say
to the rich men of Chicago, their money will not be worth much if
communism and infidelity sweep the land.... There can be no better investment for the capitalists of Chicago than to put the saving
salt of the Gospel into these dark homes and desperate centers."[32]

The promise of life after death for the poor, luxurious life here
and now for the rich—it seemed a good bargain to the capitalists.

In the small towns and villages of the Midwest and Southwest, however, the "old-time religion" that had characterized
the fluid and dynamic frontier cooled and hardened into the religion of respectable farmers and small merchants, the religion
of what has come to be known as the Bible Belt. The preachers
remained as ignorant as before, but revivals became traditional,
predictable rituals and the evangelical churches became established institutions.[33] The fundamentalism of William Jennings
Bryan, who as a Populist leader used religious imagery in his famous "cross of gold" speech to attack Eastern bankers, typifies
this religious conservatism and the loss by the Populist movement of its progressive features in its fixation upon a return to
the childhood of American capitalism.

The Civil War and Religion

The West was opened to the capitalists and to the farmers tied to
them by transportation and credit by the victory of the Northern
bourgeoisie in the Civil War. The Civil War had settled the question of whether the system of slavery or the capitalist system
would be extended there. In the clash between "these antagonistic systems," as Senator William N. Seward characterized them
in presciently describing the "irrepressible conflict" that was developing,[34] religion played an ideological role on each side.

At the time of the Revolution the abolition of slavery was
the unfinished business that was left to a later generation to
complete. There was a strong awareness of the discrepancy of
the proclaimed revolutionary ideals and the existence of slavery.
The Massachusetts Superior Court, for instance, declared that
the statement in the state constitution, borrowed from the Declaration of Independence, that "all men are created free and

equal" meant that slavery was prohibited within its jurisdiction. Moreover, some members of the Southern ruling class believed that slavery was a wasteful mode of production that exhausted the soil. Under these circumstances it was felt that accommodations could be reached and that slavery would gradually be done away with.

What altered things was the invention of the cotton gin, which expanded the production of cotton enormously and made the value of a slave, because of the increased profits that could be extracted from him as a cotton picker, quadruple in forty years. The older liberal Jeffersonian plantation aristocracy was supplanted by a new aristocracy of "cotton capitalists." It would seem not coincidental that during the same period the position of the Southern churches was turned around from hostility to slavery to defense of it. The Baptist and Methodist churches, stoutly republican, had previously taken strong stands against the South's "peculiar institution." The Virginia Association of Baptist Churches declared in 1789 that slavery was "a violent deprivation of the rights of nature and inconsistent with a republican government." The General Conference of the Methodist Church stated in 1780 that slavery was "contrary to the laws of God, man, and nature" and forbade members to possess slaves. In 1784 it presented a detailed plan for doing away with the "abomination of slavery."[35]

But the increase in the number of slave owners among their growing memberships soon changed the attitude of the churches.

> A historian of the Baptist church writes that..."the great mass of Baptists soon reconciled themselves to the existence of slavery.... Large numbers of slave-owners became Baptists.... [It was argued that] to free their slaves might have exposed them to worse evils than to retain them under gospel influences."[36]

Thus the Christian duty of Baptist slave owners was now to keep their slaves rather than to free them.

So too the historian of Southern Methodism writes: "The sensitive and excited tone of legislation on the subject all through this period [after 1784] indicates that the church had an increasing and considerable number of slaveholders." By 1836 the Methodist General Conference opposed abolitionism and denied "any right, wish, or intention to interfere in the civil and political relation between master and slave as it exists in the slave-holding states of the union."[37]

The attempt of the Baptist and Methodist churches to compromise between their Northern and Southern sections was unsuccessful. In 1844 and 1845 they split along sectional lines. Each side was able to find Biblical texts to justify its stand. The Southerners pointed to the Old Testament patriarchs' possession of slaves and to Paul's exhortation to slaves to obey their masters. The Northerners argued that the injunction "love thy neighbor" could scarcely be observed by enslaving him.

The Presbyterian and the Lutheran churches likewise underwent schisms, although there the fight was not so much over the ethics of slavery as the politics of secession. The Southern Presbyterians attacked the Northern Presbyterians for having abandoned the traditional Presbyterian doctrine of the Church's independence from the state. The Civil War, said their church paper, *The Southern Presbyterian*, was being waged "not alone for civil rights and property and home but for religion, for the Church, for the gospel."[38] The civil rights referred to were, of course, those of the slave master: the slave had no civil rights since he was his master's property. The Northern Lutherans, on the other hand, true to their doctrine of obedience to the state, denounced the Southern Lutherans not for upholding slavery but for supporting "the cause of treason and insurrection."[39]

But even the Northern churches were called by the radical abolitionist William Lloyd Garrison, whose strong voice made itself heard despite the "conspiracy of silence" about slavery, "the main pillar of American slavery" in their temporizing.[40] Garrison came from a world of artisans, laborers, and small shopkeepers, the descendants of Samuel Adams's "vulgar men."[41] When he started his campaign in Boston, the powerful clergymen there opposed his "fanatical notions," and he was able to get a meeting place for his lectures only from the Society of Free Enquirers, an organization of freethinkers. He continued to try to work with and through the churches but was bitterly disappointed. Although he was himself a Baptist, he excoriated even his own church as controlled by "blackhearted clergy" who "connived with slaveholders."[42] But if the churches were respectably moderate, there were exceptional clergymen and other men of religion such as John Brown who, inspired by the Old Testament, went beyond even the nonviolent resistance of Garrison.

Black Religion

The slave masters were uncertain and suspicious about the churches teaching their slaves Christianity, but they also saw advantages to such instruction. In 1727 the Bishop of London replied to objections that had been raised to religious missionary work. It had been argued, he said,

> that "the time to be allowed for instructing them would be an abatement from the profit of their labor," "that making them Christians only makes them less diligent and more ungovernable," and that baptizing slaves automatically destroys the owner's property rights in them.

The worthy bishop reassured the slave masters on each of these scores, stating that "Christianity and the embracing of the Gospel does not make the least alteration in civil property or in any of the duties which belong to civil relations."[43]

So too the Episcopalian Bishop of Georgia stated in 1847: "There should be much less danger of inhumanity on the one side or of insubordination on the other between parties who knelt upon the Lord's Day around the same table and were partakers of the same communion."[44] Converting the slaves to Christianity made the slave owners feel that they were being humane towards the men and women they kept under duress and was designed to teach the slaves docility.

The slaves and the Black freedmen of the North, for their part, appropriated those elements of Christianity which best suited their class feelings and amalgamated them with the remnants of the African religions that survived the stamping out of their culture. A deposition against Denmark Vesey, a literate ex-slave who with a number of others was executed in 1822 for leading a conspiracy of revolt, stated: "His general conversation was about religion which he would apply to slavery, as for instance, he would speak of the creation of the world, in which he would say all men had equal rights, blacks as well as whites."[45] In addition to referring to the Bible and echoing the Declaration of Independence, Vesey won support by including among the conspirators a conjurer who promised protection for those engaged in the dangerous enterprise.

So too "Appeal to the Colored Citizens of the World" by the Black free man David Walker has been said to be "one of the most remarkable religious documents of the Protestant era" and in its attack upon the white man's religion the "most devastating" critique of Christianity "since Voltaire's *Catechisme de l'honnete homme.*"[46] White men, said Walker, act "more like devils than accountable men" and would dethrone Jehovah if they could.

> They want us for their slaves and think nothing of murdering us in order to subject us to that wretched condition—therefore, if there is an attempt made by us, kill or be killed.... [T]he man who will stand still and let another murder him is worse than an infidel.[47]

There is nothing of "turn the other cheek" religion here.

The Black folk religion that developed on the plantations under the eyes of the masters could not be thus openly insurrectionary, but it was subtly rebellious. The spirituals, for instance, were often ambiguous in their meaning. Frederick Douglass, the great ex-slave abolitionist, comments, "A keen observer might have detected in our repeated singing of 'O Canaan, sweet Canaan, / I am bound for the land of Canaan,' something more than a hope of reaching heaven. We meant to reach the *North*, and the North was our Canaan."[48] "Freedom" could mean freedom from the bondage of slavery as well as freedom from spiritual bondage, and the flexibility of the spirituals, stemming from African communal song, permitted improvisation in accordance with the occasion. The slave owners were uneasily aware of this when they jailed slaves at the beginning of the Civil War for singing, "We'll soon be free, / When de Lord will call us home."

The Biblical story of the deliverance of the children of Israel from Egyptian slavery had the most intense significance for Black slaves. A Union Army chaplain who worked with freedmen during the war expressed distress concerning this unfortunate emphasis, which made Jesus merely another Moses: "I think they have been accustomed to regard Christ not so much in the light of a *spiritual* Deliverer as that of a second Moses who would eventually lead *them* out of their prison-house of bondage."[49]

Religion, the only means by which slaves could gather together that was at all tolerated, became a vehicle for their struggle, as the mosques did under the Shah of Iran. Slave preachers had a rapport with their audience that was unusual. In their sermons they kept alive the hope of liberty and at the same time exerted a restraint on its premature expression.[50] This is beautifully epitomized in "An Ante-bellum Sermon" by Paul Laurence Dunbar, a Black poet, the son of slaves, who undoubtedly made use of oral tradition. In it the preacher tells the story of the freeing of the children of Israel, saying, "Now, de Lawd done dis fu' Isrul, / An' his ways don't nevah change." At the same time he is cautious enough about the "mastahs" being told that he's "preachin' discontent" to state: "But fu' feah some one mistakes me, / I will pause right hyeah to say, / Dat I'm still a-preachin' ancient, / I ain't talkin' 'bout to-day." At the conclusion, however, he is transported by his fervor but checks himself just in time: "An' we'll shout ouah hallelyas, / On dat mighty reck'nin' day, / When we'se reco'nized ez citiz'— / Huh uh! Chillun, let us pray!"

Worried by the slaves' prayer meetings and terror-stricken by the Nat Turner revolt, concerning which the governor of Virginia wrote, "I am fully convinced that every black preacher in the whole country seat of the Blue Ridge was in the secret,"[51] the slave owners passed legislation forbidding slaves to learn how to read and write, to preach or to hold unauthorized prayer meetings. Night patrols scoured the plantations to prevent such meetings, and Black men discovered to have been sufficiently presumptuous to preach the gospel were severely whipped.

Although religion was thus a vehicle for the slaves' struggle for freedom, it should be noted that some slaves completely rejected Christianity. Frederick Douglass stated that the discrepancies between the whites' religious professions and their behavior "awakened in my mind a distrust of all religion and the conviction that prayers were unavailing and delusive." Other ex-slaves also made clear that they regarded Christianity as a sham and a slave owner's religion.[52]

Because of the leading positions of the preachers many of them were among the Blacks who held office during the Reconstruction period. With the deal between the Republican representatives of the Northern capitalists and the Democratic representatives of the former slave owners in the Hayes election of 1876, white supremacy was restored in the South and Blacks were disenfranchised. Under these conditions Booker T. Washington advanced his program of industrial education, acceptance of the social status quo combined with efforts toward personal uplift, and silence concerning the absence of civil rights. This program received the support around the turn of the century of a stratum of skilled artisans and of teachers in the Black schools, colleges, and industrial institutes, government workers, and Northern church dignitaries.[53]

Black churches in the North had split off before the Civil War from the white churches of which the Blacks had been members. Aside from the desire of Blacks to express themselves in their own forms of worship, they had been segregated within the churches, being consigned to galleries or "nigger heavens." The founders of what was to be the African Methodist Episcopal Church stated that in leaving the Methodist Church they "had no other view therein but the glory of God and the peace of the Church by removing what was in a measure treated and esteemed as a nuisance on the one hand and an insult on the other."[54]

Following the Reconstruction period the churches of the North received an influx of new members from the South. This was the "Migration of the Talented Tenth," which preceded the migration of poor farmers and agricultural laborers. These churches became imitative of the white conservative evangelical churches, with their hostility to radicalism. A patiently suffering Christ fitted in with Booker T. Washington's politics of accommodation. The element of restraint that had been present in Black religion now came to the fore. As had happened in history before, revolutionary expectations of a messiah became transformed into otherworldly quietism. The influence of clergymen in the civil rights organizations was so much on the side of moderation that the Black Church came to be said to be "the NAACP on its knees." Black clergymen followed the lead of white liberal clergymen who talked about the fatherhood of God and the brotherhood of man but deemed themselves to be the big brothers.

During the Second World War the ruination of Black farmers by disastrous floods and the boll weevil and the lure of promises of high-paying jobs made by recruiters for Northern industrialists producing war goods brought the biggest internal migration in American history. Some of the new migrants joined the Baptist and Methodist and other orthodox churches. Many of these churches were of the middle class, particularly those in the Methodist Episcopal Church, whose clergy was better educated than that of the Baptist Church. This was even truer of the Presbyterian, Episcopal, Congregational, and Roman Catholic churches.

Far more migrants joined the storefront Pentecostal and Holiness churches and the various cults that had sprung up and that continued to grow during the Depression of the 1930s. Alienated by the more sophisticated ways and the middle-class values of the orthodox churches, they found in the small churches a means of adjustment to the bewildering complexities of the big city. Amid the proliferation of churches various cults flourished that were recognized by Ira Reid in 1940 as enormously significant, being more attuned to the "bitter realities of race" than "the prayerful procrastinations of the church institutions they now supplant."[55] These cults, especially the Black Jews, who regarded Blacks as the only true descendants of the Biblical Israelites, and the Moorish Science Temple adherents, who were the precursors of the Black Muslims, expressed the Black nationalism of the ghetto masses and their opposition to Christianity as the white oppressor's religion foisted upon Blacks. They were the continuators of David Walker, who, Christian though he was, indicted the Christianity of his time and assailed the white rulers as "devils," as the Black Muslims were to do.

A large and increasing number of the disillusioned masses of the ghettos regarded religion cynically and ceased to go to church at all. Gayraud Wilmore, himself a member of the staff of the Council on Church and Race of the United Presbyterian Church, but a religious radical and an honest and thorough scholar whose book is invaluable, states:

> There is probably no place in the world where the Christian Church has been under a more sustained and determined attack from those who once were within it than in the Black ghettos of the United States. The attack has been intensifying since the end of the First World War. It was joined in the twenties and thirties by the Black intelligentsia who identified religion with ignorance and superstition and looked upon Black preachers as the "lickspittle of their white masters."[56]

The members of this intelligentsia, who were in the anti-religious tradition of Frederick Douglass, people such as Claude McKay and Langston Hughes, were often influenced by Marxism.

Opposed by the unchurched street-wise people of the ghetto, by intellectuals identifying with the masses, and by Black nationalists and other activists, the church was no longer the focus of ghetto life. As Fauset noted in 1944:

> It is no mere fortuitous circumstance that with the decline in the proportion of orthodox churchgoers indicated by Mays and Nicholson, there is an increase in the proportion of Negroes who are entering the trade unions...and those who are otherwise girding for political action.[57]

The political action, which he foresaw, took place in the 1960s; unexpectedly, however, it began in the South. The demands of former soldiers who had fought in a war supposedly directed at racism, the beginnings of a Black proletariat in the war-spurred industry of the South, the influence of the worldwide rise of the colonial movement, the development of a new breed of student in the Black colleges, the revival of a folk religion of struggle—these were some of the elements that set the process going. Martin Luther King, although he had a doctorate from Boston University, knew how to address the Southern masses in their own idiom. But he himself, as he stated in his autobiography, came to Montgomery without any notion of struggle and was impelled by the action of the masses.

Rosa Parks, who sparked the Montgomery bus boycott by refusing to give her seat in the front of the bus to a white man, was not, contrary to legend, a politically uneducated tired, Black woman. She was the secretary of E.D. Nixon, a Black trade union leader, and had just completed a seminar at a labor training school conducted by the labor organizer A.J. Muste. Nixon was one of the Black union and community leaders cited by Daniel Guerin in his *Negroes on the March*, published in its French edition in 1951, four years before the boycott.

Nixon, knowing that clergymen were the traditionally accepted leaders of Southern Blacks, asked for their aid. Among those who assented was the young King, who became the orator, as Nixon was the behind-the-scenes organizer, of the boycott. King's Southern Christian Leadership Conference was dominated by Baptist clergymen, but it received its impetus from poor Blacks, many of whom were not church-goers, who brought the struggle into the streets.[58]

The Student Nonviolent Coordinating Committee militants carried the movement a stage further with the more direct confrontations of the sit-ins and the freedom rides. They were attracted to King as a charismatic leader but did not expect much from the Black churches, many of which refused to co-operate with them. As time went on, the rift between SNCC and the churches widened.[59]

King himself became increasingly aware of the foot-dragging of the orthodox churches. He avoided making public complaints but at times did comment that "too many Negro churches...are so absorbed in a future good 'over yonder' that they condition their members to adjust to the present evils 'over here.'"[60]

However, the pressure of the masses, as the struggle came to the ghettos of the North and the cry of "Black Power" rang through the land, politicized many Black clergymen, particularly the younger ones.[61] The herald of the Black Power movement was Malcolm X. Malcolm began as a convert to the Nation of Islam. This conversion was indispensable to him as a means of gaining a sense of racial solidarity that supplanted his previous individualistic attempts to escape from an oppressive environment. While never giving up his religion, he was expelled from the Nation of Islam for insisting that it involve itself in Black political struggle and went on to form a political organization that was open to those of any religion or of no religion. Although this organization was destroyed, Malcolm's idea of militant struggle under a Black leadership independent of the white power structure is a legacy to his people. "I've never heard of a non-violent revolution or a revolution that was brought about by turning the other cheek," he said, "and so I believe that it is a crime for anyone to teach a person who is being brutalized to continue to accept that brutality without doing something to defend himself."[62]

The Protestant Churches and Labor

The relations between the Protestant churches and labor in the

U.S. followed much the same course that they did in England and Germany. The prevalent economic doctrine in the first part of the nineteenth century was what might be called clerical *laissez faire*. The laws of economics were, in the words of a textbook written by Alonzo Potter, who later became an Episcopalian bishop, "nothing less than laws of God."[63] Labor unions, which "artificially" raised wages, hurting employers who provided workers with jobs and thereby throwing people out of work, violated these natural laws ordained by God.

The Civil War brought a tremendous acceleration of industrialism. Between 1860 and 1890 the national wealth increased almost five-fold, of which 0.3 percent of the population possessed more than half.[64] The robber barons gave munificent sums to churches and church colleges. The churches were duly appreciative. When John D. Rockefeller, the most hated man in America for his ruthlessness against his competitors and against labor, gave a large sum of money to a Cleveland Baptist Church, the pastor declared, "People charge Mr. Rockefeller with stealing the money he gave to the church, but he has laid it on the altar and thus sanctified it."[65] Boards of trustees of colleges and of denominational governing bodies increasingly became dominated by wealthy laymen instead of by ministers, as previously.[66]

In the fiercely fought labor battles that attended the rapid post–Civil War industrialization the Protestant churches were solidly on the side of capital. The newspapers of the churches of the Prince of Peace declared that strikes must be crushed in blood. During the great railroad strike of 1877, the *Independent* stated, "Compromises are not in order when men *are fighting* for higher wages or against a reduction of wages," and added, "Napoleon was right when he said the way to deal with a mob was to exterminate it." The *Congregationalist* warned of the "fervid apostles" of "the most fiendish excesses of the days of the Commune in Paris" and proclaimed: "[L]et the mob know, everywhere, that for it to stand one moment after it has been ordered by proper authorities to disperse, will be to be shot down in its tracks." When the Chicago anarchists were condemned to be hanged for having "incited" by their editorials unknown persons to throw a bomb at the police in Haymarket, the *Christian Advocate*, expressing the unanimous opinion of the religious press, declared: "To talk about pity, sympathy or delay in connection with such demons, is to encourage their kind."[67]

In the face of this onslaught, labor, a large part of which was in any case made up after 1880 of immigrants from Catholic countries, was understandably not too friendly to the Protestant churches. Samuel Gompers, scarcely a flaming radical, stated in 1898: "My associates have come to look upon the church and the ministry as the apologists and defenders of the wrong committed against the interests of the people."[68]

As in England and Germany, however, when trade unions grew in strength and the ruling class felt it necessary to make an accommodation with the labor aristocracy, the churches followed suit. In the United States this movement has gone by the name of the social gospel. Walter Rauschenbusch, the chief propagator of the social gospel, spoke of the need for the churches to regain the workers it had lost to the working-class movement:

> There is no doubt that in all the industrialized nations of Europe, and in our own country, the working classes are dropping out of connection with their churches and synagogues, and to a large extent are transferring their devotion to social movements, so that it looks as if the social interest displaced religion.[69]

The social gospel, however, has been unable to gain adherents among workers. The evangelical preachers of the nineteenth century talked to their own kind among the frontier farmers, but the social gospel clergymen have been middle-class people who have talked to workers as conciliators between classes, urging good will and moral improvement. Although perhaps not to the same degree as in Europe, there is still by and large working-class alienation from the major Protestant churches. Yinger states: "While no definitive study has been made of the class distribution of church membership, the consensus of expert opinion is that the rolls are weighted in favor of the middle and upper classes and the nonurban lower classes in most of the large denominations, the Catholic Church being the chief exception."[70] Argyle and Beit-Hallahmi, citing various studies, amplify on this, stating that workers are "less likely to be church members, but those of this class who are, are more likely to have fundamentalist religious beliefs."[71]

Protestant fundamentalism is particularly prevalent among

Southerners who have moved to industrial centers. It has had a conservatizing, racist, anti-union effect. However, in the wake of the social transformation wrought by industrialization and the defeat of the Jim Crow system by the civil rights movement, religion has lost some of its grip. The role the church played in the famous 1929 Gastonia strike in running the union "outside agitators" out of town is not one it can now sustain.

American Catholicism

Aside from the Catholic "old families" of colonial America, who had wealth and social position, American Catholics in the nineteenth century were peasant immigrants from Ireland and Germany in the early part of the century, and from Italy and Poland in the latter part. The Irish, driven by English oppression and by famine, came in great numbers and established early hegemony over the American Church. Since their Catholicism was a part of the national identity to which they clung in resisting national oppression, they were especially attached to their religion. They identified themselves with it even more strongly because of the racist and religious bigotry they encountered in the United States, where notices of jobs were often listed with the statement "Irish need not apply," where their churches and homes were burned to the ground, and where they themselves were often brutally attacked and sometimes killed by mobs. They got only the lowest pay and dirtiest jobs, including dangerous jobs in the South for which the slave owners did not want to risk such valuable property as their slaves.

After the Civil War the Catholic Church received some of the munificence of the robber barons. The railroad magnate James J. Hill, who employed thousands of immigrants, stated in donating a million dollars for a Catholic seminary, "Look at the millions of foreigners pouring into this country, for whom the Roman Catholic Church is the only authority they either fear or respect. What will be their social view, their political action, their moral status if that single controlling force should be removed?"[72] William Howard Taft asserted that the Catholic Church was "one of the bulwarks against socialism and anarchy in this country, and I welcome its presence here." Even the

Bishop of the Episcopal diocese of Albany forgot about doctrinal differences to state that the Catholic Church must be given "every opportunity" to retain its influence over "the most turbulent element in our citizenship."[73] The popularity of Leo XIII, who accommodated the Church to bourgeois democracy, helped to promote good feeling. A Catholic priest wrote in 1888 that those who "a quarter of a century ago looked upon the Pope as a spook with which to scare children and Puritans, now consider him the champion of the rights of property."[74]

At the same time the Catholic Church could not forget that its membership consisted almost entirely of workers. When the Vatican was contemplating condemning the Knights of Labor, a 700,000-strong predominantly Catholic organization of trade unions led by the anti-clerical Catholic Terence Powderly, Cardinal Gibbons wrote a memorandum to Leo advising against it. It is true, he declared, that "great numbers of ecclesiastics were alarmed at the revolutionary principles which undoubtedly disgraced some members of the trade unions," but "many other Bishops...were equally alarmed at the prospect of the Church being presented before our age as the friend of the powerful rich and the enemy of the helpless poor."[75] One could not hope, he added, for Church-organized unions in the United States, and the leadership of the Knights of Labor did act as a restraining force upon militancy. Condemnation of the Knights of Labor would encourage anti-Romanist feeling among non-Catholic workers. Moreover, the Catholics in the organization, who "continually give their means" to the Church, would be alienated so that the amount of Peter's pence received by Rome would probably be diminished.[76] Leo was guided by the memorandum.

As time has gone by, with Catholics no longer being at the bottom of American society, developing an important middle class and even entering the top economic and political circles, their voice in world Church affairs has steadily grown more powerful. American Catholicism, it was estimated in 1944 by the well-informed *New York Times* correspondent Camille Cianfarra, probably furnished over 50 percent of the revenue contributed to the Vatican, a percentage which Catholic commentators agree has almost certainly grown greater, and, with less than 10 percent of the world's Catholics, it furnished in 1966 almost half of all seminary students.[77] Consequently, American Catholics have not been so ready to go along unthinkingly with the pronouncements of the Pope and indeed feel that they have some lessons in modern American efficiency to teach. At Vatican II, although American bishops displayed a provincial deference, American Catholic theologians and laymen, despite the undemocratic nature of the proceedings, played an important role.

Nevertheless, with the different ethnic groups no longer having to huddle together in the Church for survival, the Church has lost influence among the formerly faithful. Father Andrew M. Greeley, the director of the National Opinion Research Center at the University of Chicago and the Doctor Gallup of the Catholic Church, states that the percentage of American Catholics attending mass at least once a week fell from 71 percent in 1964 to 55 percent in 1976 and that the percentage of those so alienated as to be considered "unchurched" was at least 20 percent. He adds that 75 percent support the liberalizing changes of Vatican II and that there would have been more desertions if it were not for the Church's modernization. Most of the defections, he asserts, came from the 1968 encyclical reaffirming the prohibition of birth control other than through the uncertain rhythm method, which has come to be known as "Vatican roulette." Moreover, the authority of the Pope has so declined that surveys show that the use by Catholic churchgoers of contraceptives is almost as great as its use by non-Catholics.[78]

American Judaism

Although a small number of Spanish and Portuguese Jews came to colonial America on being exiled, the first wave of Jewish immigrants came from 1830 to 1870 from Germany and central Europe, looking for civil rights and economic opportunity. They spread throughout the country as peddlers and merchants with the advancing frontier. Some rose to be bankers and merchant princes.

As the German Jews became assimilated, intermarriage and a dropping away from Judaism occurred in great numbers. The *American Israelite* warned in 1854 that unless Judaism accommodated itself to American ways, "we will have no Jews in this country in less than half a century."[79] The Reform movement accordingly introduced changes borrowed from Protestant church services: more restraint and decorum, no segregation of women, sermons in English, mixed choirs, organs, modification of the dietary and Sabbath laws. It transformed messianic memories into an acceptance of the idea that Jewish dreams would be realized by the progress of Western civilization, above all in the United States.

But both the fears of extinction and the hopes of the survival of Judaism as a reformed religion in what it hailed as "the modern era of universal culture of heart and intellect"[80] proved illusory. Beginning in the 1870s, a far greater wave of Jews, driven by the violent winds of anti-Semitism in tsarist Russia and the Austro-Hungarian Empire, landed on the shores of America. This wave was halted only by immigration restrictions in 1924 and consisted of Orthodox Jews from the ghettos. The men wore caftans and had ear locks and beards; the married women wore wigs. To the consternation of the native Jews they altered the image of the Jew in America.

These Jews, coming as artisans, *luftmenschen*, traders, and small merchants, settled in slum neighborhoods in large cities, particularly in New York and the Northeast. They entered the garment and needle industries as cheap labor. Others made use of their artisan skills to become carpenters, painters, glaziers, printers and jewelry workers; many became peddlers and junk-dealers.

Jews seeking jobs in other industries met with discrimination. Employment ads commonly specified "Christian only." An ad for stenographers that stated the jobs were for "well-groomed Christian American young women" is typical. The New York Telephone Company explained that it could not "take on Jewish women as switch-board operators because their arms are too short," but Wall Street firms did not seek to explain why they could not take Jews for any kind of job. No doubt their legs were not long enough for them to be messengers.[81]

The native-born Jews of German and central European extraction were scarcely less hostile. They called their Eastern European co-religionists "uncouth," "lazy and shiftless," and "repulsive ill-bred savages." B'nai B'rith would not charter a group of Russian immigrants because—this was before it founded the Anti-Defamation League—they were "not yet civilized." The most influential Jewish fraternity, the Harmony Club, excluded East Europeans, its unofficial motto being "more polish and less Polish." The *Hebrew Standard* stated that "the thoroughly acclimated American Jew...is closer to the Christian sentiment around him than to the Judaism of these miserable darkened Hebrews."

Indeed, the charity of American Jewry was all too close to the Christian charity extended to the immigrants. The United Hebrew Charities of Rochester declared: "The Jews have earned an enviable reputation in the United States, but this has been undermined by the influx of thousands who are not ripe for the enjoyment of liberty and equal rights, and all who mean well for the Jewish name should prevent them as much as possible from coming here." It is not surprising that the anti-Semitic epithet "kike" originated with the German Jews as a contemptuous term for the East Europeans, whose names often ended with "ki."[82]

The comfortably established native Jews did not know whether to be more embarrassed by the phylacteries of the East European Orthodox Jews or the pamphlets of the East European radical Jews. The *Jewish Messenger* told its readers to have nothing to do with the "moral hydrophobia" of the Jewish "Nihilists, socialists or anarchists." At the Educational Alliance of New York native Jews did their best to explain Americanism to the newcomers. Professors and clergymen, Jews and non-Jews, lectured there on the evils of socialism and delivered sermons on the vanity of the things of this earth.[83] Oddly, it was the German Jews who had the earthly goods and the East European Jews who had none.

As the twentieth century progressed, however, the Eastern European Jews learned American ways and rose on the social scale. With their mercantile traditions and their zeal for learning, more and more became businessmen ("A Jew would rather earn five dollars a week doing business for himself than ten dollars a week working for someone else," it was said), salesmen, office workers, and, finally, professionals (teachers, doctors, lawyers). Hostility between the "Russians" and "Germans" subsided, and cultural and ethnic amalgamation took place. Religious practices also came more and more to converge, as Orthodox Jews accommodated themselves to American life.

Nevertheless, a substantial portion of the immigrant Jews remained working class and radical until the prosperity of the Second World War years and the 1950s virtually completed the process of de-proletarianization. There are, however, many aged and poor Jews left in the old Jewish neighborhoods of New York, Miami Beach, Chicago, and Philadelphia. About a quarter of a million Jews in New York, most of them over sixty-five, live at less than the poverty level of $3,500, and about 150,000 more live at just above this level with an annual income of $3,500 to $4,000.[84]

With the decline of the radical organizations, Jews have become more tied to the synagogue. However, the synagogue itself, like the Christian churches, has become secularized, a social meeting place whose concern for religious doctrine is minimal. The bar mitzvah, the ceremony for consecrating a boy to Judaism at the age of thirteen, is now, unlike a few decades ago, observed by virtually every Jewish family, but it is a party, often exceedingly lavish, with only a nominally religious significance. There has also, however, recently been a counter-movement toward Orthodoxy by Jews, who, more secure in their American identity, have become concerned with retaining their Jewish identity in reaction to the Holocaust and in their pride in Israel.

As a result not only of their de-proletarianization but of the anti-communism engendered by the anti-Semitism of the regime in the Soviet Union and of the frequent stifling of criticism of American foreign policy entailed by Jewish support of Israel, Jews in the main have become conservatized, although many pride themselves on being liberal. However, to the dismay of such neo-conservative Jewish intellectuals as Norman Podhoretz, the tradition of the radical Jewish intellectual is not altogether dead. If the average middle-class Jew feels comfortably at home in the United States, as did the average middle-class Jew in pre-Hitler Germany, many Jewish intellectuals, like other American intellectuals, feel alienated from a society that is spiritually sick.

The Religious Situation Today: The Three-Religion System

The United States is far ahead of the European countries in the percentage of its population who are church members, and that percentage is increasing, not declining, as is true of the European countries. There are a number of factors that account for this phenomenon.

The United States is a country of immigrants. German, Swedish, Norwegian Lutherans; German Methodists; Armenian Congregationalists; Irish, German, Italian, Polish Catholics; German, Russian, Hungarian Jews—all found their churches and synagogues to be cultural institutions that bound their ethnic communities together in a new and bewildering world. When they lost their languages and other aspects of their cultures under the pressure toward homogenization of American life, they retained their religions, the one feature of their cultures that received social approval. By the latter part of the nineteenth century this was fairly true even for Catholicism and Judaism, which were regarded as less foreign than the poisonous "un-American" socialism for which they were antidotes and which became quite integrated into the religious establishment after the Second World War. In a vast country with a geographically mobile population the churches and synagogues became social centers to which those coming to a new city could go to meet people with whom they had "something in common."

The acceptance of different sects and religions was furthered by the separation of church and state effected during the Revolution and its aftermath. This was perceived by De Tocqueville, who stated that, since there is in the United States no official religion that bears the opprobrium of unpopular measures taken by the state, religious belief is not undermined, as it is where state and church are joined together. Consequently, "Christian sects are infinitely diversified and perpetually modified; but Christianity itself is an established and irresistible fact, which no one undertakes either to attack or to defend."[85] Although De Tocqueville's observation must be modified by the fact of the existence of earlier popular free thought, which was submerged by the religious tide, and by the fact of challenges to religion in the latter part of the nineteenth century and the early part of the twentieth century by bourgeois rationalists such as Colonel Ingersoll and Clarence Darrow, it remains basically true.

The diversity of religions was due not only to the influx of immigrants from different countries but to the small farmers on the frontier, who set their imprint on American religion. These small farmers were not like the peasants of the Old World, content to maintain their inherited religion. American agriculture was a commercial capitalist agriculture, and the religion of its farmers was highly individualistic. But with the competitiveness of the sects there was, as De Tocqueville asserts, the assumption that the existence of religion as such was to be taken for granted.

De Tocqueville also stated that in the United States religion is "mingled with...all the feelings of patriotism, whence it derives a peculiar force."[86] We have seen how the Puritan heritage made the American capitalist ideology present the American nation as a chosen people. The sharp rise in religious membership and church attendance that took place immediately after World War II was undoubtedly connected with the inception of the cold war. "In God we trust": on the side of the "good guys," God had never let us down, and He would not do so now. Religion was acclaimed as America's "secret weapon," "more powerful," as one religious leader put it, "than the H-bomb"[87]—which didn't prevent the government, of course, from stockpiling H-bombs.

The factors accounting for the durability of American religion are interrelated. In the last analysis the distinctiveness of American religion is derived from the distinctive features of American capitalism: the destruction of relatively feeble feudal institutions, making it unnecessary for the bourgeoisie to engage in a stultifying compromise, as in Britain and Europe, with throne, altar, and landed aristocracy; an immense amount of cheap land available to freehold farmers; imported cheap foreign labor, each new generation of which was successively subjected to super-exploitation; the dominance since World War I of American imperialism over other capitalist countries. These have up until now militated against the development of a mass socialist movement and Marxist party, which in turn has affected the religious situation.

While industrialism and the dissemination of scientific knowledge have given European churches a diminished membership, in the United States they have secularized religion itself. Religious beliefs do not have very much to do with ordinary everyday living. What one does six days a week is one thing; what one hears in church on Sunday is something else. This is due not so much to conscious hypocrisy as to confusion and superficiality of thought. Doctrines and dogmas having broken down, religion is but a shell with very little content. It serves primarily as reinforcement for the ritualized abstractions of the Rotary Clubs and the Kiwanis—"democracy," "free enterprise," "community service," "positive thinking"—which are the secular faith of American capitalism.[88]

Three religious faiths—Protestantism, Catholicism, and Judaism—are the "official" religions in the United States today. The three-religion system may be compared with the two-party system, which is designed to ensure political monopoly for the parties of capitalism. Through the tax-exemption laws, by which the churches do not have to pay taxes on their enormous property holdings and investments, the American state actually gives greater support to religion than the European states with religious establishments. Of course, the storefront Black cults, which do not have such property holdings and investments, do not get such aid. This is the same kind of process as that in political campaigns, in which the state gives great sums of money to the wealthy Republican and Democratic parties but none to small, poor parties.

Peter L. Berger, therefore, rightly characterizes the separation between church and state that prevails as being not so much a divorce between those who had been previously married as a "polygamous arrangement in which all wives share equally in the favors dispensed by the husband-state" (although, he might have added, the wealthier wives in practice enjoy greater favors). The "wall of separation" serves to keep out from the political harem "certain of the less respectable candidates" and "separates from respectability those few belligerent secularists in our midst who would have nothing to do with this religious-political marriage at all."[89] Against these secularists, religious bodies acting as agencies in such matters as the adoption of children or the selection and screening of political refugees are able to impose various sanctions.

The system of chaplains in the armed forces best illustrates the relationship between church and state. Clergymen get preferential treatment in that they are exempt from a military draft. Those who enter the armed forces are automatically commissioned as officers. In addition to holding religious services, they are required to give "character guidance" lectures and to act as bolsterers of morale. If a clergyman were to advise soldiers that a war in which the country was engaged was evil and that they could show their strength of character by opposing it, he would not last long in his post. In return for special privileges, the Church is expected to serve the state.

"Jesus Freaks," Mormons, and Evangelicals

When, during the Eisenhower years, Will Herberg wrote of the "official" religions of the United States, these religions seemed entirely unchallenged. But the undermining of the stability of this era meant the growth of new religious movements.

During the 1960s disaffected middle-class youth turned to Zen and Eastern mysticism. But under the influence of the dominant Christian culture many of them then turned to a countercultural form of Christianity, which, after all, had begun in the Middle East and whose early adherents had practiced communal living. They became known as "Jesus freaks," a phrase derived from "freak out," meaning, in the drug culture of which they were a part, "to behave bizarrely under the influence of drugs." It is an appropriate enough designation. The "Jesus freaks" or the "Jesus People," as they have been more decorously called, have been in good part absorbed by the evangelistic movement, where they are in the unorthodox wing.

One church that grew greatly in the 1970s, increasing its membership in the United States from 1.7 million at the beginning of the decade to 3.1 million by the end of it was the Mormon Church. Mormonism was born as a Utopian communal movement of theological inspiration during the religious ferment of the 1820s. In its emphasis on the central place of the United States in the divine scheme of things and in its optimistic doctrine of progress, in which man is capable of endless development until he becomes literally a god with the power to create worlds, it is a peculiarly American religion. This is indeed the apotheosis of the common man: not just every man a king, as Huey Long was to say, but every man a god. The statement proverbial among the Mormons was: "As man is now, God once was; as God is now, man may become." To the doctrine of the self-made man, Mormonism added the doctrine of the self-made god: "Mormonism has developed the notion of a self-made deity, who through activism and effort has achieved a relative mastery over the world.... God's relation to the world is that of a powerful artificer, a projection of the relation of American man to the American continent."[90]

Mormonism's radically different theology, its polygamy, and its claim to be delivering to humanity a new Bible[91] made it an object of hate. It attracted to itself, however, poor farmers and those displaced from land which had become too expensive. Driven west by persecution, the Mormons eventually came to Utah. Here, in the course of time, especially after the Mormon Church accommodated itself to the demands of the United States government, in order for Utah to become a state, its early egalitarianism was lost. Joseph Smith had received the revelation that "every man may receive according as he stands in need," but the rest of his earning was to go to the Church to give to those who did not have enough and to be used to buy land for the New Jerusalem.[92] This became modified to the payment of a tithe of one-tenth of one's income which, invested and reinvested, is today the source of the Church's immense wealth.

The contemporary Mormon Church, according to Gordon Weil, Maine's Commissioner of Business Regulation, is among the nation's top fifty corporations and has at least $2 billion total assets. The Quorum of the Twelve Apostles, who advise the president—still regarded as a divinely inspired prophet—and run the authoritarian structure of the Church, are often on the boards of directors of corporations in Utah associated with the Church.

Historically, the Mormon hierarchy has had close ties to the Republican Party since the granting of statehood. The senior member of the present Quorum, who traditionally is elected president after the ruling prophet has passed on to his reward, is Ezra Taft Benson, a leader of the John Birch Society. Despite his objections to "big government" and its bureaucratic meddling in economic life, Benson, as Secretary of Agriculture under Eisenhower, disbursed vast sums of money to corporations and millionaires engaged in agribusiness for them to withhold production while the majority of people on earth were suffering from malnutrition. Apparently, Mormon leaders now believe in socialism for the rich and capitalism for the poor.

The social conservatism of the Mormon Church has been especially manifested in its fight against the Equal Rights Amendment. But the dispersal and urbanization of the Mormons, now in good part middle class, has subjected the Church to new pressures and influences. "Divorce is increasing.... Some critics inside the church believe that church members follow the leadership too blindly; and the impact of feminism is unsettling the Mormon pattern of strictly defined sex roles, with family and church life dominated by men."[93] These, however, are only undercurrents: the ruling elite is at the moment firmly in control.

An even more powerful reactionary force than the Mormon Church is concentrated in the evangelical movement. While evangelicals are present in large numbers in the mainline churches as well as in the smaller churches, they are opposed to the kind of secularized religion represented by the leadership of the mainline churches. What distinguishes the evangelicals is the claim to have been "born again" through a commitment to Christ and the desire to spread the good word. Generally, they are fundamentalist in their reading of the Bible. Largely made up of members of the middle class who are dismayed by social unrest in the United States manifested in the Black, feminist, and youth movements,[94] many of them are strongly conservative (the Black evangelicals are not). They came forward openly as a political power in favor of Ronald Reagan in the 1980 presidential campaign, although Carter and Anderson as well as Reagan call themselves "born again" Christians. In the 1984 presidential campaign they played an even more prominent role in the Republican convention. At a prayer breakfast, Reagan told these zealots that those opposed to school prayer were "intolerant" of religion. Reagan's own tolerance extends to religious bigots, as indicated by the fact that Reverend James Robison, who delivered the opening prayer at the Republican convention, once defined an anti-Semite as "someone who hates Jews more than he's supposed to."[95]

Evangelicalism in our time may be said to have got its start with Billy Graham's campaign to gain commitments to Jesus in 1949, notable for its warnings of the menace of communism and of a coming Armageddon. The campaign got a great boost from the wire by William Randolph Hearst to the editors of his newspaper chain to "puff Graham."[96]

Today various evangelical organizations associated with the extreme right receive heavy financial backing from some of America's wealthiest men. Nelson Bunker Hunt, the Texas oil magnate who is on the governing board of the John Birch Society, pledged more than $10 million—he would not say how much more—toward a $1 billion fund-raising effort by the Campus Crusade for Christ, and acted as a fund-raiser in getting other donors to pledge $1 million or more.[97] The Heritage Foundation, a conservative "think-tank," was started by Robert Billings, the director of television-evangelist Jerry Falwell's Moral Majority and the religious liaison representative of Reagan, with money from Joseph Coors of the Coors brewing family, who also contributed to the John Birch Society. The Christian Freedom Foundation, an "educational lobby," is financed by J. Howard Pew, the founder of the Sun Oil Company and "other businessmen who espouse the free enterprise system."[98] They evidently are determined to remain espoused to it until death do them part.

Evangelicalism, which cuts through many churches, has made bedfellows of ancient enemies, including new Catholic evangelicals and evangelists of Protestant sects that formerly declaimed against the Catholic Church as the "Whore of Babylon." There are even some Messianic Jews who keep Saturday worship, observe Jewish holidays, and wear skullcaps, but accept the divinity of Christ. Evangelical Christians have also established ties with more orthodox Jews. Fourteen prominent evangelical ministers in a full-page advertisement in the *New York Times* and other newspapers voiced their support for Israel, including its "right" to an undivided Jerusalem and the occupied territory of the West Bank. The Reverend Carl D. McIntyre, who supported the racists George Wallace and Lester Maddox and defended the fascist Minutemen, did the same in a similar ad of his own. This support for Israel stems from anti-communism and the belief derived from a reading of the Bible that the gathering of Jews in Israel is preliminary to the Second Coming of Christ.

Jews for their part have responded warmly to the fundamentalist Protestants, who were often in the past pronouncedly anti-Semitic. "Since 1967," says Kenneth A. Briggs, the religious editor of the *New York Times*, "the American Jewish Committee has devoted its principal resources in the area of interreligious affairs to building bridges with evangelicals. In so doing, the agency largely has turned its back on liberal Protestants on the ground that they have not been forthcoming in support of Israel."[99] The American Jewish Committee should, however, be wary in its flirtations: old habits of thought die hard. At a meeting of 15,000 fundamentalists, mostly ministers, on August 22, 1980, the president of the Southern Baptist Convention, Bailey Smith, exclaimed: "God Almighty does not hear the prayer of a Jew, for how in the world can God hear the prayer of a man who says Jesus Christ is not the true Messiah?" The Reverend Smith may deem it fortunate for Israel that those such as he, who have the ear of God, pray for it, but Jews had better take heed of this manifestation of anti-Semitic prejudice.

And not only the Jews: this reactionary movement, whose growth marks a shift to the right among religious forces, is the enemy of all oppressed classes and races.

PART III

The Social Roots of the Chief Religions of Asia and the Middle East

CHAPTER EIGHT

Hinduism and Buddhism

The Two Chief Asiatic Religions

Buddhism was a reaction in the India of the fifth century BC against the Vedic religion brought by the Aryan invaders of northwest India between 2000 and 1500 BC. It was from Vedism that what has come to be called Hinduism originated. This term, which was used by the conquering Muslims many centuries later to refer to the religion of the unconverted Indians, has largely superseded the term "Brahmanism," which is now generally confined to the religion of the Vedic period and of the period of the *Brahmanas*, the prose commentaries on Vedic rites and invocations.

Buddhism retained many features of Brahmanism and in turn influenced Hinduism. It came to be eclipsed in India by Hinduism by about AD 1200, but it had previously spread to China, Korea, Ceylon, Burma, Tibet, and other Asian countries. Since Hinduism and Buddhism were so long intertwined, they may be considered together.

The history of Hinduism and Buddhism has suffered from their being lost in the mists of time, with religious texts surviving through oral tradition and being written down only centuries after composition, from the paucity of historical records, from the fact that religious texts are in Sanskrit, Chinese, Japanese, and other languages. The sparseness of historical records, which, together with the comparatively slow pace of change in Indian society, has given rise to the misleading aphorism that India has no history, is in good part due to the official ideology of the time that historical change is unimportant compared to the unchanging eternal verities. Archaeology has helped the historian in recent years, but even there the ancient Hindu practice of cremation deprived the historian of the funeral inscriptions on burial-places of other ancient civilizations. Nevertheless, the work of Marxist and other historians has shed much light on the social origin and development of Hinduism and Buddhism.

Aryan Culture and Vedic Religion

The Aryan-speaking tribes who invaded India from Iran were a semi-nomadic cattle-breeding warrior people. Cattle was the measure of wealth, and the word for "to fight" meant "to search for cows," an indication that cattle-raids and rival claims for lost cows were a major source for intertribal conflict. A central feature of the religion of the Vedas, the religious texts of the Aryans, is the sacrifice to the gods. In earliest times this was human sacrifice, as it was among the ancestors of the Hebrews; later it was sacrifice of cattle and other animals.[1] This was a kind of investment, as from this sacrifice was expected to come prosperity in peace and war.

The gods to whom sacrifice was made were many, but the chief gods were Indra, the war god, who, as the Rig-Veda puts it, looted the "treasure-houses of the godless,"[2] and Igni, the god of fire, the sacred element. These gods are projections of the destructive force, which the Aryans visited upon the superior culture of the Indus cities that they found.

The Development of Brahmanism

In time the Aryans developed their own agricultural settlements, clearing the forests and ploughing the land. Agricultural cultivation brought about private property, and in the settlements occupations such as carpentry, metalworking, pottery, and weaving sprang up. The wealthier landowners engaged in trade with other settlements, using cattle as a means of exchange.

With the decline of tribal society, three social divisions emerged: the Kshatriyas (warriors), the Brahmans (priests), and the Vaishyas (cultivators).[3] When to these were added the Sudras, consisting of the conquered indigenous Dasas or those of mixed Aryan-Dasa origin, the beginnings of the caste system came about. The Sudras, like the medieval Jews of Europe, were both a class and a people who were regarded as beyond the pale. They became the cultivators, and the Vaishyas became landowners and traders. The other three castes were called twice-born castes because after their physical birth they were initiated into their privileged caste, but the Sudras, excluded from the Brahman-conducted Vedic ritual, were, like Christians in contemporary America who have not made an evangelical commitment to Christ, not born again. Their punishment if they even listened to the religious recitals was to have their ears filled with molten lead, and they continued to worship their own gods.

Since the level of production was low, with comparatively little occupational differentiation, and since there was a desire to retain racial privileges, caste became hereditary and central in religious doctrine. As occupational differentiation increased and more and more native tribes were integrated into society, sub-castes came into being and proliferated into the thousands. "The lower one goes in the economic scale, the lower the caste in the social scale on the whole"[4]

A powerful reinforcement of the caste system was the doctrine of the transmigration of souls. This doctrine is not to be found in the Vedas although some vague statements in the later hymns have been used by Hindu "modernists" to authorize it. Indeed there is only one reference to caste in a very late hymn, for the Vedas were the product of a pastoral, egalitarian society. But the Brahmans, the custodians of the Vedas, only certain sections of which they imparted to the high castes, as the Catholic Church used to withhold knowledge of the Bible from the laity, developed doctrine supposedly sanctioned by the Vedas as society changed. Thus was born Brahmanism.

The doctrine of the transmigration of souls stated that upon death the soul entered the body of one being born. The caste into which the soul now entered was dependent on one's conduct in previous life. Each caste had its own law of what was right that it had to observe. Naturally, the primary law of conduct for the Sudras was obedience. As is stated in the *Laws of Manu*, one of the sacred books of Hinduism, "One occupation only the lord prescribed to the sudra—to serve meekly these other three castes....

For him...are prescribed truthfulness, meekness, and purity."[5]

The doctrine of the transmigration of souls thus provided justification for caste: the Sudra should not blame the system: he was only being punished for his transgressions in a previous life of which he had no memory. If he rebelled, he would only make it worse for himself in his next life, for there were still worse things than being a Sudra: the soul could inhabit the body of an animal, even becoming "a worm in the intestine of a dog," as one text graphically put it.[6] Thus too the epic *Mahabharata*, another part of the canon of Hinduism, whose stories were orally developed over a period of centuries (c. 200 BC–AD 200), when the authority of the Brahmans was being challenged, has a jackal say, "I used to refute the brahmins and was hostile to what the brahmins said.... This life of the jackal which I am now suffering is the result of all this."[7]

On the other hand, by performing one's caste obligations one could ascend to a higher caste in a future life and even, as later Hindu doctrine said, become a god—for even the gods are not immortal, and undergo reincarnations. Everything is subject to change—except for the caste system, which goes on forever. Instead of the everlasting reward and punishment in another world, which the medieval Catholic Church used to maintain the social order, the Brahmans used an eternity of successive rewards and punishments in this world, with some transitory sojourns in another world.

Just as the doctrine of the medieval Catholic Church was concerned not only with maintaining the social order but its own authority, which was bound up with the social order, so was the doctrine of the Brahmans.

> The power of the Brahmins was strengthened by the fact that the religious ritual had become so complicated that only professional priests could successfully conduct it. Even the priests had to have textbooks. The Brahmanas became those textbooks, which every Brahmin learned by heart, as he also learned the Vedas.... In one passage it was asserted that the individual's salvation depended on paying fees to the priest. In another the claim was made that the sun would not rise without the performance of the appropriate sacrifice.... Says the Shatapatha Brahmana, "Verily there are two kinds of gods; for, indeed, the gods themselves are gods, and the Brahmins who have studied and teach the sacred lore are the human gods."[8]

The Rise of Kingdoms and the Origin of Buddhism

Caste loyalties replaced tribal solidarity, and tribal chiefs became kings. By about 600 BC kingdoms were firmly established in northern India. With agriculture building greater surpluses from the rich soil of India, the kings levied taxes on the land, generally one-sixth of the produce, and sought to expand their kingdoms. As the might of the kings increased and the expanses of their kingdoms became greater, the traditional tribal assemblies were held less frequently and became less meaningful. There were, however, also republics, consisting of individual tribes or of confederacies of tribes, which kept more of the tribal ways, including the assemblies.

Kingships became hereditary, and kings were regarded as being reborn on their coronation and invested with divinity. The sacrifices to the gods on these occasions became royal spectacles, in which hundreds of Brahmans were employed and huge numbers of animals were killed. The Brahmans conferred divinity upon the kings; the kings bestowed munificence upon the Brahmans.

To extend their kingdoms, the kings had to clear the jungle and suppress the food-gathering tribes who inhabited it. The theoreticians of the great kingdom of Magadha "proposed a relentless conduct which might have caused any Borgia to blench; but their openly declared principal aim was to change the face of the land.... This sort of kingship had to burst all barriers of tribal privilege, property-sharing, and exclusiveness."[9] It produced a political doctrine of utter cynicism in which society was seen as characterized by "unbridled competition in which the powerful preyed upon the weak without restraint, or, to use the language of the text—'where the big fish swallowed the little fish in a condition of anarchy.'"[10]

Under the shock of monarchic despotism after the freedom of tribal society, numbers of individuals renounced society, seeking salvation in ascetic practices and becoming wandering mendicants. This was an expression of nostalgia for nomadic tribalism and a counter-cultural rejection of conventional society. One of these seekers was Siddhartha Gautama (c. 563–483 BC), who came to be known as the Buddha ("the Enlightened One").

The Buddha was the son of the chief of a republican tribe, but he was active as a teacher of salvation in the kingdoms of Magadha and Kosala. He renounced society as an ascetic who starved himself to gain truth, but then he decided that salvation lay in "the middle path" between the extreme asceticism of the Jainist sect, founded somewhat earlier, and the self-indulgent luxury of the rulers of society. The order of monks that he founded was governed by the same democratic and egalitarian principles as the tribal assembly. Buddha himself said, when a king was considering a campaign against a confederacy of tribes, that as long as this confederacy would "act in accordance with the ancient institutions" and decide things together in harmony, so long would they prosper and then added that this was also true of his monastic order.[11] The initiation of new monks into the order also resembled the tribal ceremonies of adoption.

One Buddhist text, evidently making use of folk memories of tribal communism and of observation of the patches of primitive communism that remained, found the origin of kingship to reside in the institutions of private property and the family. Before the cultivation of the land, there had been no private property, and there was a golden age of harmony and brotherhood. With the development of private property there came contention as to who owned what. Finally, it was agreed to choose a supreme arbiter, the king, who in return for his services was given one-sixth of the produce.[12]

In essence the Buddhist monk was seeking to return to the period of nomadic food-gathering before agriculture brought private property and the family.

> A monk possessed almost no private property at all.... The life of the monk is described [in Buddhist texts] as the *homeless life*, and in order to enter upon it he had to *leave the home, filled with faith*. The original rigor of the monastic rules seems to have demanded that a monk lived in the forest, in the open, at the foot of a tree.... Food should be obtained by begging.[13]

The monastic brotherhood—similar in many respects to the tribal brotherhood—replaced private property and the family.

The Social Conditions for the Rise of Buddhism

Buddhism was, however, more than an attempt to return to the past on the part of its monks. It came into being at a time when the agricultural surplus had brought about the flourishing of trade. Urban centers of production grew up, mainly of luxury goods, whose products went to the upper classes and to export markets, first the Roman Empire and then, when the Roman Empire collapsed in the third century, China and the Arab world. Buddhism's influence grew, as the mercantile community, which was its chief support, grew in wealth until its gradual decline toward the end of the first millennium AD.[14] At the same time the vastness of the sub-continent, the remaining jungle, and the ease of food-gathering made possible the continuing survival of primitive food-gathering tribes despite the advance of civilization.

The fabled riches of the upper classes and the splendid civilization made possible by it was, to use the title of A.L. Basham's well-known book, "the wonder that was India."

> [W]hen Alexander of Macedon was drawn to the East [in 327 BC] by the fabulous wealth and magic name of India, England and France were barely coming into the Iron Age. The discovery of America was due to the search for new trade routes to India.... The Arabs, when they were intellectually the most progressive and active people in the world, took their treatises on medicine and a good deal of their mathematics from Indian sources.[15]

The immensely rich merchants and financiers of the cities were the early patrons of Buddhism.[16] Many of Buddhism's features must have appealed to these members of the Vaisya caste, which, though economically powerful, did not have the status of the landowning Brahmans and Kshatriyas. Buddhism denied the authority of the Vedas and of the Brahmans who had monopolized knowledge of them. It rejected animal sacrifice, which was a source of power for the Brahmans, and instead propounded the doctrine of nonviolence that opposed the taking of any life, animal as well as human. The doctrine of nonviolence was undoubtedly congenial to those engaged in trade, who did not want it to be interfered with by intertribal warfare or other violence. Moreover, unlike the Brahman texts, which forbade Brahmans to associate with those who engaged in trading in money, Buddhism did not condemn usury.

Buddhist monasteries were built near towns to make begging easier. "Wealthy merchants," comments Thapar, could accumulate a "credit of merit" through grants to the monasteries, and adds, "The analogy with the accumulation and transference of capital can hardly be overlooked."[17] While the monk avoided the things of this world in order to gain the blessedness of nirvana, the "pious laity" who did not seek "complete salvation" could gain "worldy goods...such as riches, a good name, good company, death without fear and betterment of rebirth opportunities" through such "merit-making" grants.[18]

Although Buddhism boasted of its converts and patrons from the higher castes, the monks were chiefly drawn from the lower castes—artisans, fishermen, basket-weavers.[19] The Buddhist order was a means of entering a non-caste sect, for Buddhism did not believe that caste stood in the way of personal salvation. While the Buddhist order accepted members of all castes, it did not condemn the caste system in society, just as it did not condemn the family although its members left their families, for the renouncers of society were dependent upon society for their support. So too women, mostly from urban centers and royal households, were accepted into nunneries. The adoption of a new name by both monks and nuns was indicative of a new birth into an order in which caste and sex were irrelevant, but this order did not seek to change society.

Buddhism therefore supplied a safety valve for society. This commended it to Asoka, the ruler of the Mauryan empire from 268 BC to 231 BC, under whom Buddhism flourished. He saw it as a unifying ideology that would lower the tensions generated by such social problems as "the status of the mercantile community, the power of the guilds in urban centers, the strain of a highly centralized political system, and the sheer size of the empire."[20] Instead of the tyrannies of petty kings there would be the benevolent despotism of an emperor who ruled in accordance with the Universal Law of Righteousness and regarded his subjects as his children, preserving peace within the family. But, while he spoke to his subjects about the virtues of harmony, tolerance, and nonviolence, he claimed that "there were occasions when violence might be unavoidable, as for instance when the more primitive forest tribes were troublesome" or when it was not possible for rulers to conquer save by force, in which case "conquest" should be "conducted with a maximum of mercy and clemency."[21] The "middle path" in conquest as well as in everything else!

Buddhist Philosophy and Its Milieu

Despite its talk of the "middle path" in the conduct of life, Buddhism is in its essence a doctrine of salvation. Early Buddhism, however, denied the existence of a god who created the universe and dispensed rewards and punishments. Many have asked how an atheistic philosophy can be called a religion. Do we have to revise our idea of religion or do we have to say that Buddhism is not a religion? Another question, not so frequently asked, is how did Buddha come to propound atheism in the fifth century BC.

Thapar's description of Buddha's social and philosophical milieu is helpful for arriving at answers to these questions:

> The changing features of social and economic life, such as the growth of towns, expansion of the artisan class, and the rapid development of trade and commerce were closely linked with changes in another sphere: that of religion and philosophical speculation. The conflict between the established orthodoxy and the aspirations of newly rising groups in the urban centers must have intensified the process, which resulted in a remarkable richness and vigor in thought which was rarely surpassed in the centuries to come.... [P]hilosophical speculation ranged from determinism to materialism.... There was a wide variety of atheistic sects, many of which, such as the *Charvakas*, preached total materialism.[22]

Buddha himself was very much a part of this milieu. "Most of the Buddha's public activity," says Conze, "took place in cities and that helps to account for the intellectual character of his teachings, the 'urbanity' of his utterances and the rational quality of his ideas."[23]

Buddha's intellectual milieu bears many points of resemblance to the milieu of Greek philosophy, which George Novack finds originated in the commercial centers of Iona.[24] Like Indian philosophy, Greek philosophy

> moved along the two opposing paths of idealism and materialism which intersected and interacted upon each other.... [T]he idealist tendency...[was] a rationalized reconstruction of religious views

and an ideological instrument of patrician domination.... The materialist tendency...was the distinctive outlook of the historically
new and socially dynamic forces in the Greek city-states...the merchants, manufacturers, shipowners, along with sizeable bodies of
artisans, miners, and maritime workers.[25]

Buddhism, as we have seen, while providing in its monasteries an escape for members of all castes from the society of the
time, was expressive of the outlook of merchants and artisans. It
was a largely materialist philosophy which denied the creation of
the universe by a god and the existence of a soul.[26] But, just as
Greek materialism and idealism "intersected and acted upon
each other," so did Indian materialism and idealism. The thought
of the Greek materialist philosophers, says Novack, "was subjected to the influences and pressures exerted from above by the
aristocrats and from below by the discontented peasants, soldiers, plebeians, foreigners, freedmen, and even slaves in their
city-states."[27] Just so, Buddhism, despite its materialism, retained
with some modification the Brahman ideas of reincarnation and
of the changeless bliss attained by the wise men of Brahmanism.
We may say, therefore, that early Buddhism was essentially a materialistic philosophy[28] that, however, deviated from materialism
in rationalizing features of the inherited religious belief. Later it
adopted many beliefs of the tribes that had been assimilated into
the caste system, and it degenerated into a religion.

The idea of reincarnation in Brahmanism was dependent on
the idea of the soul, which migrated from the body on death to
another body being born, but Buddhism rejected the idea of the
soul and yet retained the doctrine of reincarnation. It explained
reincarnation by asserting that desire for life in this world exists in
all beings except saints and that this desire is a vital process,
which passes from one body to another. The Buddhist texts compare this transference to one lamp lighting another lamp: the fire
is transferred, but no part of one lamp goes into the other lamp.[29]

Buddhism accepted the idea that the predispositions and place
in existence of a being were conditioned by the character of the
being from which the vital process was transferred. This, it held,
was an automatic process, the wheel of rebirth, which needs no
presiding divine spirits. Why the process worked this way and
how it did so without the transference of something that is un-

changing it did not explain. It declared that the sexual act was the necessary but not sufficient cause for a new life since the fertilized egg had to develop a body and acquire a mind, a process imparted to it from outside, but it did not explain hereditary resemblance between parents and children. As a historian of Hinduism and Buddhism has noted, "Unless we accept a materialist explanation...that mind is merely a function of matter, the birth of a mind is not explicable as a mere process of cell development: something pre-existent must act upon the cells."[30] But the Buddhist texts, like the Brahman texts, do not take up the question of whether mind is a function of matter and do not present any evidence for reincarnation, simply taking if for granted.

So too Buddhism accepts the idea propounded in the Upanishads, the Brahman works of idealistic philosophy which were composed, it is believed, starting about 600 BC, that a saint may by rising above this world of flux attain a state of changeless bliss; but it gives different grounds for belief in that idea. The Upanishads spoke of the universal soul, Brahma that animates the universe and is manifested in the different gods. Brahma alone is the Real, which cannot be described or intellectually comprehended. The saintly person who rises above the material forms of this world can, however, attain mystic union with it, experiencing the ecstatic state in which there is, as the Mandukya Upanishad says, "the cessation of all phenomena; It is all peace, all bliss...."[31]

Buddhism also spoke of a state of bliss, nirvana, even though it did not believe in a universal soul. Life is characterized by suffering, which is the result of the desire for the things of life. The struggle of the saint to rid himself of this desire may extend over several births. The saint who persists in this struggle "will be born again on earth or in some heaven but not more than seven times before he attains nirvana."[32] Seven, which cannot be divided by any number other than itself, is of course, like three, a mystic number, as is known to gamblers ("seven, come eleven").

And what is nirvana?

[T]he Buddha emphasizes the fact that his teaching is not a variety of the Brahmanic doctrine about the Atman [soul]. Shortly afterward in the same sutta [text purporting to give the words of Buddha himself] he even more emphatically says that he does not teach annihilation.[33]

In another dialogue Buddha tells a monk named Vaccha,

> Vaccha, the theory that the saint exists (or does not exist and so on) after death...does not conduce to distaste for the world, to the absence of passion, to the cessation of evil, to peace, to knowledge, to perfect enlightenment, to nirvana.... The saint who is released from what is styled form is...like the great ocean. It does not fit the case to say either that he is reborn nor not reborn.[34]

Vaccha, we are informed by the text, was satisfied by this statement.

Apparently, as Eliot says, the idea is that a wave in the ocean which stops struggling to continue as a wave cannot be said to continue to exist and yet it cannot be said to be annihilated since the water that composed it is still there. But, Vaccha might have retorted, the wave, unlike a human being, does not think or feel. The material elements of a human being may not be lost to the universe on his or her death, but it is rather difficult to say of the person who no longer thinks and feels that he or she has gained peace and perfect enlightenment.

The Development of Buddhism

Buddhism underwent a development similar to that of ancient Christianity. The monasteries, which it received from its wealthy patrons, became huge, opulent complexes which employed slave labor, as the Christian monasteries of the Middle Ages employed serf labor. A Chinese traveler in AD 630 described what he saw:

> Six kings built as many monasteries one after the other.... Precious terraces spread like stars and jade pavilions were spired like peaks.... Streams of blue water wound through the parks; green lotus flowers sparkled among the blossoms of sandal trees, and a mango grove spread outside the enclosure.... In India there were thousands of monasteries, but none surpassed this one in magnificence and sublimity. Always present were 10,000 monks, including hosts and guests.... The king gave them the revenue of more than 100 villages to support them.

This was a little different from being a wandering mendicant receiving leftover food and sleeping under a tree in the forest.

The Buddhist order split into two sects in the second century AD, the Mahayana sect and the Hinayana sect. The Mahayana sect accepted the new monasticism without apology. The Hinayana sect kept some external forms of the old austerity, but it too received lavish grants, which came to be administered in the course of time by families that headed the abbeys.

The Mahayana sect borrowed from the idealistic philosophy of Brahmanism. Nagarjuna, a Buddhist philosopher from a Brahman family, taught that everything in this world, including of course the splendid monastic complexes, is an illusion. For centuries Buddhist philosophers debated Brahman philosophers on fine points of metaphysics. On the other hand, however, Buddhism, eager not to lose its support among the masses, assimilated some of the features of Tantricism, a primitive fertility cult. Tantrists held, among other things, that "the sage is not defiled by passion but conquers passion by passion" and that "nirvana can be attained by sexual union here."[36] Buddhism did not accept these doctrines, but it took over Tantric rituals and magic. Miracles, which Buddha had derided, became a dime a dozen.

One doctrine that was developed by later Buddhism was that of the bodhisattva, one who is in the process of becoming a Buddha through successive reincarnations. The bodhisattva forgoes nirvana for the sake of teaching humanity, becoming a "suffering savior" like the Jesus celebrated by the Christians. But, characteristically, Mahayana Buddhism provided for superimposed heavens, each higher than the other in which dwelled numberless bodhisattvas. Eventually there would come the Maitreya Buddha, a messianic Buddha who would save the world.

These seem to be late borrowings from Christianity, just as aspects of Christianity seem to be indebted to early Buddhism. These seemingly Christian borrowings from Buddhism include stories about Christ that parallel stories about Buddha—the supernatural birth (Buddha chose to descend from heaven and to be born by his mother without his supposed father being his progenitor), the temptation by the Demon of Evil, the ability to walk on water. Other aspects of medieval Christianity that seem to be indebted to Buddhism include monasticism, asceticism, relic-worship, and the use of the rosary. The production of "relics" was fully as great in medieval Buddhism as it was in medieval Christianity. "[R]elics of the Buddha's mortal body, worshipped everywhere," comments Kosambi caustically, "grew in size and quantity till they would have done credit to a whole troop of elephants."[37]

Again, characteristically, however, Mahayana Buddhism admitted a pantheon of gods, including the Siva and Vishnu of Hinduism, over whom presided Buddha. A well-known gibe at the philosopher George Santayana has it that his religious belief was "There is no God—and Jesus Christ is his son"; the religious belief of the Buddhists may be said to be "There are no gods—and the chief one of them is Buddha."

As is true of the Christian rulers of society, who have paid no heed to the biblical injunction "Blessed are the peace-makers," Buddhist rulers were little affected by the Buddhist doctrine of nonviolence. For instance, says Kosambi, "the devout Buddhist emperor, Harsha Siladitya (AD 605–655) of Kanauj, fought incessantly for at least thirty years to bring most of India under his sway."[38]

The Development of Hinduism

Brahmanism was influenced by both Buddhism and primitive tribal magic, evolving into that conglomerate of cults that is Hinduism. During the classical period of the Gupta dynasty (c. AD 300–500) Hindu culture achieved definite form. The Guptas continued the work of the Mauryas in clearing the jungle, but because of the vast extent of the settlements, which were no longer on the fertile plain of the Ganges and therefore involved more difficulties, had to adopt a different method than that of force in subduing the tribes.

Max Weber describes how the tribes were assimilated. In return for handsome gifts, primarily that of land, Brahmans "provided the necessary 'proofs' of genteel descent for the Hinduized ruling stratum of an area undergoing assimilation." This "not only endowed the ruling stratum of the barbarians with recognized rank in the cultural world of Hinduism, but, through their transformation into castes, secured their superiority over the subject classes with an efficiency unsurpassed by any other religion." But even the subject classes found advantages in being received into the caste system instead of being pariah workers outside of the system, "untouchables," as they were later called. Since they were "impure anyway, and obliged by restrictions to keep their place," it was "advantageous to secure a monopoly over their work opportunities by recognizing them as a legitimate 'caste,' however underprivileged, rather than an alien people."[39] The state, moreover, put down intertribal warfare, instituted waterworks, and policed trade routes between the villages.

Thus the Brahmans built a Hindu society with a minimum of violence. In doing so, they had to accommodate themselves to tribal cults, acting as priests for the masses of people, which they were the more ready to do insofar as there were now too many Brahmans to maintain themselves by ritual services for kings and chieftains. Just as the caste system was able to absorb more and more native tribes by proliferating castes into subcastes, so the Hindu religion absorbed the tribal cults.

This accounts for the confusion of belief and the combination of subtle metaphysics and gross superstition of Hinduism, of which Eliot says:

> Any attempt to describe Hinduism as one whole leads to startling contrasts. The same religion enjoins self-mortification and orgies: commands human sacrifices[40] and yet counts it a sin to eat meat or crush an insect, has more priests, rites and images than ancient Egypt and yet outdoes Quakers in rejecting all externals.... Neither the devil-worshipping aborigine nor the atheistic philosopher is excommunicated, though neither may be relished by average orthodoxy.[41]

Buddhism's attack on the Vedic gods and the sacrifices made to them caused the Brahmans to emphasize the pantheistic doctrine of the Upanishads that Brahma, the Universal Soul, permeates the universe. Yet Hinduism venerates the images of many gods. The two main gods are Vishnu, the Preserver, and Siva, the Destroyer, who periodically annihilates the universe when it has been overrun by evil, and the two main Hindu sects consist of the worshippers of Vishnu and the worshippers of Siva. Vishnu, Siva, and Brahma, the Creator, at one time formed a kind of trinity, but Brahma faded away.

The worshippers of Siva and the worshippers of Vishnu each regard their god as the supreme god but do not deny the god of the other sect. The doctrines of each sect are much the same, and "the general inclination" is "to make the two figures approximate by bestowing the same attributes on both."[42] Each is an aspect of the Hindu cyclical theory of time in which the universe is successively created, destroyed, and recreated, as the seasons recur in nature and as reincarnation takes place among living beings, and consequently the god regarded as the supreme god takes on the attributes of the others.

> Thus the Vishnu Purana [the Puranas are the latest of the Hindu sacred writings, originally popular legendary histories but rewritten by the Brahmans] extols Vishnu as being "Hiranyagarbha, Hari and Sankara (i.e., Brahma, Vishnu and Siva), the creator, preserver and destroyer...."[43]

Vishnu therefore differs from his competitors only in name, but the adherents of Vishnu, unlike Shakespeare's Juliet, who asked, "What's in a name?" seem to regard the name as of importance.

The gods, like human beings, show themselves in many incarnations. A popular incarnation of Vishnu was Krishna, a hero of one of the epics, which from being secular bardic poetry were made into religious literature by the Brahmans to suit popular requirements. The Hebrews progressed from "My god is more powerful than your god" to "There is no god but mine"; the Hindus may be said to have progressed from "My god is more powerful than your god" to "Your god is only a manifestation of mine."

The worship of Siva assimilated tribal fertility cults, notably the worship of the lingam or phallic symbol, which is to be found in Hindu temples throughout India. The worship of the mother goddess, derived from tribal matriarchy, in which women tended the communal land while men hunted, also became a part of Hinduism, and the cow became a sacred animal whose very urine was regarded as purifying, as Catholics regard holy water. The gods were now given wives who were themselves worshipped and who, like the gods, appeared in different manifestations. In southern India, where there were many tribal matriarchies, Vishnu obligingly took the form of a woman in order to have a son by Siva.

Kosambi points out that while Brahmanism played a progressive role in bringing the tribes into society and in acquiring a knowledge of astronomy and mathematics useful for forecasting the coming of monsoons, it came to be disabled by the great increase in number of village settlements. The village Brahmans, unlike the earlier Brahmans, were often illiterate.

> The apparent failure of brahmanism...was in fact the complete victory of the helpless, apathetic, virtually self-supporting and self-contained, disarmed village...the productive basis of state power and of the king's treasury.... The unlimited growth of superstition showed...the necessity for the ruling class to subject itself to formal disabilities and restrictions in order to make religion effective in control of society. The advance of culture needs exchange of ideas, growing intercourse, both of which depend in the final analysis upon the intensity of exchange of things: commodity production. Indian production increased with the population, but it was not commodity production. The village mostly managed to subsist upon its own produce.... This curious isolation of village society accounts for the fantastic proliferation of medieval Indian systems of religion and religious philosophy.[44]

The self-contradictions of Hinduism, its derogation of material reality, its adherence to tradition and to a manufactured authority, supposedly from the past, wrought havoc upon Indian science. Brahmanical literature of the period of 800–1200 criticized subcastes in professions demanding medical or mathematical knowledge and decried mechanical occupations, including the building of embankments for controlling rivers, as education in Brahmanical centers of learning became ever more theological. Medical works became commentaries on earlier works, with little attempt at acquiring new empirical knowledge, just as medieval European medical writing consisted largely of commentaries on Galen. So too what was known of astronomy came to be mainly used for astrology.

There was also regression in other areas. The practice of suttee, the suicide of a wife by casting herself upon the funeral pyre of her husband to demonstrate her grief and faithfulness, was revived and given religious sanction in about the sixth century through a corrupted Vedic text. It was a high caste ritual, especially of the Rajputs, the warrior caste of assimilated barbarian invading chiefs claiming Kshatriya status, who were governed by a code of honor similar in many respects to that of medieval European chivalry and whose wives had to be as ready to die as their husbands were ready to be killed in battle. It must be said, however, that honor or no honor, it was a rite that was not often practiced. Later it was not always voluntary—widows sometimes being drugged or coerced by relatives.

At the other end of the social scale there were the rites in the cult of Juggernaut (a corruption of Jagannath, "Lord of the World"), a form of the Krishna incarnation of Vishnu. In these rites a great wooden image of Vishnu was annually drawn in a huge car—"the car of Juggernaut"—supported on sixteen wheels seven feet in diameter, by many tens of thousands of people from the god's temple, originally constructed in the twelfth century, to his "country house" a mile away. Although the distance was short, the dragging of the heavy car by ropes through the deep sand took several days. In the thickly packed throng of straining, fervent worshippers, serious accidents often occurred (the rites are still held, but now on the main street of the city of Puri), but the horror stories of worshippers throwing themselves underneath the wheels in a religious frenzy were unfounded.

British imperialism, intent on justifying itself by pointing to the barbarism of the natives, exaggerated what happened. Imperialism, however, did not materially alter the backwardness of Indian society that produced "the car of Juggernaut." It may also be pointed out that the Christian world is not devoid of such sorry spectacles: thousands of Mexican peasant women each year painfully crawl on bleeding knees to the shrine of the Virgin at Guadelupe Hidalgo. Nevertheless the rite of Juggernaut illustrates the figurative, if not literal, crushing of human beings under the giant wheels of religion.

The Decline of Buddhism in India

The victory of the self-contained village society, which meant the transformation of Brahmanism into Hinduism also meant the decline of Buddhism, as the mercantile community, which was its chief support, weakened. The growth of a self-sufficient village economy brought a dwindling of trade. This made the tribute collection for a large central army more difficult and led to the disintegration of empires and the reemergence of regional kingdoms, which engaged in frequent wars that further decreased trade. Wealth was concentrated in a few ports and capitals, but other cities declined. Patna, which had once been the greatest city in the world, became a mere village.

In overseas trade Arab merchants increasingly cut out Indian intermediaries, sailing directly to China and Southeast Asia. The overland trade with China slackened when Persian and west Asian merchants opened up central Asia, and it came to an almost complete halt in the thirteenth century with the Mongol invasions. Nevertheless, trade with Southeast Asia remained sufficient for eastern Indian towns to remain relatively prosperous, although the debasement of the currency shows the weakening of the mercantile economy. These developments were reflected in religion:

> In the contest for primacy between the Brahman and mercantile communities, the Brahmans, having acquired political power by becoming landowners, were emerging as victors. The decline of the mercantile community led to a lowering of the status of Buddhism, since the Buddhists were largely dependent on it for financial support.[45]

Buddhism retained its strength longest in eastern India, where the decline in the mercantile economy did not proceed so rapidly, and where it had royal patronage.

The Buddhist monasteries were an important element in overland trade. They were substantial customers, buying fine cloth for the monks, costly incense for the rituals, and metal images and lamps. Moreover, they were

> important stages on the journey, resting-places for the caravaneers, as well as supply houses and banking houses.... The system and the monasteries it supported passed away when Buddhism had become a drain upon the economy instead of a stimulus.... The long caravans gradually dwindled.... [T]he immense amount of precious metal, brass, and bronze locked up in the monasteries was badly needed for currency, utensils, and tools.... King Harsha of Kasmir (AD 1089–1101) systematically melted down all metal images throughout the length and breadth of his kingdom.... The work was carried out under a special "minister for uprooting gods...." The metal was needed to finance the king's desperate and expensive wars against rebellious Damara barons.[46]

The weakening of the network of monasteries led to the absorption of Buddhist laymen by Hinduism, which was made all the easier because Buddhism and Hinduism had borrowed so much from each other, Hinduism having accepted the doctrine of nonviolence and the sacredness of animal life and even having accepted Buddha as an incarnation of Vishnu. It was a gradual process of assimilation, as in osmosis. Buddhism largely died out in India about 1200, although in some areas it continued to breathe for another 200 or 300 years.

The final blow was the invasion of India in the eleventh, twelfth, and thirteenth centuries by the iconoclastic, monotheistic Muslims, who found the images of the gods in the Buddhist monasteries offensive and the wealth contained in them attractive. They looted the monasteries and killed the monks, who were not in a position to hold out, particularly since they were convinced that the world had entered a cycle of destruction and religious decline. But even in regions of India uninvaded by the Muslims, Buddhism gradually expired.

Islam in India and Its Effects on Hinduism

The culmination of the steady succession of invasions and conquests and of the setting up of dynasties by Muslim Turks, Afghans, and Mongols was the Mogul Empire. This empire ruled most of northern India from 1526 to 1857, when the English crown, following the Sepoy Rebellion of 1857, took over the domain of the British East India Company, which had maintained a puppet emperor. The consequence was that India, prior to the separation of Pakistan, probably had more Muslims than any country in the world, and yet it remained solidly Hindu. Even today the Muslims constitute 13 percent of the Indian people.

The vastness of the country and the hugeness of its population prevented the Muslim armies from swiftly overrunning India, as they did with the countries of the Middle East, and the difference in cultures made the task of converting the people to Islam more difficult. The first stage of conquest was marked by deliberate terrorization to discourage resistance, systematic slaughter, forcible circumcision, mass enslavement, destruction of temples, and enormous looting. The chronicler of Mahmud of Ghazni, the first of the Muslim conquerors, who set the pattern, writes of one victory, "Many infidels were slain or taken prisoner, and the Muslims paid no regard to booty until they had satiated themselves with the slaughter of the infidels and the worshippers of sun and fire." What the chronicler evidently regards as exemplary restraint in completing the business of slaughter before the seizure of booty is all the more notable since, as the modern Christian missionary historian Murray T. Titus comments, "The dividing up of booty was one of the special attractions to the leaders as well as to the common soldiers of these expeditions."[47]

The second stage of conquest was when the Muslims were faced with the problems of administration as an occupying power. They then followed their customary practice of permitting their subjects to observe their religion, exacting from them in return the tribute-tax paid by unbelievers, and retaining the old state apparatus, employing Hindu chiefs and minor administrative officials. Hindus were governed by their own laws if these did not constitute a danger to the rulers. Thus, although Muslim law forbade suicide, Hindu women were magnanimously allowed to practice suttee.

There were, however, advantages to conversion, and the great majority of Muslims were, before too long, Indians. Although the villagers generally went along with their work, indifferent to changes at the top of society, many low-caste Indians who were reached by the Muslim missionaries were won over to a religion that spoke of the equality of its believers.[48] Also, opportunistic high-caste Indians changed their religion to seek to worm their way into the ruling elite even though the foreign nobility regarded them as Johnny-come-latelies.

A point of contact between Islam and Hinduism was Muslim Sufism and Hindu Bhaktism. The Sufis were a popular cult who sought union with God through ascetic practices and mystical rituals, including the inducing of trances through whirling about. There were various Sufi orders, which followed the teaching of different sheiks or religious guides. In India, as in the Middle East, these orders were rooted among the artisans and peasants.

The Bhakti too was a devotional cult that spoke of direct communion with a god without the mediation of priesthood. The followers of the Bhakti gurus were primarily the artisans of the towns and those in the villages who were in touch with them. They were opposed to the Brahmans, attacked the caste system, welcomed women, and did their teaching in the vernacular. They were influenced by Sufism, and one of their cult leaders, Nanak (1469–1539), for a while joined the Sufis before founding an order that became the Sikh religion, which blends elements of Islam and Hinduism, accepting the ideas of reincarnation and the determination of one's actions in a previous life but rejecting the caste system, the Brahman priestly monopoly, and the polytheism, images, and much of the ritual of Hinduism.

But, although there was social and intellectual intercourse between Muslims and Hindus, the adherents of each religion overwhelmingly maintained their own forms, rituals, and beliefs, the priesthood of each being intent on keeping its own following. The arrogance of the Muslim elite, the indignities that Hindus continued to suffer as second-class citizens, the resentment Hindus felt toward collaborators with the occupying power, particularly that of high-caste Hindus toward low-caste Indians who had advanced socially by becoming Muslims—these things left a bitter memory.

The Spread of Buddhism Through Asia

Before Buddhism died in the country of its origin, it spread to other countries of Asia, taken there by Buddhist merchants. As has happened frequently in the transmission of Christianity, religion and commerce went hand in hand. In taking root in other societies, Buddhism adapted itself to their cultures.

Theravada Buddhism, which was derived from the Hinayana sect, was strongest in South India and Ceylon (now Sri Lanka) and went on from there to the Indianized areas of Southeast Asia. Mahayana Buddhism was strongest in North India and went on from there through central Asia to China, the Sinicized Indo-Chinese peoples, and Japan.

Theravada Buddhism stressed the maintenance of monastic discipline; Mahayana Buddhism stressed the interpretation of Buddha's doctrine. The difference between the two sprang not only from their origins but from the fact that in Southeast Asian kingdoms Buddhism was the state religion tending to become petrified, but in China and Japan it had to compete with other religions.

Mahayana Buddhism in its concern with doctrine split into many sects. These wore different colored robes to distinguish themselves from each other, unlike the Theravada monks, who retained their saffron robes. Many Mahayana sects did not require celibacy, and their monks married. The difference in cultures produced other differences. In the more developed economy of China, the monks found that they could not abide by the rule not to carry money. Even such a trivial monastic requirement as that underwear might not be worn proved not to be practical in Japan: the climate was too cold.

Buddhism in Ceylon, Burma, and Siam

Theravada missions reached Ceylon by the third century BC. As in India, Buddhism assimilated the local magical beliefs, giving broader support to the monarchy, which promoted it. By the power of the Buddha, it was said, "myriads of snake-spirits were converted to the Three Treasures [Buddha, his doctrine, and the monastic community] and moral precepts."[49] Part of this superior magical power was derived from the tooth of the Buddha, which had been allegedly brought from India and was accorded appropriate honor. The Portuguese invaders in the sixteenth century as part of their campaign to convert the natives to the true religion of the cross publicly burned what they said was Buddha's tooth, but the monks claimed that it was really a false tooth palmed off on the conquerors, and so, Buddha's tooth—or at any rate a tooth—is still an object of veneration.

In meeting Hindu Tamil invasions, the kings relied on Theravada Buddhism as the national religion. When a king of the second century BC expressed suitable repentance for having caused the death of millions in these wars, he was assured by the Buddhist monks that most of those slain were "unbelievers and men of evil life...not more to be esteemed than beasts." "Thou wilt illumine the doctrine of the Buddha in many ways," they added. "Therefore dispel care from thy mind."[50] In their desire to console "the defender of the faith," they forgot the traditional Buddhist regard for the sacredness of animal life, to say nothing of human life.

As the official state religion, with a centralized hierarchy, the order acquired ownership of over one-third of the land. It became the center for Theravadin orthodoxy. The monarchs of Burma, Siam (Thailand), Cambodia (Kampuchea), and Laos followed the model of Ceylon. It may be said of them what Donald Eugene Smith said of the Burmese kings: they were,

> with few exceptions, arbitrary and cruel despots whose absolutism was qualified only by the inherent difficulties of building a highly centralized bureaucracy in the country and to a lesser extent by the influence of the Sangha [Buddhist monastic community].[51]

The Buddhist monks, whose temples were the centers of social welfare, education, and local administration in the villages, served the interests of the monarchy, the monastic community and the monarchy being mutually dependent on each other, even though the monks often served as a vehicle for village complaints.

In foreign affairs, with the support of the monastic communities, "Buddhist kings in Thailand, Burma, Cambodia, and Laos (to name no others)" waged wars for "conquest and expansion."

> From the Burmese king Anawrahta's campaign of expansion in Mon territory in the eleventh century onwards, the list of battle honors gained by the armies of the many Buddhist kingdoms is one which would not disgrace such great shrines of military glory as Canterbury Cathedral or Westminster Abbey.[52]

They did not engage in religious discrimination in conducting these wars: while they mostly fought against other Buddhists, they also fought against Hindus, Muslims, and Christians—just as did the European Christian rulers.

Buddhism in Tibet

Tibetan Buddhism was a fusion of Buddhism, both Mahayana and Hinayana, Tantricism, and native magical animism. The exceedingly harsh geographical features of Tibet caused this native animism to take the form of a "labyrinthian demonaltry" (*sic*) that included

> the walking dead, vampires, hundreds of malevolent spirits, each with a specialized talent to inflict sickness, torture, and death. Even the Tibetan hearth god, the sacred companion of every home, was

a choleric spirit. Trivial neglect—a hair in an offering of butter or a pot that boils over—could provoke remorseless punishment.[53]

A line of strong kings in the seventh century brought Buddhism to Tibet from China, with which they effected alliances through state marriage, and from India. It was opposed by the old provincial nobility and the old shaman priesthood but received the support of newer aristocratic and mercantile groupings. This struggle continued for some centuries, eventually bringing into being a theocratic state in which the priest-king was regarded as a bodhisattva. A legend symbolically describing this conflict tells of how Tibet's chief culture-hero, the Buddhist monk Padmasambhava, "the greatest sorcerer in India," conquered "all the most furious and fearful evil spirits, 21,000 devils male and female...making them serve the cause of religion."[54] Buddhism won at the price of incorporating much of the old animism.

The demons, whose images in the Buddhist temples are adorned with human skulls, inhabited not only the earth but the eighteen hells where sinners were punished. Bad deeds, which included disrespectful behavior toward monks and nobles, were punished by the state by such means as eye gouging and maiming, and after death by tormenting demons in one of the hells. There was no escape for the sinner since if he committed suicide he went to the worst hell of all, in which he was continually torn apart and reassembled in order to be torn apart again. Fortunately for the Tibetans, there was the theocratic ruler, the Dalai Lama, who in his great compassion delayed his entrance into nirvana in order to teach his people to be good.

The method of choosing the Dalai Lama was unique to Tibet. Since the Dalai Lama was reincarnated as an infant shortly after he died, a council of regents chose the newborn infant in whom the Dalai Lama was reincarnated by an elaborate ritual. The procedure eliminated the rivalries of competing families and had an element of democracy: any Tibetan infant might become the ruler, just as any American child may grow up to be president. Another advantage of the procedure was that

> it was open to carefully planned manipulation, since the rites of divination could be adjusted—chiefly through the state oracle—to accommodate a suitable family, and the young boy could then be carefully supervised as he matured.[55]

The system, however, did not always work: the ninth to the twelfth designated Dalai Lamas, who, unfortunately for them, lived at a time when the council wielded an unusual degree of power, mysteriously disappeared before they came of age. In fact, only the fifth, seventh, thirteenth, and fourteenth Dalai Lamas reached maturity.

Buddhism in China

Buddhism in China existed as early as the first century AD, but it was restricted to foreign enclaves in the commercial centers of the north. It was only with the later arrival of Mahayana missionaries that proselytization took place. It found its early adherents among petty merchants and the urban gentry, landowners who were outside the major landowning families. It was opposed by the Confucian literati, the ideologists of the Han empire (AD 25–220), who saw it as a threat to family piety and devotion to the state, the values promoted by them.

Buddhism gained further adherents among lower social classes by adopting the practices of local cults. As it grew in popularity, it received the recognition of the more powerful families and of the court, which wished to avail themselves of its authority. The unification of China through conquest by the Sui dynasty (581–618) was justified by reference to the Buddhist idea of the universal benevolent monarch.

By the fifth century many monasteries had acquired great wealth. The income from donated land was invested in various enterprises such as water mills, oil presses, and hostels. In operating these enterprises, the monasteries behaved like the powerful families, charging the same rent and the same exorbitant interest for loans as they did.[56]

The emperors sought to prevent the monasteries from becoming too independent centers of power, at times by taking repressive measures against them and at times by regulating them. The state ordained monks and defrocked them for dissoluteness (it was said in the fifth century that monks "compete with each other in extravagance and lewdness"), rebelliousness, and tax evasion.

> Just as the imperial armies served as the military arm, and the imperial bureaucracy as the political arm, so the sangha [the Bud-

dhist order] served as the religious arm of the government....
[T]he national monasteries established by the imperial government...were charged with the celebration of those aspects of the
imperial cult connected with the royal birthday, anniversaries, and
memorial services for departed ancestors.[57]

The peak of Buddhist power was the eighth century, but the
ninth century witnessed a decline.

> The main factors in this decline were the rise of Taoist political
> power in the royal court and the renewed importance of Confu-
> cianism among the gentry class, including the restoration of the
> bureaucratic examination system under neo-Confucian leader-
> ship. Internal rebellions and barbarian pressures on the frontiers
> contributed to the collapse of the great family systems on which
> Buddhism had relied.[58]

The need for a standing army and for payment of tribute to the
barbarians resulted in straitened finances. The imperial government resorted to the same kind of measures in 845 as did the Indian king Harsha of Kasmir. The images of bronze, iron, gold,
silver, and jade in the Buddhist temples and monasteries were
confiscated, as were millions of acres of tax-exempt land.

Monasticism continued under strict government control.
The Mongol emperors supported Buddhism of the Tibetan variety, but precisely because of Buddhism's identification with alien
dynasties it lost its appeal to the upper classes and intellectuals.
It did, however, remain as a popular religion, engaging in welfare activities and performing such functions as praying for the
souls of the dead, not necessarily for professed Buddhists. Buddhism, Taoism, and the ancestor worship and animism of the
folk fused in popular religion.

Buddhism in Japan

Buddhism did not come to backward Japan until the sixth century, when it was brought in Sinicized form from Korea together with medical science, astronomy, and other features of
the superior culture of China. It was taken up by the emperor
and an aristocratic clan closest to his court but resisted by the
provincial clans. In a royal proclamation in the seventh century
Buddhist religious belief and Confucian civic morality were pronounced to be the guiding philosophy of society under an in-

creasingly centralized government:

> Sincerely reverence the Three Treasures—the Buddha, the Law
> and the Monastic orders [which] are the supreme objects of faith
> in all countries.... When you receive the imperial commands fail
> not scrupulously to obey them. The lord is Heaven and the vassal
> is Earth.... The ministers and functionaries should make decorous
> behavior their leading principle.... Every man should have his
> own charge, and let not the spheres of duty be confused.[59]

The court grew in splendor, as did the monasteries.

> Bishops and abbots shared the brilliant life of the court nobles....
> [T]he mutual acceleration in corruption of the court nobles and
> the ecclesiastical prelates was the chief feature of the time (c.
> 800–1200), though at first hidden under the parade of pomp and
> glory.[60]

The palace intrigue of the court was mirrored in the rivalry of
monasteries and religious schools tied to the court factions. The
consequence was that "centralized imperial control, always ten-
uous at best, slowly gave way to centrifugal provincial loyalties.
Clan conflict was frequently defined along 'religious' lines with
the great families supporting one feudal monastery against another."[61] Buddhism, which was to have mitigated clan hostility
in the service of the emperor, itself succumbed to it.

The monasteries, intent on defending their rich properties
and asserting their claims, organized bodies of warrior-monks
who engaged in warfare, even threatening the government itself.
Buddhism had assimilated the Shinto cult of nature deities and
of hero and ancestor worship, regarding the Shinto gods as
bodhisattvas, and now the monastic fortresses had their Shinto
warrior deities to call upon.

During an extended period of feudal warfare (c. 1200–1400),
the seat of power moved from the court to the provinces, which
were under the domination of a new class of warriors, the samurai.
Buddhism ceased to be tied to the court, and in this time of turmoil
ministered to the general malaise. "The fateful days have arrived,"
it was said. "We, the weak and vicious people of the 'Latter Days,'
could not be saved but by invoking the name of the Lord Amita."[62]

Amita ("Unlimited Light") was the embodiment of the infinitely compassionate Buddha. He provided the "easy way" of
salvation. Degenerate man could no longer engage in monastic

self-discipline or gain merit through offerings to those engaged in such self-discipline. He could, however, attain the Pure Land of heavenly bliss in which Amita resides through believing in him with all his might while fervently repeating his name over and over. Like the evangelical Christian, the Pure Land Buddhist is saved through faith and faith alone.

This doctrine appealed of course especially to those of the lower classes, but troubled persons of all classes found solace in it. As a learned Buddhist who turned away from orthodox Buddhism wrote,

> Final salvation...is nothing but the mere repetition of Amita's name without a doubt of his mercy.... Those who believe this, though they understand all the teachings of [the Buddha] should behave like unlettered and ignorant people...whose faith is implicitly simple.[63]

The devotees of Zen Buddhism, introduced like Amita Buddhism from China, held, on the other hand, that in this time of degeneracy it was all the more necessary to cultivate spiritual self-discipline. Through identifying one's self with the cosmos, one rose above the vicissitudes of life, becoming like a rock in a stormy sea of troubles. The Zen Buddhist, like the aristocratic Roman Stoic, was distinguished by the fearlessness and resolution which never left him. Zen Buddhism was taken up by the new rulers, the samurai, who made it a part of their warrior code. Through them it spread among the common people, among whom it acquired magical practices essentially foreign to it.

When Japan was unified by force at the beginning of the seventeenth century, a military dictatorship over the feudal states was set up. Under this dictatorship there was a revival of Shinto in alliance with Confucianism. The emperor's descent from the sun-goddess was said to preclude his activity in worldly matters, his function being to act as mediator between his heavenly ancestors and his people. No one except his principal ministers (and his consorts) was even privileged to see his face. The business of the state was conducted by the military dictator, the Shogun, and by the samurai, who from warriors had become administrators.

Confucianism had been cultivated by the Zen monks, but it now took on a life of its own, coming into conflict with Buddhism, which was identified with clan particularism.

> Emphasis was laid on the gradation of classes and on the subordi-
> nation of the individual to the social order imposed from on high.
> A breach between this ethic of subordination and the individual-
> ism of Zen culture was inevitable, and most of the orthodox Con-
> fucianists, deserters from Buddhism, sharply attacked their former
> religion.… One of the consequences was…a division of creeds and
> ideals according to the classes, the creed of the Samurai being
> Confucianism and that of the people Buddhism.[64]

When the Shogun, whose official title was "Generalissimo
for Expelling Foreign Barbarians," under military pressure from
Western imperialism had to open Japan to commerce in
1854–58, his prestige was impaired. A section of the feudal
landowners effected a revolution from above through which
Japan was industrialized and the nation unified. It was a com-
plicated process in which both "renovation" and "restoration"
were the watchwords of the day. As a symbol of national unity,
the emperor was taken out of cold storage, and the rites of
Shinto were revived. At first this meant the abolition of the Buddhist monks' privileges and the confiscation of much of the
monastic property, Buddhism, despite its millennium of activity
in Japan, being regarded as a foreign religion as against Shinto.

But Buddhism proved to be too firmly rooted among the
masses. Moreover, the European nations and the United States
pressed for freedom of religion in order to halt the persecution
of Christians. Consequently, the 1889 constitution—the "gift"
of the emperor to his people—drew a distinction between "religion" and "national faith." Buddhism, Christianity, and various
Shinto sects were designated as religions which were granted
freedom except, it was stated, if they were "antagonistic" to the
Japanese "duties as subjects," but traditional shrine Shinto,
with its insistence on the sacredness of the emperor, was the
"national faith."[65] Thus Buddhism, like Christianity, was tolerated, but state Shinto was promoted.

Asian Religions and the Blocked
Development of Capitalism

The fact that Japan became an advanced capitalist nation raised
the question of why other Asian nations did not. As Samir
Amin says, customarily to answer this question "religion is in-

voked (Max Weber and the Protestant ethic), or else race (the specific qualities of democracy among the Germanic peoples, or more subtly, Europe's 'Greek heritage')."[66] Even more crude are statements by Western journalists about the indolence and irrationalism of the people of the East.

In the wide-ranging and highly condensed first chapter of his book, Amin gives his own answer. He makes use of Marx's suggestive comments about "the Asiatic mode of production," which actually existed on four continents, correcting their errors and shortcomings rising from the insufficient knowledge of Marx's time. His thesis is that the birth of capitalism occurred in the periphery of the great precapitalist systems, just as today socialist revolutions have started in the periphery, not the center, of world capitalism, the chain of world capitalism, as Lenin put it, snapping at its weakest links.

The "tribute-paying" mode of production, which "adds to a still-existing village community a social and political apparatus for the exploitation of this community through the exaction of tribute" is, he finds, the most widespread form of the precapitalist modes of production. The feudal mode of production is

> a "borderline" case of the tributary mode, in which the community is especially degraded, since it loses the *dominium eminens* of the land. This borderline character entitles us to describe the feudal formations as "peripheral" in relation to the "central" tributary formations.[67]

> Because Barbarian Europe was backward in relation to the areas of ancient civilization, a full-fledged tribute-paying mode of production did not become established there: feudalism took shape as an embryonic, incomplete form of this mode. The absence of a strong central authority to centralize the surplus left more direct power over the peasants to the local feudal lords...whereas in the fully developed tribute-paying system of the great civilizations, the state protected the village communities. In those civilizations it was only during periods of decline, when the central authority weakened, that society became feudalized, and thus feudalization appeared as a regression, a deviation from the ideal model: peasant revolts reestablished the tribute-paying system by reconstituting state centralization through destroying the feudal lords, thus putting an end to their "abuses."[68]

The backwardness of European feudalism in relation to the fully developed tribute-paying economies of China and India became its strength. The absence of political and economic centralization gave greater freedom to the merchants in the cities.

> The peasants who fled from feudal tyranny, and later those whom the lords themselves evicted in order to modernize the organization of production, formed in the free cities a proletariat that was at the disposal of the merchants who controlled these cities. Commodity production by free craftsmen and by wage labor developed, both being dominated by the merchants.... The trade no longer consisted merely in collecting the products that the local societies could offer; these societies were directly subjugated so that they might be organized to produce goods for sale in Europe.[69]

Japan in the nineteenth century was also at the periphery of a system of tribute-paying societies.

> In the region to which Japan belongs, China was the finished model in all respects—a model that was faithfully reproduced wherever natural conditions made this possible: in Vietnam, in Cambodia in the Khmer period, and in Korea. In Japan, however, the natural conditions presented serious obstacles: the feudal fragmentation of the country and the autonomy of the trading cities limited the degree of state centralization.... True, Japanese society did not give rise to capitalism until it had received a jolt from without. But when the time came, it became capitalist with the greatest of ease. In fact, this evolution might not have taken place if Japan had been so unlucky as to have become integrated in the periphery of the capitalist system [as did China with "its substantial centralized surplus"]. It did not suffer this fate, because it was a poor country.[70]

Amin's answer to the problem, it will be clear from just these few quotations, is far better than the answers given by those whose opinions he is contesting. After all, Japan was neither Germanic nor of Greek heritage nor Protestant. Moreover, medieval Christianity was just as otherworldly as Hinduism or Buddhism. The official doctrine was *de contemptu mundi*, contempt for the things of this world, which are dross compared to the treasures of the life to come. The three great temptations were the world, the flesh, and the devil. The medieval wheel of fortune symbolized the uncertainties of this world, attachment to which must bring misery, just as the Buddhist wheel of rebirth symbolizes the ever-recurrent cycle of life, attachment to the things of this life, inevitable loss, and inevitable death. Of course, the development of capitalism in Asia would have brought either great changes in Hinduism and Buddhism or new religions or both, just as the development of capitalism in Europe brought, first, the Protestant Reformation and, then, a modification and readjustment in Catholicism itself. But we have seen the capacity for Hinduism and Buddhism to change and for new religions to rise in Asia.

Buddhism in Asia Today

Under the impact of Western imperialism, Buddhism became the vehicle of nationalism in the same way that the Catholic Church in Poland and Ireland did. Since the monasteries were not maintained by the colonial governments, impoverishing the monastic order, the monks, leaders in their communities, furnished a focus for rebellion. A militant minority of monks led anti-imperialist struggles in Ceylon, Burma, and Indo-China.

The weakened state of British imperialism at the end of the Second World War resulted in the British reaching a *modus vivendi* with the native bourgeoisie of Ceylon and Burma, as with the bourgeoisie of other colonies, by granting them formal political independence and commonwealth status. The Singhalese and Burmese bourgeoisie, like those of some other countries in the colonial world, were able to effect "semi-revolutions from above."

"Semi-revolutions from above" are "characterized by a Bonapartist leader with broad popular support who implements some important reforms." Their achievements, however, whether in radical agrarian reform or in significant economic independence from imperialism or in democratic freedoms, are "incomplete, limited and often ephemeral."[71] Under the guise of constructing a distinctively native form of socialism, industries requiring heavy investment beyond the means of individual capitalists are built with state revenues in order to provide the necessary base for the growth of capitalism while the managers of the enterprises in the public sector enrich themselves as members of a "bureaucratic bourgeoisie" bribed by private businessmen dealing with them.

As in other countries where a "semi-revolution from above" occurred, the Singhalese and Burmese bourgeoisie have sought to use religion as a unifying ideology but to adapt it to the needs of modernization. Intellectuals have called upon Buddhism to reform itself by returning to the ideals and values of the past, which supposedly will enable it to cope with the present. But the monastic community, whose ancient prerogatives are tied up with traditionalist society, remains a conservative force permeated by corruption.

"The conservative priests" of Sri Lanka, says the *Time* correspondent Schecter, "come from the goyigama caste—'the cultivators,' traditionally the highest caste[72]—and have a vested interest in their temple lands, which are often rented to laymen .... Buddhism in Ceylon...has...some very worldly attributes in its practices."[73] The West German Ernst Benz, who is a strong Buddhist sympathizer and anti-communist, speaks of the "sordid and degenerative aspects" of "the present-day Ceylonese Sangha," which includes many "quack doctors, astrologers, soothsayers, exorcists, and so on," but places his hope in "the strong reformist trends which are endeavoring...to put an end to the politicization and secularization of the Sangha."[74]

In Burma the nationalizations of the Ne Win military regime produced rumblings of discontent among the monks, who were distrustful of the government and felt that it could not be counted on to patronize the monastic order as private businessmen had done.[75] The government for its part, while taking care to speak of its devotion to Buddhism, sensationally presented evidence of corruption within the monastic order, bringing to trial "rogues in yellow robes" who had been caught sleeping with women or with liquor, drugs, or large sums of money in their possession.

After their founding, both Sri Lanka and Burma had coalition governments that were led by bourgeois parties and included communist parties. The 1965 election in Sri Lanka, held after the assassination by a Buddhist monk of the coalition leader, S.W.R.D. Bandaranaike, an English-educated former Christian who had embraced Buddhism, was fought on the issue of Buddhism versus Marxism, with dire warnings about a Chinese Communist takeover in which Sri Lanka would suffer the fate of Tibet. The "middle path" of "dynamic neutralism" in foreign affairs of the coalition was not to the liking of the monks, most of whom opposed the new prime minister, Mrs. Bandaranaike, the widow of the former prime minister.

The consequence was the victory of the United National Party, which had been defeated in 1956 because, led by an English-speaking and English-educated elite, it had failed to gain Buddhist support but which now proclaimed its devotion to Buddhism and criticized Mrs. Bandaranaike for not taking the advice of elder monks. Today the Sri Lankan government is engaged in repressing the Tamils (the Hindu minority descended from natives of southern India brought into the country by the British as plantation workers in the nineteenth century) as the conservative Buddhists had desired.

In Burma, after the disintegration of the coalition between the bourgeois nationalists and the Communists, the bourgeois nationalists turned to the monastic community and promoted a revival of Buddhism. U Nu, the prime minister, made Buddhism the state religion and built new shrines for the nats, the animist spirits worshipped in Burma before Buddha that had been incorporated into Burmese Buddhism. But the government was beset by troubles, including insurgencies by the minority peoples, the Hindu Tamils and the Karens, many of whom had given up their animistic religion to become Christians, regarding the imperialist rulers as their defenders against their Buddhist masters.

In 1962 General Ne Win made a coup d'etat to carry through the government's program by military authoritarian means. One of his first actions was to conduct a campaign of extermination against the pests—stray dogs, rats, and mosquitoes—whom U Nu had permitted to flourish because Buddhism forbids the taking of life. He also attacked nat worship as foreign to Buddhism. Submerged tensions between the government and the monastic order remain, but the pattern of using a modified religion as a unifying ideology in the midst of modernization prevails.

The bourgeoisie of Vietnam and Thailand did not effect a "semi-revolution from above" but instead acted as the servants of American imperialism. After the division of North and South Vietnam by the Geneva Conference of 1954 (a division that was intended to be temporary but that American imperialism perpetuated, knowing that the Communists would win the election the Conference provided for), Ngo Dinh Diem, a Catholic, took power in South Vietnam with American backing. He made use of the 400,000 refugees from North Vietnam, 80 percent of them Catholic, as a political base and favored Catholicism as against Buddhism.

The monastic community became a focus for mobilizing the masses' resentments against the regime. Particularly effective in its effect on public opinion in Vietnam and indeed all over the world was the self-immolation by one monk after another, pouring gasoline over himself and then striking a match. Self-immolation had numerous precedents in Mahayana Buddhist tradition, which tells of how Chinese and Japanese Buddhists burned themselves to death, sacrificing themselves for a principle in order to gain merit and to illustrate their extirpation of physical concerns. For Mahayana Buddhists it was an act of martyrdom that inspired them to resist a government, which was carrying on a war of which they were profoundly weary. The remarkably callous statement of Madame Ngo Dinh Nhu, the influential sister-in-law of Diem, "If another monk barbecues himself, I will clap my hands," which outdoes Marie Antoinette's "Why don't they eat cake?" only increased the distance between the government and the people.

However, the fact that the monks, divided among themselves, were unable to present a clear political program caused their mass support to dissipate. Even the self-immolations no longer galvanized the people onto the streets. "The horror of the act was still strong but the impact was weakened by the monks' open grabbing for power and their inability to present their movement's purposes in terms that aroused widespread sympathy."[76]

Thailand, although it had been subject to the pressures of imperialism, had never been occupied by an imperialist power, and the monastic community there had retained traditional ties to the state. It had served as a tool of the government during the postwar period when, under a facade of monarchy, a military elite supported by the United States ruled the country.

A democratic government was established by students and workers in 1973, but it was suppressed in a brutal coup by the military in 1976. "There were Buddhist monks from rural areas among those who during the brief period of democracy from 1973 to 1976 sought better conditions for the mass of Thailand's cultivators.... But while village Buddhist monks supported demands for reform, the royal monks of Bangkok appeared to have other loyalties."[77] These other loyalties came from family relationships with the royal family and from the power granted them through the centralized structure of the monastic order established by the military dictatorship in 1962.

Hinduism and the Nationalist Struggle

What is called in Western popular histories the Sepoy Rebellion or the Indian Mutiny of 1857 is usually described as a result of a misunderstanding on the part of the ignorant native soldiers, who were incensed because of the spreading of a rumor that the paper covers of their cartridges, which had to be bitten off before their guns were loaded, were greased in beef fat and pork lard. For Hindus biting into them would mean a loss of caste, for Muslims it would mean the violation of their religious law. Actually, the evidence is that although many cartridge covers were indeed greased by the fat of these animals, the soldiers had many other grievances and the greased cartridges were only a precipitating factor. Above all, the widespread revolts in northern and central India, in several cases before the mutiny of the sepoys, showed the general discontent.[78]

G.W. Forrest, the British historian of the mutiny, stated shortly after it occurred: "Among the many lessons which the Indian Mutiny conveys to the historian and the administrator none is of greater importance than the warning that it is possible to have a revolution in which Brahmin and Sudra, Mahommedan and Hindu, were united against us."[79] This was a lesson on which the British acted.

Before this the British had sought to build up a pro-British elite from the Hindu upper classes. But after a period of repression of Muslims after the mutiny, the government adopted the policy of playing off Muslims and Hindus against each other. As Sir John Strachey, a member of the council of the secretary of state for India, wrote in 1894,

> The better class of Mohammedans are a source to us of strength and not of weakness. They constitute a comparatively small but energetic minority of population, whose political interests are identical with ours, and who, under no conceivable circumstances, would prefer Hindu dominion to our own.[80]

Muslim intellectuals therefore came to the growing national-ist movement late. Some joined the predominantly Hindu Indian National Congress, but more formed their own Muslim League. The Indian National Congress included secular nationalists (no-tably, Jawaharlal Nehru), what Donald Eugene Smith calls Hindu universalists (notably, Mohandas K. Gandhi), and what he calls Hindu communalists (notably, Bal Gangadhar Tilak).[81]

Gandhi was the acknowledged leader of the Congress from 1919 until his death in 1948. He declared himself an orthodox Hindu and stated that his politics were inextricably bound up with his religion. He accepted the idea of reincarnation and the accompanying idea that one's caste was determined by one's be-havior in previous life. He "long defended the regulations that prohibited caste interdining and intermarriage," and, although "his views on caste restriction gradually became more liberal... he never rejected the fundamental idea of *varna* [caste] as the ordering principle of society."[82]

Gandhi crusaded against India's treatment of the untouch-ables, calling them the "children of God," but his stand, when a delegation asked him to appoint untouchables to the managing committee of his league against discrimination toward untouch-ables, was that, since "the welfare work for the untouchables is a penance which the Hindus have to do for the sin of untoucha-bility...the Hindus alone must run the Sangh." The untouch-ables in this view, as Roy-Burman comments, are "the passive objects for the practice of virtue by the caste Hindus."[83]

Whereas for many of his lieutenants nonviolence was merely a tactic, for Gandhi it was the center of his religious creed and political doctrine. Nonviolence was in reality much more central historically in Jainism and in Buddhism than it was in Hinduism, with its Vedic animal sacrifices and its Gita presentation of the rightness of killing in accordance with the moral law of one's caste. However, as Donald E. Smith says, Gandhi, "as a Hindu working within his own tradition...stood in a long line of religious reformers who had functioned by a process of highly selective emphasis and reinterpretation."[84]

Gandhi called for Hindu-Muslim unity, asserting that "the God of the Qur'an is also the God of the Gita."[85] This "univer-salism" was in accordance with traditional Hindu eclecticism and ahistoricity, in which religious differences are transcended at a higher level of reality. The trouble was that, as a Hindu, he spoke in Hindu terms, and so he did not always stay on this lofty plane. Although Gandhi on occasion was able to mobilize great masses of Muslims as well as Hindus, his use of Hindu phraseology, in speaking for instance of the future independent India as Ram rajya, the wondrous kingdom of Rama, who with his half brothers constituted a collective incarnation of Vishnu, was not the best way of appealing to Muslims.

Even more alienating to the Muslims was the Hindu communalist movement ("communalism" is an Indian term meaning a bellicose religiosity that brings conflict between religious communities). Hindu revivalism at the beginning of the twentieth century served as a vehicle for anti-imperialism, as Buddhism did in other countries. Mother India was a new aspect of the traditional Hindu goddess, to whom one must be ready to sacrifice everything. Like the Buddhist revivalists, the Hindu revivalists called for a return to the purer religion of a splendid distant past, which would act as a guard against Western imperialism. Their slogans were "Back to the Vedas" and "aryasthan for the Aryans." Hindu revivalism, however, often had anti-Muslim overtones.

Despite Hindu and Muslim communalism, however, which was much stimulated by the British reservation in 1909 of separate Muslim seats in the Indian Legislative Council and the provincial councils, candidates for which could only be voted for by Muslims, Hindu-Muslim anti-imperialist unity was manifested in times of revolutionary upsurge. In the wake of the Russian Revolution there were great demonstrations and strikes from early 1919 to early 1922, in which Hindus and Muslims fraternized. Hindus forgot about ritual purity to publicly accept water from Muslims, and Muslims invited a Hindu leader to preach at the greatest mosque in India. The Sikhs, whom the British had given preference in their army as being a "martial race" (and a religious minority to be used against the nationalist movement), joined the nationalist struggle to practice civil disobedience by the thousands, allowing themselves to be beaten into unconsciousness without resistance.

But at the crucial moment Gandhi called the mass civil dis-

obedience movement off because in a small village angry peasants, who had been fired on by police constables, stormed the
police station, killing twenty-two policemen. "I know," he
wrote, "that the drastic reversal of practically the whole of the
aggressive program may be politically unsound and unwise, but
there is no doubt that it is religiously sound."[86]

In the ensuing bitter disappointment communalism flourished. Nehru, who defended Gandhi's action, nevertheless admitted: "It is possible that this sudden bottling up of a great
movement contributed to a tragic development in the country....
The suppressed violence had to find a way out, and in the following years this perhaps aggravated the communal trouble."[87]

Following the Second World War, with the disintegration of
the British Empire, there was a replay of events. Again, there occurred giant Hindu-Muslim demonstrations, abysmal British
brutality, and heroic determination upon the part of the masses.
Congress, Muslim League, and Communist flags flew side by
side, and the Indian armed forces fraternized with the demon-
strators. Professor Frank Richard, the leader of a British all-
party parliamentary delegation that toured India in January and
February 1946, told Prime Minister Atlee, "We must quit India
quickly. If we don't we shall be kicked out."[88]

For their part the Indian leaders feared the mighty power
they were seeking to ride. Gandhi, whose service to the Indian
bourgeoisie was that he could mobilize India's masses but keep
them under control, said, "A combination between Hindus and
Muslims and others, for the purpose of violent actions, is unholy
and is bad for India."[89] Nehru was concerned that the Bombay
demonstration, the greatest in history although held despite
Congress disapproval, was due to the Communists' influence.

Fearful of revolution, the Congress leaders accepted the
offer of an independent India shorn of Pakistan, where the
British, according to one of the Indian negotiators, Congress
president Azad, thought that a British base would force India to
pay more attention to British interests.[90] The Muslim League
leaders also agreed, although they wanted more territory. The
announcement of partition was a signal for the renewal of a
frenzied communalism, which brought, before it ended, thousands of dead and millions of refugees fleeing from one country

to the other. This was the price of the Indian bourgeoisie's deal with British imperialism. It was also the burden placed on the shoulders of India, a burden of hatred and suspicion, under which it threatens to founder.

Hindu Communalism Today

For a period after independence, communalist riots slackened, but they have increased in the last twenty years. The loss of lives between 1950 and 1964 was far less than that in the fifteen years after 1964, when they went into the thousands. Since 1977 communalist violence has grown tremendously.[91] The pogrom killings of Sikhs following the assassination of Indira Gandhi were, therefore, no mere aberration.

How did a people with a religion widely regarded as especially tolerant of other religions, a people who were somewhat patronizingly referred to in the nineteenth century as "the mild Hindu," come to be possessed by this fury? A partial answer is that many Hindus have not succumbed to it. In 1983, when the Muslims in a shantytown of Bombay were attacked by a communalist mob, the Hindus also living there helped the Muslims to resist, and this occurred in a number of places elsewhere. Many Hindus at the risk of their lives aided Sikhs after Indira Gandhi's assassination.

But this answer does not explain the frenzy of the communalists. This frenzy comes from a seething but misdirected mass discontent. The "semi-revolution from above" India has undergone has produced only limited gains. The rising expectations of the masses have been disappointed. At the same time among the Muslims, who suffered a "middle-class vacuum" when the educated went to Pakistan, where they would have greater opportunity, there developed some real estate entrepreneurs and other newly rich, ministering to communalist feeling.

Communalism must be fought through thoroughgoing socioeconomic change and also ideologically. The ruling Congress Party (I)[92] cannot do the first and does not wish to do the second. The state that was established at independence, although supposedly secular, from the beginning had elements of communalism built into its structure, symbolized by the fact that the walls of parliament buildings have quotations from Hindu sacred texts inscribed on them but not quotations from Islamic, Sikh, or Christian texts.

Today, in addition to the growth in number and influence of rabid communalist organizations, the Congress Party (I) is turning more and more openly to communalism. It and the national government remained quiet when the police in various districts were passive onlookers or even active participants in communalist riots. Rajiv Gandhi, when the attention of the world press was fixed on India, called out the army only after 2,000 Sikhs in Delhi alone were killed, with the police doing nothing to stop it. The escalation of violence, which began as being spontaneous, was organized by second-rank Congress leaders and their gangs of hoodlums.[93]

With the erosion of the mass base of the Congress Party (I), it has made more and more use of diversionary communalism, thus ironically using the same tactic as British imperialism. But just as Hindu unity with the Muslims and Sikhs was greatest during upsurges of anti-imperialist struggle, so is it greatest during times of acute class struggle. "In general, communal riots do not take place when strong movements of the toiling masses are taking place. During the textile strike [of 1982], communalism in Bombay was down to a minimum and the influence of Shiv Sena [an anti-Muslim communalist organization] was at an all time low."[94] But anti-communalist forces need to unite on a program of opposition to communalism.

CHAPTER NINE

Islam

The Social Origins of Islam

Islam was born in Arabia in the seventh century AD; it was a religion that had its genesis in Mecca, an important urban center on the existing trade routes.

A complex relationship existed between the town dwellers and the nomads, who, since pasturage was scarce in the desert, went in groups from one spot to another on camels, which were able to travel great distances with little food and water. The swift camels of the warlike bedouins enabled them to make raids on the trade routes and to exact protection from the town dwellers in the form of what is still in parts of Arabia today wryly referred to as the "brotherhood tax."[1] At the same time townspeople often bought herds, which were privately owned but with collective access to pasture, to be taken care of by the nomads, who frequently became indebted to the rich merchants. Conversely, bedouin families, which had grown wealthy, bought property in the towns, from which some of the chieftains ruled their wandering tribesmen.

Theoretically, all members of a tribe were equal, with chieftains elected by the tribe. But by the time of Muhammad, tribal society had begun to disintegrate, with a nomadic nobility having been established and individual clans or subtribes being ranked in accordance with the closeness of their kinship to the nobility within their tribe. Moreover, not all tribes were the same. Small tribes were dependent on large tribes and acted as buffers between them in intertribal conflicts.[2]

The power of both the towns and the bedouin tribes was related to the power of the outlying states, which vied for the control of the Arabian peninsula. It was the mutual exhaustion of the Persian and Byzantine empires in their struggle with each other that brought Mecca, the birthplace of Muhammad, to the fore as a trading center.

> The decline of Al-Yaman [in South Arabia] as the dominant commercial power in the peninsula, the northern migration of nomads and the rise of Mecca as a trade center must be seen both within the context of international state relations and in the setting of town and desert relations.... The lengthy wars between Persia and Byzantium had, in addition to weakening their economies, made trade routes in the Gulf and Red Sea unsafe. The result was that coastal trade through Mecca and Yathrib [later renamed Medina] became increasingly important. This influx of wealth into Mecca brought about fundamental changes in its social, political and cultural life.[3]

These changes effected an undermining of bedouin egalitarianism and other bedouin values. The wealthy merchant might be the chief of a clan, but his wealth came not from tribal raids but from his own enterprise. He did not, therefore, feel the traditional obligation to take care of the poorer members of the clan. His business came before his clan solidarity.

The Effect of Its Social Origins on Islam

Muhammad, who began life as an orphan of a declining clan, became a moderately prosperous trader after his marriage to a widow of substance. The first followers of Muhammad shared his social position. "The simplest way of describing the main body of Muhammad's followers," says W. Montgomery Watt,

> is to say that they were the strata of society immediately below this topmost stratum [of "the leading, richest and most powerful merchants,"].... The younger brothers and cousins of the chief merchants must have been wealthy young men [but lacking great influence in their families and clans], while the men from other clans, like Abu-Bakr, were probably struggling to retain such independence as still remained to them.[4]

The Koran reflects Muhammad's outlook as a trader but a trader who had been a poor orphan and was not a member of the inner circle of great merchants. It is, as Maxime Rodinson says, citing a study by Charles C. Torrey, "spontaneously studded with commercial expressions."

It will suffice here to give Torrey's summary of the practical theology of the Koran, which concludes his precise study of its vocabulary and concepts: "The mutual relations between God and man are of a strictly commercial nature. Allah is the ideal merchant...the pattern of honest dealing. Life is a business, for gain or loss. He who does a good or evil work ("earns" good or evil), receives his pay for it, even in this life. Some debts are forgiven, for Allah is not a hard creditor. The Muslim makes a loan to Allah; pays in advance for paradise; sells his own soul to him, a bargain that prospers. The unbeliever has sold the divine truth for a paltry price, and is bankrupt.... At the resurrection, Allah holds a final reckoning with all men."[5]

The individual thus has value in himself as one who can attain salvation, not merely as the member of a clan, and his value increases as he grows in wealth justly earned. This is a religion of merchants, and Allah himself, in accordance with the predilection that humanity has for making God in its own image, is appropriately the idealized merchant, just-dealing but also compassionate, not like the mighty mercantile chiefs.

Thus the Koran counsels men not to inveigh against inequality as such, but it denounces the arrogant rich who do not live just lives, thinking only of amassing more money and not giving anything to the poor.

Nay, nay! But ye / Honor not the orphans! / Nor do ye encourage / One another / To feed the poor!— / And ye devour Inheritance [of women, minors, and other weak clan members]— / All with greed, / And ye love wealth / With inordinate love! (Koran, lxxxix, 17–20)

The denunciation of the rich who paid no heed to the poor as well as other aspects of Islam made it congenial to the bedouins after it had established itself in the oasis settlement of Medina and had triumphed over Mecca, whose ruling tribe dominated by great merchants had originally rejected the Prophet. Islam, "a temporary fusion of urban skills and leadership with nomad power,"[6] answered to the needs of the Arab people generally. The great empires of Persia and Byzantium had played the different tribes against each other for their own advantage and used the bedouin warriors as mercenaries to buttress themselves. Islam acted as a cohesive force which served to protect from tribal raids the commerce that had grown up and turned the restless bedouin energy outward.

After Muhammad's death, the nomad chiefs of the confederation he had effected, for whom their profession of faith was an insignificant article of a treaty by which they no longer felt bound, rebelled. They were, however, reconquered by the zealous band that had a genuine religious fervor and were welded together into a community with a common faith and a common interest in booty.

Islam and the Tribal Ethics and Religion of the Arabs

The religion of the bedouins, like that of the ancient nomadic ancestors of the Hebrews, consisted of belief in local deities, spirits inhabiting sacred places, and fetishistic objects of various kinds. Muhammad, who knew the monotheism of the Christians and the Jews, representatives of civilizations superior to that of the Arab tribes contending against each other, proclaimed to his fellow Arabs that there is but one God—and that this God is Allah. Allah, the creator of heaven and earth, was the god of the shrine of Mecca. Just as the Israelites made the tribal god Jehovah into a universal God, so did Muhammad do the same for Allah. But Allah, the one God, the Lord of the universe, had a special connection with the Arabs, as Jehovah had with the Israelites.

Muhammad denounced the local idols and fetishes of the Arabs, but he did not do away with all of them. Just as the Jews had their fetish in the temple of Jerusalem's sacred "Covenant Box" that supposedly contained the tablets Moses received from Jehovah, so the followers of Muhammad continued to regard with reverence the sacred Black Stone, probably a meteorite, in the great shrine in Mecca, the Prophet himself kissing it whenever he approached it. One reason that Mecca had become a trading center was that pilgrimages were made to visit the shrine, and on four months of the year the blood vengeance of the desert was forbidden in the city. Muhammad made the pilgrimage to Mecca a basic part of the Islamic religion, to be undertaken if possible at least once in one's life.

But Islam modified the values of the nomads. Vengeance should as much as possible be left to Allah, who would punish transgressions in the next world. Various rules were laid down that cut the amount of feuding among believers. At the same time Islam provided for mutual aid and a solid front against unbelievers. One believer in Allah could not kill another believer to avenge a related unbeliever, and in war believers could not make individual peace with the enemy. There had before this been alliances of tribes, but now there was a sense of community based on religious belief.

So too the careless generosity of the nomadic nobility, which was considered a mark of honor, and the hospitality which each tribesman was expected to practice were in good part absorbed by the organized charity run by the religious community. Very early on this community began to build a political structure in the stateless tribal society. The head of this structure—first the Prophet and then his successors, the caliphs—was the religious guide as well. Basic tribal characteristics were preserved in this rudimentary state, in which administrators were few, the repressive apparatus limited, and the state treasury, used to pay for the standing army, by no means clearly differentiated from the private wealth of the leader.

Islam, Judaism, and Christianity

Islam was in large part an Arabization of elements of Judeo-Christian belief. Just as the Jews regarded the Old Testament as the Word of God and Christians regarded the New Testament as a sequel to the Old Testament, Muslims regarded the Koran as the recording of God's voice, as transmitted by the angel Gabriel to the prophet Muhammad. That Muhammad was indeed the messenger of God was "proven" by the fact that his coming had been predicted in the Bible, as Paul and the author of the Epistle to the Hebrews had "proved" in the same way that Jesus was the long-awaited messiah.

Zealous Christians before our own time considered Muhammad to be a madman, for of course it was lunacy to assert that one was the messenger of God's word since that word was contained for all time in the Bible. The Western Enlightenment thinkers, on the other hand, with their propensity to regard religion as an upper-class conspiracy, considered him to be a clever imposter who practiced upon the credulousness of his people. It is far more likely, however, that, although he may have occasionally purposefully heard what he wanted to hear in making immediate practical decisions, he really believed that he received messages from Above.

His hallucinations were of the same kind as those of Saint Teresa and others certified by the Catholic Church as having been in communication with God. They were induced by periods of solitude and intense meditation and prayer in a cave in the barren uplands outside Mecca, a practice in which Muhammad, like other Arabs of the time, was following the Christian hermits of the desert. What he heard and saw in these hallucinations was, unknown to him, the product of his unconscious working on his ruminations on the Arab condition and on what he had picked up from Christians and Jews in Mecca and in his caravan journeys.

But Muhammad was not unique. Just as the Essenes had anticipated much of the teaching of Jesus, so Arab seekers of a new faith preceded Muhammad. Just as there were other self-proclaimed messiahs in the time of Jesus, so in Muhammad's time there were other prophets among the Arabs. One of them, Maslama of Yamama, also received revelations in the rhymed prose used in the Koran, formulated prayer rituals, and preached of a god called Rahman, meaning "merciful," the name given by the South Arabians to the Jewish and Christian God. Muhammad also called Allah "the merciful" at the same time that he was saying, as the Jews and Christians said of their God, that his justice was rigorous and dire. The "revelation" Muhammad received was in short not confined to him: others were voicing similar ideas.

Abraham, according to this revelation, was the forefather of the Arabs, whose line was descended from his son Ishmail, as the Jews were descended from Abraham's son Isaac. Abraham was a prophet, as was Jesus, whom the Jews wrongly rejected. But so too were the Christians wrong in regarding Jesus as the son of God. To regard God as having children was to bring the incredibly awesome and distant deity down to earth. In the words of the Koran (iv, 171), "Far exalted is He above / Having a son." The Christian Trinity was, Muhammad pointed out, a rejection of the idea of one God. Moreover, the widespread Christian veneration of icons and relics was really the worship of idols. In proclaiming that there is but one God, the Muslims were harking back, they believed, as numerous other faiths have believed, to an originally pure religion. In their case it was the alleged monotheism of Abraham, who was discovered to have a special relationship with Arabs.

However, Islam retained the heaven, hell, resurrection, and day of judgment of Christianity. As the Christian church fathers had pictured the blessed in heaven looking down mockingly upon the tormented in hell, so did the Koran exultantly contrast heaven and hell, each of which is given an Arab coloration. All that the damned have to relieve the parching thirst of the desert is boiling water. Heaven, however, is like a delightful oasis with cool springs and shady orchards of palms and fruit trees, where the blessed, reclining on rich carpets, are served delicious food. In these Gardens of Bliss there will be maidens (Koran, lv, 56–58), "Chaste, restraining their glances, / Whom no man or Jinn [a spirit or genie] / Before them has touched;— / Then which of the favors / Of your Lord will ye deny?— / Like unto rubies and coral."

Modern Muslim commentators state that this passage has nothing to do with sex and is to be interpreted allegorically, just as Christian modernists seek to explain away as allegorical those passages in the Bible embarrassing to them. They overlook the statement that the young, demure virgins have not been touched by any one "before them," that is, before the blessed of the Lord, indicating that the blessed indeed will touch them. As the Koranic scholars Jane Idleman Smith and Yvonne Yazbeck Haddad point out, the hadiths, the traditions about Muhammad, supposedly derived ultimately from his companions, which have been accepted in Islam as second only to the Koran in authority, show that in the centuries immediately after Muhammad the passage was taken to refer to sexual enjoyment:

> References [in the hadiths] to the increased sexual prowess of those male believers for whose pleasure the *hur* [the houri, the beautiful "gazelle-eyed" virgins] are intended are numerous; the reports make it clear that the *hur* are created specifically as a reward for males of the Muslim community who have been faithful to God.[7]

This picture of paradise, which has shocked Christians who prefer sexless angels strumming on harps, undoubtedly owed greatly to the view of life of the bedouins, whose values were assimilated in modified form into Islam. Bedouin poets, who sang, "You are mortal; therefore enjoy life," traditionally celebrated the joys of sex with women like gazelles.[8] But the Islamic picture of paradise was probably also indebted to "a very old and deep-rooted strain in popular Judaism and Christianity"[9] which regarded the delights of heaven as quite physical, including sexual. So strong was this current of belief that some Christian theologians sought to assimilate it by permitting sex after death until the resurrection on the day of judgment, after which pleasures would be entirely spiritual—an odd restriction upon the body reunited with the soul.

Bedouin belief also included the idea of fate, the acceptance of drought and sandstorms as part of the harshness of life to which humanity was consigned, a harshness from which it could escape only through transitory pleasures. The idea of everything being preordained was incorporated into Islam although it contradicted Islam's emphasis on moral responsibility. This doctrine of predestination imbued Islamic warriors with the religious fervor of those who knew they were chosen by God, as it was to do for Cromwell's army.

The rituals of Islam, apart from those of Meccan origin, were borrowed from Christianity and Judaism. Religious devotions were performed while prostrating one's self and bowing from the waist in the fashion of the eastern Christians. They were held at sunrise and sunset, as were those of the Christians of the Nestorian heresy, who, driven out of Constantinople, were evangelizing in Persia. Later this was changed to an obligatory five times a day.

Initially, prayers were uttered while the worshippers turned towards Jerusalem, as the Jews did, and the Jewish fast day of atonement was adopted. Special prayers were held on Friday, the day when Jews were making preparations for the Sabbath on the following day, even though Muhammad rejected as ridiculous the biblical idea of the Sabbath that almighty God had to rest after his six days labor of creating the universe. Although Muhammad, like the Christians, regarded the dietary restrictions of the Jews as God's punishment upon them for their transgressions, he did adopt them to a limited degree, forbidding the eating of pork. The Jewish practice of circumcision was an ancient tribal ritual that was continued.

After Muhammad gave up his efforts to have the Jews acknowledge him as a prophet like Abraham and Moses (the Jews of Medina perceived the errors and distortions of his references to the Old Testament and, moreover, regarded him as a menace to their own attempt to extend their political influence), he abandoned much Jewish ritual. Instead of turning toward Jerusalem, Muslims were now to turn toward Mecca. Instead of observing the Jewish day of fast, they were now to fast from sunrise to sunset during the month of Ramadan, probably in commemoration of the victory over the Meccan army in that month.

The Expansion of Islam

Through political negotiation and religious proselytizing, through military might and bribery of chieftains, Islam spread throughout Arabia. Muhammad used the customary methods of tribal chiefs, but beyond this he offered the power of Allah, to which he attributed his triumphs, as the ancient Israelites had attributed their triumphs to Jehovah. With this he offered the idea of a united Arabia no longer dominated by foreigners but held together by an Arab religion. "Become Muslims, / And cease to dress after the fashion of strangers," his poet Hassan ibn Thabit told a delegation of tribesmen come to parley with the new power.[10]

The Muslims now turned their gaze toward the rich lands of the Fertile Crescent, the countries of Mesopotamia, Syria, and Egypt, where some Arabs were already living. The increasing aridity of their own country with the resulting paucity of grazing land had driven the bedouins to attack these peoples before without success, but now they had the mighty and unifying force of the new religion behind them.

> The Arab conquests were not the realization of ideas conceived by the Muslim leaders. On the contrary, the roving Arab tribes on the border of Babylonia began the invasion and later applied for help to the Muslim leaders at Medina.... Although hunger and avarice were the driving forces, the new religion was the rallying factor.[11]

Beyond these countries Islam expanded like a compressed force that had been released. Within a century of Muhammad's death (AD 632) it conquered the vast expanse between the Himalayas and the Pyrenees, an empire larger than the Roman Empire at its height. The great cities of Damascus, Jerusalem, Aleppo, and Antioch were taken. Alexandria, the foremost commercial city in all the world, fell after a siege lasting over a year. The border of China was reached; North Africa was added to the Islamic empire; Spain was acquired; Europe itself seemed threatened, as it was for centuries. Nothing had ever been seen like this amazing series of victories.

How was it achieved? Religious zeal contributed greatly to the victories. But beyond this there was the inner decay of existing empires that made them fall like overripe fruit.

> There was every reason why the Arabs should be hailed as deliverers by the older populations of the Semitic World of Syria and Mesopotamia and by the Egyptians.... [T]hey had long been in subjection to Rome, then to Byzantium in the West, and to the Persian Sassanid Empire in the east. They were in a state of permanent revolt...and this revolt...had a religious tinge and a social basis.[12]

The Christianity brought by the Byzantine Empire to these peoples was bubbling with the ferment of many heresies, as was the Zoroastrianism brought by the Persian Empire. The denunciations of the arrogant powerful that appealed to the Arab bedouins also appealed to them. Moreover, the urban centers of these countries were quite willing to turn to any power that would promise them protection from depredations and war.

The Islamic power absorbed these and many other peoples at first as subjects, then as Muslims who in theory (but not in actuality) had the same rights as earlier Muslims. This was in accordance with the bedouins' strategy of accepting less powerful tribes as clients.

> Arab customs accepted and encouraged the adoption, by every clan, of peoples of all kinds and every nationality, which then became wholly Arab. The tide of conversions swelled slowly and then became an irresistible torrent. Persians, Syrians, Egyptians, Berbers, Goths, Greeks, and a host of others joined the Arabs, considered themselves as Arabs and really became Arabs. But still greater numbers became Muslims.[13]

The Islamic army took these peoples into its ranks as new forces, which carried its drive further. Syrians and Egyptians took North Africa, North African Berbers took Spain and Sicily, and Persians invaded central Asia. Thus Islam expanded from its center in Arabia in a series of concentric circles, as new peoples became avid for booty.

Contrary to the view of Islam widely held in Europe and the United States since the nineteenth century that it is an inherently fanatical religion that is committed to enforced conversion at the point of the sword,[14] there were no religious persecutions or forced conversions during this period.[15] Jews found life much easier under Islamic rule than under Christian rule, for the Muslims had the tolerance of enlightened people who did not care particularly if the benighted remained in their ignorance.

The conquerors insisted on only one thing, the payment of a special tax to be levied by the notables of the conquered communities upon their people. In return for this "the religious authorities guaranteed...freedom of worship and freedom to engage in economic activity."[16] Escaping this tax and raising oneself up in society were reasons for seeing the light and embracing the true belief. So far were the Muslims from forcing conversions that in the early period of Islam "some Christians, Jews or Mazdeans [Zoroastrians] who wanted to be converted to Islam were flogged,"[17] a rather severe means of protecting the purity—and the revenues—of the faith. But Arab custom and the recognition of the need for strengthening the base of the empire precluded the continuance of this exclusiveness.

The Zenith of Islamic Civilization

As the Hellenistic provinces of the Roman Empire contributed to Roman civilization, so did the conquered portions of the Byzantine Empire, with their cultural heritage of ancient Greek science and philosophy, contribute to Islamic civilization. Persia contributed more sophisticated (and more autocratic) methods of political organization. India contributed its knowledge of medicine and mathematics. Finally, the Arabs, who absorbed the superior culture they had conquered and at the same time left their stamp on it, contributed their share to this civilization.

Islamic civilization was the richest and foremost in the world in the early Middle Ages, particularly from the mid-eighth to the mid-eleventh centuries, perhaps reaching its highest point in the ninth century. Compared to it, the commerce and culture of Europe crept far behind. Beside the fabled opulence of the great cities of the "East" such as Baghdad, Cairo,

Palermo, and Cordoba the towns of the European Dark Ages were small and squalid indeed.[18]

The Islamic Empire was, in the words of Perry Anderson, "a vast, catenary system of cities separated by a neglected or despised countryside"[19] or, in the words of Maurice Lombard, a "superb urban organization" consisting of "a series of urban islands linked by trade routes."[20] So sophisticated was the commercial and financial network that a letter of credit drawn in Baghdad could be cashed in Morocco.

The extremely rapid growth of great cities was largely based on the monopoly of trade between the Far East and the West. The desert Arabs not only used and improved overland routes but assumed command of the seas with amazing speed. For the first time since the Hellenistic period the Mediterranean Sea and the Indian Ocean were joined together in commerce as parts of a maritime system, and Muslim ships plied their way between the Atlantic Ocean and the China Sea. The wealth realized in these transactions stimulated an extensive trade in luxury goods (spices, jewelry, silk) and the manufacture of textiles, paper, and pottery.

During this flowering of culture, Greek philosophy was highly influential and affected religious thinking among the cultural elite. The celebrated philosopher and physician Avicenna, who recognized that disease could be spread by drinking water and whose *Canon* "remained a medical bible" in Europe "for a longer period than any other work,"[21] and the equally celebrated philosopher and physician Averroes were among many who "felt that the truth learned from rational study and philosophy was also revealed to less sophisticated people through the symbolic language of religion."[22] As sophisticated Christians were to learn to do with the Bible, they interpreted the Koran "allegorically" when they found it to be in conflict with reason.

Some members of the cultural elite went beyond this. Rhazes, also a philosopher and physician (he was the first to use mercurial ointments and sutures of animal gut) opposed the acceptance of miracles and prophets. Although he was a deist, he "maintained that all misfortunes came from tradition and custom, that religion was the cause of wars and was hostile to philosophy and science. He believed in the progress of science and he considered Plato, Aristotle, Hippocrates much greater than the holy books."[23] Here the halfway house of the compatibility of religion and science is destroyed, the concept of fate and the authority of tradition is denied, and the validity of the Koran is rejected. Such thinking was inconceivable in tenth century Europe.

Rhazes and others like him were able to get away with their freethinking because of their social position and academicism. "It should be noted," says Rodinson, "that the people who wrote such blasphemous things about the Muslim religion died in their beds, some even held important positions in government and played an important role despite their extremely unorthodox ideas."[24]

The Development and Decline of Islamic Civilization

Brilliant as was the Islamic culture, the development of Islamic civilization soon reached its limits.

> Despite the soaring commercial prosperity of the 8th and 9th centuries, few productive innovations in manufactures were registered, and little technological progress was yielded by the introduction of scientific studies.... The very volume and fever of mercantile activity, outstripping any impetus from production proper, appears to have led to a series of explosive social and political tensions in the Caliphate. Corruption and mercenarization of the administration went hand in hand with increased fiscal exploitation of the peasantry.... While the internal security of the regime deteriorated, professional Turkic guards increasingly usurped power at the center, as the military rampart against the rising tide of diverse social revolts from below.[25]

This state of affairs in the tenth century inaugurated a long-range process in which waves of expansion followed periods of recession, with the center of gravity shifting from one part of the Islamic world to another. The military might of Islam, for a long time superior to that of the rest of the world, gradually weakened, as its economic strength became less. The chief blows that it received in this long-range process were the overrunning of Persia and Mesopotamia by Turcoman nomads in the middle of the eleventh century; the Crusades, which were a vital thrust into the Middle East, in the twelfth century;[26] the European voyages of discovery in the sixteenth century, which gave Europe direct access to the East and outflanked the Islamic world.

The Islamic society of the Middle East was a tribute-paying society which in relation to India and China had a small internal surplus, but it was what Amin calls a "tribute-paying and trad- ing formation," that is, its prosperity was dependent on a sur- plus transferred from outside, first through booty and then through its monopoly control over long-distance trade circuits. With the loss of this monopoly control, it declined, although this decline was at first masked by continuing military expansion.

Turkish, Mongolian, and other nomads invaded the core areas of Islam, became overlords, were assimilated into Islam, and became soldiers of Muhammad against Christendom or Hindustan. Economic life in the core areas was damaged, but Islam in the middle of the sixteenth century took most of the Balkans and threatened Vienna. These conquests, however, were only preliminary to what seemed to be a sharp reversal of the course of history that set in with the loss of most of Hun- gary at the end of the seventeenth century. But from the incep- tion of the period of the three empires (Ottoman Turkey, Safavid Persia, and Mogul India), 1500–1800, these Islamic states had been subject to the economic pressure of Europe be- fore European imperialism triumphed in the nineteenth century.

As a result of shrinking trade and the further militarization of Islamic society in the twelfth and thirteenth centuries, it could no longer afford the luxury of tolerance that characterized the previ- ous centuries. Schools for the official interpretation of religion and the law based on it were established, free philosophical and theological inquiry was not permitted, and a more hierarchical re- ligious structure was constructed. Earlier theologians had "en- dorsed the secularization of politics in return for a pact of mutual assistance between the government and the Ulema [scholars of Is- lamic law]."[27] Now al-Ghazali, Islam's Thomas Aquinas, and his successor Ibn Jamaa propounded the Doctrine of Necessity, which stated that even the worst of rulers is better than civil strife.

As with brahmanical literature of the same period, scientific compendia replaced the search for new knowledge. The spirit of intellectual curiosity was renewed in the courts of the new em- pire-builders of the fifteenth and sixteenth centuries, but it soon flickered out.

> Something like the spirit of the Italian Renaissance had been abroad in the courts of Mohammed the Conqueror [Ottoman sultan, reigned 1451–81] and Akbar [Mogul emperor, reigned 1556–1605]; but Selim the Grim [reigned 1512–20] and Suleiman the Lawgiver [reigned 1520–66] undertook to suppress dangerous thoughts in the Ottoman empire; and Aurangzeb [reigned 1658–1707] attempted to do the same in India. Suleiman was so far successful that no revival of the inquiring, innovative spirit which in seventeenth-century Europe gave birth to modern literature and science ever occurred in the Ottoman empire (or in any other Moslem state).[28]

Imperialist apologists attribute the failure of the Islamic world to develop into capitalism to the intellectual sterility of Islam.[29] But this sterility was an effect, not a cause. Islam had produced a culture far surpassing that of Europe during the Dark Ages and a commercial market that was only surpassed by the world market of modern capitalism. Indeed it gave Europe such devices for the advancement of capitalism as Arabic numerals, which facilitated arithmetical computations, including the use of percentages for the taking of interest,[30] and double-entry bookkeeping. That the brilliant Arab civilization at its zenith did not develop into capitalism is to be attributed to its structure as a tribute-paying and trading society, not to the religion of Islam.

Islamic Sects

Before its ossification, Islam was marked by a proliferation of sects, which split off from the orthodox Sunni religion or from previous sects. These sects were the religious expression of rebellious social movements against the existing order.

Shiism began as a political grouping of the followers of Ali, the cousin and son-in-law of Muhammad, who were opposed to the Meccan tribal chiefs. The Kharidjites, who objected to Ali's allowing himself to be pressured into giving up the caliphate, were a split-off from the Shiites. They represented the pre-Islamic egalitarian tribal tradition, declaring "every believer who is morally and religiously irreproachable to be capable of being raised to the supreme dignity of the imamate [the leadership of the Shiite Moslem community], 'even if he were a black slave.'"[31] They won a wide popular following, particularly among the Berbers of North Africa, and for three centuries the caliphs sought to exterminate them. Today they survive as the Ibadite sect in southern Algeria. Known as "the Puritans of Islam," they maintain themselves as a minority which has turned to trading, often acquiring substantial wealth.

The victorious Abbasid movement of the eighth century included Shiites, who gained the support of the discontented bedouin masses and of the Mawali, the newly converted Muslims of Persia, Mesopotamia, Syria, and Egypt. The Abbasid revolution was made by a coalition of Arabs, particularly southern Arabs, outside of the inner circle of the tribal aristocracy, and of Mawalis, whose "driving force" were "the Mawali merchants and artisans who throve in the garrison cities established by the Arabs."[32] The Abbasid rulers on coming to power turned against their radical followers and suppressed many Shiite groups.

Under the Abbasid dynasty the main divisions of the Shiites came into being—the "Fivers," the "Seveners," and the "Twelvers." The "Fivers" hold in special reverence the Fifth Imam in the line of Ali. The "Seveners" and "Twelvers" differ on the line of succession after the Sixth Imam.

The imam was a necessary mediator between Allah and the unlettered masses, who could not study the Koran. The imam, who increasingly became regarded as "divinely protected ...against all error and sin,"[33] was a guide through the mystery of life, making his pronouncements not so much on the basis of sophisticated legalistic reasoning about the Koran as of direct apprehension of the revelation that it contains.

Sunni doctrine, on the other hand, stressed that it was the Koran and not divinely inspired men which was a guide for all areas of life. Fine points of law not explicitly dealt with in it could be interpreted from it by the learned in accordance with its fundamental principles—rather like an Orthodox rabbi determining in moot instances whether a food or a plate is ritually unclean, or like the United States Supreme Court determining whether a twentieth-century law is in accordance with the 200-year-old constitution. "When, at any time, its [Sunni Islam's] qualified scholars...have come to an agreement" on "any point of Islam," "that point is assured and the acceptance of it as faith is binding on all [Sunni] Muslems."[34] Since the qualified scholars were more or less manipulated by the caliphs, Sunni doctrine was a buttress for the social order, as Shiite doctrine tended to be a challenge to it.

Some Shiite sects, however, were more accommodationist and others were more militant. The "Fivers" or Zaidis, who are nowadays the dominant religion only in North Yemen, did not regard their imams as infallible and were able to cooperate with the caliphs. The "Twelvers" or Imamis believed that the infant son of the Eleventh Imam went into "occupation" (or suspension outside of the realm of material being) in the nineth century, from which he would some time re-emerge to institute the justice which the Koran demands but Islamic countries have been unable to attain. This doctrine, which was popular among the Shiites in the Abbasid government, was an excuse for taking the caliph's orders while waiting for the Twelfth Imam to materialize in the indefinite future. However, in later times it also acted as a challenge to the legitimacy of the existing government.

The most radical of the Shiite sects in the nineth and tenth centuries were the "Seveners" or Ismailis, who constituted a serious threat to the Abbasid empire. The Ismailis appealed to different kinds of people, including dissident intellectuals, who developed the doctrine that the Koran has two meanings, the obvious one suited for ordinary people and the subtle one suited for the learned. For them Ismailism was "Greek philosophy with a religious veneer."[35] But primarily Ismailism was a movement of the oppressed, in its early period the peasants and then the artisans of the towns.[36]

But the Ismailis, on gaining power in Tunisia and Egypt, came to an accommodation with the Sunni monarchies. The "great struggle to overthrow the old order and establish a new millennium...dwindled into border-squabbles and cattle-raids."[37] Like so many radical religious sects in Islam and in the West, the Ismailis lost their anti-establishment dynamism and survived as an ossified sect. In our time the leader of one of the Ismaili branches is the Aga Khan, the jet-setting potentate and familiar of movie actresses.

In Persia the militant Safavid warriors came to power in 1501 following a popularized Twelver Shiism. Their leaders soon turned to a more conservative doctrine, sending for official Twelver theologians from Arab countries to instruct the turbulent tribesmen in the true religion. Shiism, calling upon Persian traditions of hereditary monarchy, was transformed from a messianic ideology into a means of solidifying Safavid rule and into a weapon against the rival Sunni Ottoman Empire. This is a pattern that, as Engels noted,[38] is repeated again and again in Islamic states: there is a revolt against the wealthy elite, but then the dynasty that is established itself becomes rich and conservative.

In addition to Shiism there was another movement in opposition to Sunni legalism, that of the Sufis. The Sufis resembled the Hasidic Jews who rebelled against the legalism of the Talmud-studying Orthodox Jews. Both originated among the illiterate or barely literate outside of the urban areas and followed popular leaders of a religion of ecstasy. The Sufi sheik engaged in a variety of mystic rituals through which he sought to attain ecstatic union with Allah. All sorts of magical powers were attributed to him. So revered was he that one of them himself recorded that once, when his horse dropped feces, his followers, eager to receive anything somehow emanating from him, picked it up and smeared their faces with it.[39]

Politically quietist and not formally declared heretical, although it was initially regarded by the orthodox with suspicion or contempt, Sufism came to contribute to the revival of Sunnism. It influenced the teaching in the schools and, organized in Dervish brotherhoods, took root in the cities, where it ministered to the social life of the artisans. Absorbed into the orthodox institutions, it gave them a new means of social control.

One idea taken from the Ismailis by various Shiite sects and by popular Sunnism was that of the Mahdi. The Mahdi, the divinely guided one, will appear just before the end of time, when the world will have gone completely to rack and ruin, "to fill, as it was said, the world with justice and equity as it is now filled with injustice and oppression."[40] This doctrine, which was derived from the messianism of Judaism and Christianity, animated religious radical movements of Islam as it did such movements in Christianity.

With the beginning of modern imperialism, Mahdism became an anti-imperialist phenomenon, and "there was an eruption of Mahdist movements at the turn of the [eighteenth] century, which continued on into the early, and middle, colonial period."[41] The most well known of these Mahdis is the one who led the insurrection against General Gordon in the Sudan. As late as the early 1920s the British colonial administrators of northern Nigeria stated, indignant that his majesty's Christian government be identified with the anti-Christ: "It has been the practice of agitators of late to identify the European conquerors of Muslim countries with Dajja [the anti-Christ who precedes the second coming of Nebi Isa (Jesus Christ), sometimes, as here, identified with the Mahdi in Islamic doctrine]."[42]

The doctrine of the Mahdi, however, is not, according to Maxime Rodinson, a significant factor in the Muslim world today.[43] The Mahdi means as little to most Muslims as the Second Coming of Christ means to most Christians in the West. The idea of the liberating Mahdi has been superseded by the idea of struggle for national liberation from the dominance of Western imperialism, but national liberation itself has generally spoken in Islamic terms.

Islam and the Anti-imperialist Struggle

National oppression, as in Hindu India and the Buddhist countries of Asia, caused a more firm adherence to a religion that was despised by the oppressor. As De Lesseps, the builder of the Suez Canal, said of the Algerians, "Fanaticism had not nearly so much to do with the resistance of the Algerians as patriotism. Religion was the only flag around which they could rally."[44] The struggle against European imperialism was a source of renewed vigor for Islam. The village sheiks provided local leadership in the struggle against European imperialism and its Christian missionary agents, of whom Jansen says, "How these missionaries from Holland, Britain and France, dedicated and sincere men of God, could have entered into what was basically an unholy alliance with Caesar, is not easy for us to understand."[45]

The princes, aristocrats, and landlords who worked together with imperialism in Muslim countries of the Middle East, Africa, and Asia were inveighed against not only for their immorality and impiety, as the wealthy rulers of former times had been attacked by rebellious bedouin movements in the name of Islam, but for their association with foreigners and for the influence of Westernism upon them. Ironically, the Christian West, which had caricatured Muhammad as an old lecher, and Islam, particularly the Islam of Turkey, as a religion of voluptuaries, was seen by Muslims as given over to a materialistic hedonism and sensuality. Even after their countries have attained formal independence, the Muslim poor have continued to see the drinking and high living of the wealthy foreigners in their midst and of their own upper classes as scorn for the national religion.

Islam and Modernization

At the same time many intellectuals have seen science and technology as the means for the Muslim world to emerge from its dependence on Western imperialism. They argue that it is only in its decadence that Islam is opposed to rationalism and science and that it is necessary to go back to the Islam of the golden age before it turned to obscurantism and to "rethink Islam in modern terms." Muslim society must remain Muslim, but it must become modern. This is in general the position of the radical bourgeois nationalists.

Other intellectuals are either indifferent to religion or ideologically opposed to it. A portion of these, together with members of the national minorities and advanced workers, have formed communist parties which are perceived as threats by the governments of the Muslim world but which are weakened by their ties with the Soviet bureaucracy.

The founders of the new Muslim nations were either Muslim modernists or secularists making use of the outward forms of Islam for political purposes. They include Ataturk of Turkey, Jinnah of Pakistan, Sukarno of Indonesia, Nasser of Egypt, and Bourguiba of Tunisia. They either effected "semi-revolutions from above" or at any rate were able to institute some reforms.

Ataturk, who established a republic under his authoritarian leadership after World War I, was the first of the "modernizers," and modernization meant coming into conflict with the religious authorities, who were closely bound to the old Ottoman Empire. Ataturk therefore dissolved the religious orders, instituted a Western-derived legal code that was free of the encumbrances of Islamic religious law, abolished many ancient customs incompatible with the modern world, and deleted the clause in the constitution that declared Islam the state religion. However, he insisted that he had "liberated and rediscovered true Islam," "essentially a progressive religion," freeing it from the "bigoted, reactionary clergy who exploited the people, debauched the government, and misinterpreted the faith."[46]

Subsequent leaders proceeded along his path although many did not go so far. Jinnah, whose country's reason for being was its religion, was quoted as saying after he came to power that "Pakistan is not going to be a theocratic state ruled by priests with a divine mission."[47] Sukarno's policy was "to tolerate Islam as a religion but to curb it as a political force."[48] Nasser restricted polygamy, suppressed religious courts, and instituted votes for women; however, his aim was "not...to knock down Islam but to transform it," "to 'neutralize' Islam in internal politics, while 'utilizing' it in foreign politics."[49] Bourguiba, "the most iconoclastic of contemporary Muslim rulers while instituting modernist reforms...allowed the Ulema a certain visibility and status as religious leaders."[50] In short, these Muslim rulers, like the Buddhist rulers of Sri Lanka and Burma, sought to use religion as a unifying ideology while adapting it for the purposes of modernization.[51]

Islam and Reaction

The theological specialists have long been accustomed to giving obedience to temporal authority, and the radical bourgeois nationalist governments have attempted to co-opt them at the same time that they have taken measures against them. To some extent they have succeeded.

But tensions and conflicts have continued as a result of the theologians' ties to classes opposed to the new bourgeoisie. In Libya, Qadafi called the established religious leaders, who had been one of the main supports of the monarchy, "a class of superfluous priests."[52] In Syria, as in Egypt, the military government was opposed by the big-city bazaar merchants and the professional men of religion traditionally allied with them, who "were offended both by its socialist pretensions and by the fact that the men in control," like those of Nasser's regime, "were provincial upstarts, many of whom took to feathering their own and their family's nests with little attempt at concealment."[53]

But the professional men of religion have often outlasted the radical bourgeois nationalist governments. Although, says Jansen, they "have not played a very activist or dynamic role in militant Islam," they are "of great importance as a strong, silent pressure group waiting and watching in the wings."[54] The limited and ephemeral gains of the "semi-revolutions from above" have brought disillusionment. There have then been reactions under the banner of Islam, varying in degree, against the uncompleted revolutions. Although these reactions have generally been led by laymen or military men, the men of religion have played a contributory role.

Turkey, which after the Second World War had conducted under Ataturk a war of national liberation against Allied occupation with the aid of the Soviet Union, after World War II joined NATO and became increasingly penetrated by foreign capital. Fearful of communism, the ruling class felt the need for "a moral and social force to strengthen the community against external attack and internal disruption."[55] Accordingly, it resumed the teaching of Islamic religion in the public schools, opened state schools for the training of religious functionaries, and took such measures for the promotion of religion as putting religious programs on the state radio.

In Indonesia, Sukarno's dictatorship, which balanced itself between the powerful Communist Party and the army, was overthrown in 1965 by the army, which carried on for four months one of the most extensive slaughters in history and instituted a brutal reaction that nullified Sukarno's modest land reforms but made Indonesia "a paradise for investors." In the massacre, "lists compiled by the military were given to rightwing Muslim groups, who were armed with *parangs* [large, heavy knives] and transported in army trucks to villages, where they killed with bloody mutilation." The head of the state security system told a Dutch television station that more than 50,000 had been killed, but Amnesty International estimated the dead at "many more than one million."[56]

In Egypt the reaction came under Sadat, who on coming to power proclaimed a "revolution of rectification" and proceeded to come to terms with Israel and United States imperialism. He declared the time of Nasser to have been one of religious unbelief which he was going to change and released imprisoned members of the Muslim Brotherhood[57] on condition that they did not join the outlawed organization. Although he had to keep changing course in response to the attacks of the reactionary Muslims, "he first encouraged Islamic movements as an ally against the leftist opposition and by so doing opened a Pandora's box which proved difficult to control."[58] How difficult to control were the forces he released was shown by his assassination, which occurred after this statement was written. The Muslim Sadat's assassination by a Muslim zealot parallels the assassination of the Hindu Gandhi by a Hindu communalist and the assassination of the Buddhist Bandaranaike by a Buddhist monk.

Pakistan did not have a "semi-revolution from above," but Bhutto, in the wake of the defeat of 1971 in the war with India, was voted into power on a promise of "Islamic socialism" despite the opposition of the professional men of religion. After the big landlords became increasingly influential in his Pakistan People's Party, Bhutto abandoned his timorous reformism, instituted "Islamic" measures, and dropped the word "socialism" for "the equality of Mohammed."

As happened with Sadat, Bhutto's "exploitation of Islam for political propaganda" served "to strengthen the credibility of Islamic opposition groups, since it made him more vulnerable to their charges of hypocrisy."[59] When General Zia seized power, he "praised the 'spirit of Islam' that inspired the opposition movement" and declared: "Pakistan...will continue to survive only if it sticks to Islam." His regime, however, has been, "to many of the peasants and workers," not the Order of the Prophet it has proclaimed itself to be but "a regime of landlords and exploiters...who are using Islam as a transparent veil for their crimes."[60]

Algeria and Iran have also had their reactions under forces flying the banner of Islam, but they differ markedly from the other countries we have discussed, having undergone what Löwy calls "interrupted popular revolutions." These occur "where the popular masses, workers and/or peasants, burst onto the scene of history, smash the old political structures, but are eventually neutralized by bourgeois or petty-bourgeois forces who usurp the leadership and 'institutionalize' the revolution."[61]

After the victory of the Algerian revolution, workers and peasants expropriated the industries and farms abandoned by the French and put into power a radical wing of the FLN under Ben Bella. However, the leadership, untrained in Marxism, did not follow a consistent course and, the victim of its own contradictions, was finally overthrown in a military coup.

The Boumedienne government, after the coup against Ben Bella, while continuing in many respects Ben Bella's agrarian reforms and anti-imperialist measures, took the direction of "a guided maximization of private enterprise."[62] Ben Bella had sought to join Marxism and Islam: "We adopt the Marxist economic analysis because we believe that it is the only one valid for the economic development of our country; but we do not espouse the Marxist ideology because we Algerians are Moslems and Arabs."[63] Boumedienne's opposition to Ben Bella was carried on in conjunction with the opposition of Islamic leaders. "What had begun as a crusade for the revival of Islam on the part of a small group of religious leaders was easily turned into an anti-Communist and xenophobic movement on the part of the army."[64]

Anti-communism has also been used by the Iranian Khomeini regime against its erstwhile allies, both the socialist left and the bourgeois nationalist modernizers, but whereas the Boumedienne regime is undemocratic the Khomeini regime is savagely repressive. In the first stage of the revolution the *shoras* (workers' and peasants' councils), which raised radical demands, gained great power. This power was first gradually eroded and then almost entirely crushed by the Khomeini regime. Women, who had played a vital part in the revolution, have also been turned against. Religious obscurantism is stiflingly all-pervasive, and the traditionalist bourgeoisie of the bazaars, the chief patrons of the professional men of religion, remains entrenched. The anticapitalist direction of the revolution has been halted. It is only through a "permanent revolution," that is, a socialist revolution growing out of the bourgeois-democratic phase of the revolution, that, as the history of the "semi-revolutions from above" and of the interrupted popular revolutions shows, progressive gains and democratic rights can be maintained and extended.

PART IV

Religion and the Struggle for Socialism

CHAPTER TEN

Marxist Parties and Religion

Lenin on Marxist Parties and Religion

Religion has social roots and in turn reacts upon the class struggle. How, then, should Marxists behave with regard to religion and religious people? The answer to this question was touched on by Engels and developed by Lenin.

Lenin pointed out in 1909 that Engels, "while ruthlessly attacking the slightest concession made by the philosopher Dühring to idealism and religion, condemns no less resolutely Dühring's pseudo-revolutionary notion that religion would *be prohibited* in Socialist society."[1] Such repression would be a diversion from the political struggle and would only strengthen religion, as Bismarck's political persecution of Catholicism in fighting the German Catholic Party of the "Center" only strengthened Catholicism. The German Social Democrats, following the lead of Engels, therefore demanded freedom for the Jesuits and the cessation of Bismarck's persecution.

What Marxists demand of the bourgeois state and advocate for the proletarian state is the complete separation of state and church. As Engels said in his preface to *The Civil War in France*, "*in relation to the state*, religion is a purely private affair."[2] Lenin, elaborating on this statement, wrote in 1905: "The state must not concern itself with religion; religious societies must not be bound to the state. Every one must be absolutely free to profess whatever religion he likes, or to profess no religion, i.e., to be an atheist, as every Socialist usually is."[3]

Although Lenin asserted that the state should allow complete freedom of religion, he also asserted that the revolutionary party must engage in ideological combat with religion. He pointed out that Engels had recommended that the Social Democrats publish atheistic propaganda and that he had qualified the statement "religion is a purely private affair" by the phrase "in relation to the state," italicizing that phrase. "The party of the proletariat," Lenin said,

> demands *that the state* shall declare religion a private matter, but it does not for a moment regard the question of the fight against the opium of the people—the fight against religious superstition, *etc.*—as a private matter. The opportunists have so distorted the question as to make it appear that the Social Democratic *Party* regards religion as a private matter.[4]

But if Lenin was opposed to opportunism, he was also opposed to the ultra-left phrase mongering of the anarchists. He recalled Engels's contention that "proclaiming war on religion as a political objective of the workers' party" is "a mere anarchist pose."[5] The struggle against religions is ideological, not political, and it must be subordinated to the concrete requirements of the class struggle.

"The Marxist," Lenin said,

> must be a materialist, i.e., an enemy of religion. But he must be a *dialectical* materialist, i.e., one who fights against religion not in the abstract, not by means of abstract, purely theoretical propaganda, equally suited to all times and to all places, but concretely, on the basis of the class-struggle actually proceeding—a struggle which is educating the masses better than anything else could do. The Marxist must be able to judge the concrete situation as a whole. He must always be able to determine the boundary between anarchism and opportunism (this boundary is relative, mobile and ever-changing; but it exists), not to fall either into the abstract, wordy and in fact futile "revolutionism" of the anarchist, or into the philistinism and opportunism of the petty bourgeois, or liberal intellectual, who...is guided, not by the interests of the class-struggle, but by petty, mean calculations such as: not to offend, not to repel, not to frighten; and who is governed by the wise rule: "Live and let live," *etc., etc.*[6]

Since "the roots of modern religion are deeply embedded in the social oppression of the working masses, and in their apparently complete helplessness before the blind forces of capitalism...no amount of reading matter, however enlightening, will eradicate religion" from the masses' consciousness "until these masses, themselves, learn to fight against the social facts from which religion arises in a united, disciplined, planned and conscious manner—until they learn to fight *against the rule of the capitalist in all its forms.*"[7] This does not mean that the party should not publish educational books against religion: ideology is a force in the class struggle. What it does mean is that "the propagation of atheism by the Social-Democracy must be *subordinated* to a more basic task—the development of the class-struggle of the exploited masses against the exploiters."[8]

Thus, for example, if backward workers under the influence of the church organize a Christian trade union that becomes engaged in a strike, Marxists regard the success of the strike as more important than carrying on atheistic propaganda among the strikers. "To preach atheism at such a time, and in such circumstances, would only be *playing into the hands* of the church and the priests, who would desire nothing more than to have the workers participating in the strike movement divided in accordance with religious beliefs."[9]

The subordination of the struggle against religion to the class struggle means that Marxists do not make acceptance of atheism a part of the party program. They welcome into the revolutionary party workers who retain religious beliefs, and they "are absolutely opposed to the slightest affront to these workers' religious conviction."[10] Although such cases will be extremely rare, the mass revolutionary party will even accept into its ranks priests who agree with its political program and are ready to do party work. Of course, in that event there will be a contradiction between the priest's philosophy and the party's program, but, as long as the priest works for the program, that is his problem. If, however, he devotes most of his time to religious proselytizing, the party will have to expel him.

Finally, in accordance with the statement in the *Communist Manifesto* that "communists everywhere support every revolutionary movement against the existing social and political order,"[11] Lenin asserted that Marxists support religious sects struggling against the state for their rights: "Social democrats support any revolutionary movement against the contemporary social order, any oppressed nationality, persecuted religion, humiliated estate, *etc.*, in their struggle for equality."[12] Such support, far from strengthening religion, weakens the state, the citadel of religious reaction.

The Russian Communist Party and Religion

The Bolsheviks, following the precepts of Lenin, did not deny admission to their party to religious believers. When the October Revolution awakened the backward peasant masses of Asiatic Russia, as many as 15 percent of the party members of Turkestan and other national republics adhered to the Islamic faith.[13]

The party also took up the struggle of the religious sects against tsarist persecution and worked with them, seeking to draw them into a more general struggle. A resolution of the 1903 party congress urged members to conduct "work among sectarians in order to draw them to social democracy."[14] After the Revolution, the sect of the Old Believers was given land on which to work out its communistic ideas.

After they came to power, the Bolsheviks instituted the separation of church and state that they had demanded. The decree of 1918 "on freedom of conscience and religious societies" abolished the 35 million ruble annual subsidy that the tsarist government had granted to the Russian Orthodox Church and all other privileges from the state. It also proclaimed:

> Every citizen may adhere to any religion or adhere to none. Any limitations before the law related to adherence to any kind of faith or non-adherence to any faith are abolished.... Free practice of religious customs is safeguarded in so far as it does not disturb the public peace and does not infringe upon the rights of citizens of the Soviet Republic.[15]

It thus gave the heterodox sects, which had been persecuted under the tsarist government, greater freedom than they had ever had.

The Bolsheviks pointed out that the separation of church and state was "advocated in the programs of bourgeois democracy" but "nowhere consistently carried out to the end owing to the diverse and actual ties which bind capital with religious propaganda."[16] The decree of 1918 went beyond the United States' separation of church and state in abolishing religious oaths and prayers at state functions. Above all, far from allowing churches tax exemptions on their property, it forbade them to have property. In this churches were treated like other corporate holders of property who were dispossessed. Their status was that of voluntary societies, which could accept contributions from their members to engage in their activity but not to acquire property. Church buildings used for worship were declared state properties but were provided to congregations free of rent. Unlike draft-exempt clergymen in the United States, no one was exempted from civil duties such as army service on religious grounds, but permission might be obtained from a people's court to substitute one form of civil service for another.

Under the regime that Stalin gradually introduced, no free conflict of ideas of any kind was possible. This applied also to religion. Moreover, the one-party state, a concept fundamentally foreign to Leninism, was proclaimed to be the essence of Leninism. The distinction that Lenin made between the attitude of the state toward religion and the attitude of the party toward religion was blurred where the party became the vehicle of a privileged bureaucracy that had a monopoly of state power and refused to be contradicted by anyone in any sphere.

During the time of forced collectivization, peasants came under great pressure to vote to close the churches, in which the prosperous peasants, the kulaks, often played an important role. Yaroslavsky, the head of the League of Militant Godless, boasted that such resolutions were adopted not only by disbelievers but by believers. Young Communists defiled altars and cemeteries, burned ikons, and derided and abused priests. Such actions were contrary to the March 1919 Communist Party program, which stated: "It is necessary carefully to avoid giving such offense to the religious sentiments of believers, as only leads to the strengthening of religious fanaticism."[17] Indeed, it soon became apparent they not only embittered religious believers among the workers and peasants but offended many nonbelievers.[18] Just as Stalin called a halt to the collectivization campaign with his famous speech "Dizziness From Success"—a "success" that had brought the country to the brink of ruin—so the campaign to close churches was halted.

During the war—which was conducted by the Soviet regime not in the spirit of revolutionary internationalism, with appeals to the German soldiers to come over to the side of their class brothers, but in the spirit of chauvinism—a "strange alliance," as Curtiss calls it, was effected between the state and church. A Council for Affairs of the Orthodox Church was created, whose head, G.G. Karpov, explained that its purpose was "to ensure good relations between church and state and, where possible, to satisfy the needs of the church in respect to opening new churches, arranging for theological education, and drafting legislation relating to the church."[19]

The Church for its part reciprocated by unfrocking churchmen who had hailed the invaders and by calling God's blessing upon Stalin and the Soviet regime, as it had done for the Tsar and his government during World War I and the Civil War. "Let us intensify our prayers," declared the Patriarch Alexii, "for the divinely protected Russian power and for its Authorities headed by the wise Leader, whom the Will of God chose and set up to lead our Fatherland along the path of good deeds and glory."[20] The former persecutor turned out to be the appointee of the deity.

Under Khrushchev "the favors that Stalin had granted the Church were now branded as 'departures from Leninist legality.'"[21] However, the repressive measures and the enforced mass closures of churches under Khrushchev's arbitrary rule were also departures from Leninist legality. The reformist wing of the bureaucracy had no desire to give up its dictatorial control over society.

Nevertheless there was a difference between Stalin's and Khrushchev's campaigns against the churches. As Gerhard Simon, an analyst of religion in the Soviet Union who is himself religious but makes a commendable (although not always successful) effort to maintain scholarly accuracy, says,

> while the repressions of various kinds against the Orthodox Church and other religious denominations during the years of Khrushchev's sole rule led to a loss to the institutionalized church of half its constituency in 1959, bloodshed was avoided as far as possible, in contrast to the 1930s, and the Soviet authorities in most cases tried to preserve the appearance of legality.

Moreover, "in contrast to the ruthless frontal attack in Stalin's time, the higher clergy and church leaders were—with some exceptions—left untouched."[22] After Khrushchev, the "strange alliance" between the bureaucracy and a church that had suffered the bureaucracy's rigors and come to terms with it was resumed. This alliance is

> of use to both sides and should not be evaluated solely as servility on the part of the Church.... Through the activity of the Church in the international arena, Soviet policy reaches areas of the foreign public which had previously been closed to it, and it tries—with partial success—to create the impression in ecclesiastical and political circles abroad of unhindered freedom of belief and conscience in its own land. The Church, for its part, has the chance of winning support and friends abroad who might one day exert their moral and political weight in its favour.[23]

However, the alliance has caused the rise of opposition groups within the Orthodox Church and within other churches, especially the evangelical Christians and the Baptists. These have opposed not only state interference but church submission. The regime has responded by concessions to the church to enhance the authority of the church leadership and by repression of the religious oppositionists. Thus we have a Soviet version of the tsarist domination of the church and of tsarist persecution of the religious sects.

Religion in the Soviet Union is fed by the alienation and stifled discontent of the masses. "Atheist researchers [in the Soviet Union] have shown, better than anyone else, what strong roots the churches of the Soviet Union have among the weary and heavy-laden."[24] Nevertheless, if religious sentiment persists among many in the masses, the religious opposition is not large. It publishes samizdat material and demands the rights supposedly guaranteed by Soviet laws. "In their protests against the continual and arbitrary interference in internal church affairs, the church authors appeal again and again to the 1918 law on the separation of church and state and thereby to Lenin, who is held up as a shining counterpart against contemporary Stalinist practice."[25]

Not only does the religious opposition appeal to Leninist norms; it accepts, generally speaking, the idea of socialism.

> It is normal for the great majority of the opposition intelligentsia to consider themselves socialists or Communists; they understand their critique of today's Soviet reality as a return to the true sources and intentions of socialism.... The letters of Fr. Sergi Zheludkov of Pskov show how strongly the internal church opposi-

tion feels itself to be linked with the liberal intelligentsia.... In letters to the spokesmen of the anti-Stalinist intelligentsia, P.M. Litvinov, A.D. Sakharov and A.I. Solzhenitsyn, Zheludkov has spoken of "our practical unity" to create a "socialist society" which must be "a viable combination of organized structure and creative freedom." However, said Zheludkov, present-day Soviet reality was not socialist but a "discrediting of socialism."[26]

Unfortunately, since Simon wrote this, a number of dissidents, disillusioned by continued neo-Stalinist repression, have turned away from socialism. Litvinov is a politically inactive exile in the United States; Sakharov in internal exile is oriented more than ever to the West; Solzhenitsyn has become a bitter anti-Bolshevik. More than that, Solzhenitsyn and a few others grouped about him find that the only salvation for Russia (and indeed the world) lies in the Russian Orthodox Church and a benevolent despotism that resembles an enlightened tsarism. But, points out the Marxist dissident Roy Medvedev, Solzhenitsyn's openly expressed contempt for the entire Russian intelligentsia indicates that he is aware that his words will not find an echo among them. "The only chance of success with our intelligentsia or the working class lies with preaching that is based on the demand for reform, and not on the rejection of socialist society."[27]

The Chinese Communist Party and Religion

The Chinese Communists followed much the same tortuous path as the Russian Stalinists in zigzagging between what Lenin called ultra-leftism and opportunism and in combining the two.

In 1927, in reporting on the work of the peasant associations in the areas ruled by the Red Army, Mao described approvingly how idols were smashed and religious processions, rites for the dead, and funeral gifts were forbidden. He added, however, that such prohibitions should not be enacted "arbitrarily and prematurely." "The Communist Party's propaganda policy in such matters should be, 'Draw the bow without shooting, just indicate the motions.' It is for the peasants themselves to cast aside the idols."[28]

As during the Russian collectivization campaign, it was ostensibly the peasants themselves, not the Communist Party, which restricted religious practices. Although the peasants probably actually played a much more active role than they did under Stalin, it is evident from Mao's statement that in some instances landlords exploited peasant opposition to the smashing of idols that many peasants did not care to shoot arrows from the bow drawn by the party.

The 1931 constitution of the Chinese Soviet Republic, however, closely followed the Russian 1918 decree concerning freedom of religion and the separation of church and state. The Common Program of the coalition government of 1949 and the 1954 People's Republic constitution reiterated the statement of freedom of religious belief. In 1958 the deputy director of the United Front Work Department in a statement on religious policy declared: "The state protects the legitimate religious activities of believers and forbids any act injurious to their religious feeling."[29] The party now said that it was drawing the bow not against religious activities but against those who would interfere with religious activities.

As in the Soviet Union after Lenin, the state intervened in the affairs of the churches. The 1931 constitution of the Chinese Soviet Republic, echoing the Russian 1918 decree on religion, had stated, "Adhering to the principle of the complete separation of church and state, the Soviet state neither favors nor grants any financial assistance to any religion whatever."[30] However, the state now granted, reported a high party official, "property tax reduction or exemption to centers of religious activities and to the dormitories and office buildings of religious professionals."[31]

Just as making the Russian Orthodox Church a creature of the Soviet state was a reversion to tsarist policy, so, Holmes Welch points out, making the Chinese Buddhist Association "a servant of the government, on which it depended for money and direction,"[32] was a continuation of the policy of earlier Chinese governments toward the Buddhist monastic community. Welch emphasizes, as Simon emphasizes about the Russian Orthodox Church leaders, that the Buddhist leaders were not merely "a collection of Buddhist quislings" but "widely respected monks and devotees" who found that cooperation with the government in its domestic and foreign policy served their own purposes.[33]

During the Cultural Revolution, when bitter factional struggle within the bureaucracy convulsed the country, all religious buildings were closed by Red Guards—a single mosque for foreign Muslims being the only exception. Red Guards also harassed religious believers, entering their homes and destroying religious scriptures and objects of art.

The adulation of Mao during this period took on the aspect of a religious cult that could not tolerate any other religion. Thus an account of the popular change in outlook in Tibet states:

> Whereas previously the Tibetan people carried bundles of Buddhist scriptures, everybody now holds the "red precious book."... Whereas before the Tibetan people burned joss sticks, worshipped the Buddha, and chanted lamaist scriptures, they now seek the advice of Chairman Mao every morning and report to him every evening, and sing "The East is Red" every day before Chairman Mao's portrait.[34]

One of the signs of the revisionism of the Russian Communist party was said to be its alliance with religion. The periodical *Red Flag* asserted:

> The Soviet revisionist renegade clique, beset with difficulties at home and abroad, has long sought the service of the reactionary religious forces in carrying out its counter-revolutionary revisionist domestic and foreign policies.... The number of religious rites held in the Soviet Union in the past ten years increased threefold or fourfold, the number of churches and parishes increased day by day, and the number of religious believers reached dozens of millions.[35]

But after Deng declared the Cultural Revolution a disaster, the editors of *Red Flag* marched to the beat of a different drummer, explaining that religious contact between the millions of Muslims in the country's northern provinces and foreign Muslims would "play an important role in raising our country's political influence" among the nations of Asia, the Middle East, and Africa.[36] Accordingly, party officials now graced the no longer prohibited religious rituals with their presence, declaring that they were showing respect for ethnic tradition.

Places of worship of all religions were reopened all over China. The rate of increase in the number of rites, churches, and open religious believers was much greater than that which *Red Flag* had deplored in the Soviet Union, starting as it did from a base close to zero.

However, as in the Soviet Union, controls over religion, especially for the young, have continued. "At the prestigious Peking and Qinghua Universities," reported the *New York Times* on December 18, 1983, "students were ordered this month to surrender philosophical material printed outside China, to admit any religious belief and to report religious fellow students. A Chinese source said that students concealing such information faced interrogation and possible expulsion."

The Castroites and Religion

Fidel Castro's 26th of July Movement began as a radical petty bourgeois movement. It took its radical language seriously, however, and made an insurrection. In doing so and in fighting against the attack of American imperialism, it became a Marxist party, more genuinely Marxist than the Communist Party with which it fused. Its policy toward religion, consequently, has been far more Leninist in its adherence to the principles of complete separation between church and state and absolute freedom of religion than the avowedly Leninist Russian and Chinese Communist parties.

To be sure, Castro had fewer difficulties with regard to religion than confronted the Russians. Unlike tsarist Russia, popular support in Cuba for any religious institution was small even before the Revolution. Although most Cubans nominally belonged to the Catholic Church, comparatively few practiced their religion. They were baptized and buried "in the church," but that was as far as their Catholicism went. "The people," says Alice L. Hageman, a religious sympathizer of the Cuban Revolution, "identified the interests of the church with those of Imperial Spain. After the defeat of Spain in 1898,...many priests still came to Cuba from Spain and the Catholic Church continued to identify itself more with the aristocracy than with the poor."[37]

As for the Protestant churches, which had less than 5 percent of the population as members, they were "dependent on U.S. dollars to finance their programs, and on 'the American way of life' to provide an identity." As the former director of studies for the International Missionary Council said in 1942, "The Evangelical church...is a middle-class and expensive institution in a largely lower class and poverty-stricken constituency."[38]

As a consequence of the correct policy of the revolutionary leadership and of the comparative isolation of the churches, the religious problem—which was serious the first two or three years of the revolution, when the churches engaged in a militant confrontation with the regime—has become insignificant. This policy, which Herbert L. Matthews, the former correspondent of the *New York Times*, states has been faithfully observed, was described as follows in the Declaration of the National Congress on Education and Culture in 1971:

> Not to make the religious problem the center of our preoccupations; absolute separation in all domains of Church and State and of Church and School; not to encourage, support or help religious groups and to expect nothing of them; we have no religious belief and practice, no cult; the Revolution respects religious beliefs and worship as an individual right; no one is persecuted for his convictions; obscurantists and counterrevolutionaries must be fought.

Matthews adds:

> The objectionable [obscuranist and counterrevolutionary] sects were listed separately as Jehovah's Witnesses, Seventh-Day Adventists, and Gideon's Evangelists.... After some American pastors were expelled, it was realized that the sects were politically harmless and socially commendable. So far as I could find out, they are ignored.[39]

This hands-off attitude with regard to the churches is all the more notable in that the churches had engaged in a virulent campaign against the newly established revolutionary government. The Catholic Church issued inflammatory pastoral letters with such titles as "Rome or Moscow," and "With Christ or Against Christ." It organized open-air masses at which there were chants of "We want a Catholic Cuba" and "Cuba yes, Russia no." "Many Christians," acknowledges the liberal Argentinian priest and sociologist Aldo J. Büntig,

> definitely passed to counterrevolutionary action, which increased from August of 1960 on—a prelude to the Bay of Pigs invasion.... In fact, in annexes to the churches, meetings of opponents of the regime were permitted, and there was no shortage of priests who encouraged Christians to enlist in the movement against the regime, as they did against Batista. Others clearly advised the alternative of exile. The defiance thus went beyond merely verbal dimensions.[40]

A number of priests and at least one Protestant minister participated in the Bay of Pigs invasion. Three priests from Spain who had served in Cuba were captured, together with a proclamation they were to have broadcast to the Cuban people. Since they did not have a chance to broadcast it, Castro, sure of popular support, read it in his speech of May 1, 1961: "We do not come because of hatred, but because of love; we come to bring peace even if to earn it we must wage war.... Catholics of Cuba: our military might is crushing and invincible, and even greater is our moral strength and our faith in God and in His protection and His help."[41] But the government and people of Cuba defeated the invincible military might of the invaders and showed a greater moral strength than they.

In this speech Castro announced that the permits of foreign priests to remain in Cuba would be declared invalid except for those of foreign priests who had not combated the Revolution. He also announced that all private schools, of which the majority were Catholic, would be nationalized, with indemnification for those schools which had not opposed the Revolution, and with no tuition henceforth to be paid by the students. Following these measures, says Büntig, "a mass exodus of members of religious orders and priests occurred. Except in cases of direct deportation—which were not many—they seem to have suffered from a desperate escape psychosis."[42]

Yet even while the confrontation with the Catholic hierarchy was fresh in memory, the government declared that it was genuinely committed to freedom of religious belief and practice even though it would not permit counterrevolutionary activity by religious bodies and insisted on separation of church and school. It stated on March 19, 1962: "The Revolution has taken serious measures to break up the conspiracy of the Catholic hierarchy, but it has done nothing to offend a sincere Catholic of the people. On the contrary, it has guaranteed the right of the believers to their worship and to their religion."[43]

The depth of feeling on this matter by governmental leaders is indicated by the words of Castro a few days before this statement at a commemoration meeting for a student leader who had been killed by Batista's men in 1957. On discovering that in the reading of the man's testament an invocation of God had been omitted, he exclaimed indignantly that the omission was stupid and dishonest, unworthy of socialists, and showed both a lack of Marxist understanding of history and a lack of confidence in the ideas of Marxism. "A revolutionary can hold a religious belief," he added. "The revolution does not obligate men, does not interfere with their conscience, does not discriminate against them."[44]

Büntig believes that "the position of Castro in the face of religion" reveals "ideological originality" and is "far from the texts of Marx, Engels and Lenin."[45] We have seen, however, that Engels spoke of the revolutionary spirit of the early Christians, of medieval heretics, and of Thomas Münzer, and that Lenin welcomed into the revolutionary party workers with religious beliefs and was "absolutely opposed to the slightest affront to these workers' religious convictions."

Büntig is, however, right about Castro's lack of dogmatism. Primarily a great revolutionist of action, he is not the theoretician that Lenin, also a maker of revolutions, was, but, on the other hand, he does not merely repeat consecrated formulas or cite infallible authority in the manner of the Stalinists. The spirit of Castroism makes it impossible for Castro to become an object of cult worship. Castro remains "Fidel," not the omniscient Leader or the omniscient Chairman. He himself has said:

> Because there cannot be anything more anti-Marxist than dogma...Marxism needs...to act as a revolutionary force and not as a pseudo-revolutionary church.... How, when we see sectors of the clergy transformed into revolutionary forces, are we going to resign ourselves to see sectors of Marxism transforming themselves into ecclesiastical forces?[46]

Thanks to the Castroite policy on religion and the ability of the Catholic Church to accommodate itself to reality, tension between the church and the state subsided. So much did it do so that in 1969 the bishops issued two pastoral letters, which were a far cry from the pastoral letters "Rome or Moscow" and "With Christ or Against Christ." The first one condemned the United States' economic blockade of Cuba and asked Catholics to participate loyally in the development of the country. The second counseled Catholics to have a tolerant and understanding attitude toward atheists, to use justified criticism of religion to purify their faith, and to have a positive view of their social conditions.[47] No one has charged or even suggested that these pastoral letters were issued as a result of any kind of pressure or manipulation by the government. The pressure came from the desire for popular support.

The Sandinistas and Religion

In his shamelessly lying campaign against the Sandinista government in Nicaragua, Ronald Reagan has called Nicaragua a "totalitarian dungeon" where religion is persecuted.[48] This campaign studiously ignores the fact that there are four Catholic priests in the government, who presumably are persecuting themselves. On the rare occasions that the priests are mentioned there is some mumbled comment that they are dupes or agents of the Sandinistas. The priests, however, are not obscure people used as window-dressing. Ernesto Cardenal, the Minister of Culture, is a poet famous in Central America and the author of *The Gospel in Solentiname*, which consists of a number of dialogues with the peasants of Solentiname about the Bible—dialogues through which the peasants were brought to revolutionary consciousness and which had a tremendous impact on the entire country. Miguel D'Escoto, the minister for foreign affairs, gained a great following through his housing projects for the poor.

Not only do these men have great authority and hold important positions, but they represent tens of thousands of partisans of the revolution who proclaim, "Between Christianity and the revolution there is no contradiction." Nowhere else in the world have Christians formed so integral a part of a social revolution.

On the other hand, it is true that the bishops of Nicaragua, who initially supported the revolutionary government, have increasingly come into conflict with it as polarization has grown. They have harassed priests and nuns who have remained committed to it and have received the backing of the Pope, who has demanded that the four priests leave the government. In Cuba, where the government is strong, the Church hierarchy has come to terms with it, but in Nicaragua, where the situation is unstable, the hierarchy is challenging the government.

The contras, moreover, also attack the government as anti-religious and claim to be fighting for the preservation of Catholicism. Their religious appeal to the peasantry is, however, negated by the well-documented murders and rapes by these mercenaries and ex-Somoza National Guardists. The latest report, that of Americas Watch, a private, non-political organization that monitors human rights in the Americas and takes no sides in the Nicaraguan conflict, says, reports the *New York Times* (March 6, 1985), that "throughout 1984 and as recently as early 1985...the anti-Government rebels have kidnapped, tortured, raped, mutilated and murdered numerous unarmed civilians, including women and children 'who were fleeing.'" When Reagan praises these men as "freedom fighters" for democracy and religion, it is a case of the pot calling the kettle white. To understand how this anomalous situation came about, and how the Sandinistas have responded to it, we must examine the position of the Catholic Church in Latin America.

The Latin American Church is riven with divisions. In Argentina, Guatemala, and Colombia, members of the hierarchy have attacked radical priests working with poor peasants, Indians, and slum-dwellers. In other Latin American countries, however, the "theology of liberation" has affected even the hierarchy. Archbishop Romero of El Salvador was assassinated by rightists for opposing the ruling junta and American aid to it; and Archbishop Evaristo of Brazil has supported his priests in their demands for reform.

The secretariat of the Latin American bishops' conference is controlled by conservatives, headed by Bishop Lopez Trujillo, a Colombian. Alan Riding, the *New York Times* Latin American correspondent, was told by "church sources" that

> Trujillo is closely identified with West Germany's conservative Catholic hierarchy, which last year channeled over $100 million into the Latin American church, and that he is advised by a group of conservative theologians. One of these, Roger Vekemans, a controversial Belgian Jesuit, was identified in testimony before a United States Congressional committee as having received $5 million from the United States Central Intelligence Agency to help Chile's Christian Democratic Party attempt to block Dr. Allende's election in 1970.[49]

In another dispatch Riding told of how a "worried Vatican," aided by "angry conservative bishops," had gained control of the secretariat.[50] Behind the conservative bishops of Latin America stand the Vatican, Washington, and the German Catholic Church, whose stronghold in Bavaria is the base of anti-communist conservatism.

Riding has described the dynamics of the "theology of liberation." The conservatism of the Church, "historically identified with the landed classes and ruling elites...led to empty churches and a declining priesthood." Intent on regaining its vanishing membership, the Church formally pronounced itself to be on the side of the poor and the oppressed. The result was that "the church again became a significant force in the lives of the poor. Youths were attracted to the priesthood. Masses celebrated by popular priests and bishops were crowded."[51] The new breed of priest discovered that Jesus led a movement of the poor.

The "theology of liberation," then, can be explained by the pressure of the masses, first in staying away from services conducted by conservative priests and then by acting upon the new young priests. Lenin explained this pressure of the peasant masses as follows:

> Why has the village priest—that policeman of official orthodoxy— proved to be *more* on the side of the peasant than the bourgeois liberal? Because the village priest has to live side by side with the peasant, to depend on him in a thousand different ways, and sometimes—as when the priests practice small-scale peasant agriculture on church land—even to be in a peasant's skin himself.[52]

Moreover, Lenin said, writing in 1905, a pre-revolutionary atmosphere affects the lower clergy itself.

> The disgusting red tape of the politically feudal autocracy has stirred up discontent, ferment and indignation even among the clergy. Cowed and ignorant as the Russian orthodox clergy is, even it has been aroused by the thundering collapse of the old medieval Russian regime. Even the clergy endorses the demand for liberty, protests against the bureaucracy and the tyranny of officials, against the police inquisition forced on the "servants of God." We, Socialists, must support this movement, carrying the demands of the honest and sincere people among the clergy to their logical conclusion, taking them at their word when they talk about liberty, demanding that they completely sever all connection between religion and the police.[53]

So also, we may remember, the lower clergy of pre-revolutionary France was affected by the growing ferment, harking back, as do the adherents of the "theology of liberation," to the egalitarianism of the early Christians.[54]

The Latin American clergy too have been aroused by the thunder before the storm that is brewing on their continent. When John Paul II came to Brazil in July 1980, 1,150 priests sent him an open letter that stated: "The Latin American people find it repulsive that their assassins invoked their 'Christianity' to justify their killings, and that not a few bishops and even papal nuncios are their accomplices, at least in their passivity."[55] Priests like the martyred Colombian guerrilla-priest Father Camilo Torres have been swept along into the class struggle. Other priests, working with the poor, have helped to give them a sense of dignity that has enabled them to stand up and fight.

The Sandinistas responded to this movement of the clergy in Nicaragua. They admitted priests and religious believers into their ranks, and in their historic program of 1969, whose promises they have striven to keep despite great difficulties, they stated that the revolution "will respect the right of citizens to profess and practice any religious belief" and "will support the work of priests and other religious figures who defend the working people."[56]

In October 1980, more than a year after coming to power, the National Directorate of the FSLN [Sandinista National Liberation Front] issued a statement on the role of religion in the new Nicaragua, asserting that it was necessary to do so because reactionaries were seeking to spread the idea that the Sandinistas were using religion now but planning to suppress it later. The statement begins by paying tribute to the many Christians who served as fighters in the Sandinista Front and to the many lay Christians and clergy who were not members of the FSLN but nevertheless "professed and practiced their faith in accord with our people's need for liberation." It states also that "on various occasions the Catholic bishops bravely denounced the crimes and abuses of the dictatorship.... Because of their brave participation in the struggle, the Catholic Church and Christians in general suffered persecution and death."

The statement goes on to say that in different historical epochs religion has served to justify exploitation, citing the part that the missionaries played in the Spanish imperialist rule over the Indians of Nicaragua. But "we Sandinistas state that our experience shows that when Christians, basing themselves on their faith, are capable of responding to the needs of the people and of history, those very beliefs lead them to revolutionary activism." This being so, "all those who agree with our objectives and proposals, and have the personal qualities demanded by our organization, have every right to participate actively in our ranks, whatever their religious beliefs."

However,

> within the framework of the FSLN, there is no place for religious proselytism. This would undermine the specific character of our vanguard and introduce factors of disunity, since the Sandinista Front includes companeros of various religions and none. Outside of the framework of the FSLN, Christian activists...have the right to express their convictions publicly. This cannot be used to detract from their work in the FSLN or from the confidence that they have gained as a result of their revolutionary activity.

The statement rejects the accusation that the Sandinista Front is interfering in the internal affairs of the Catholic Church, seeking to split it. "We do not foster or provoke activities to divide the churches. That question is the exclusive concern of the Christians and does not involve political organizations. If divisions do exist, the churches must look for causes within themselves and not attribute them to supposed malicious outside influences."[57] Important political occurrences in the past also caused members of the Catholic Church to take opposing positions. For instance, Bartolomé de las Casas, the Spanish Dominican known as the "protector of the Indians," defended the rights of the natives while the missionaries "used the cross to consecrate the slave labor that had been initiated by the sword."

Finally, the statement takes up the matter of priests and members of religious orders in the government:

> In regard to this, we declare that every Nicaraguan citizen has a right to participate in carrying out political affairs in our country, whatever their civil state, and the Government of National Reconstruction guarantees this right, which is backed up by the law.... It especially needs those who had the chance to receive higher education, which was denied to the majority of our people.

In the Somoza government, it comments, "there were priests who proudly paraded their military ranks and official positions—of course no one demanded that they give up their posts."[58]

If we examine these positions, we find that, as is true of those of the Castroites, they are not really "far from the texts of Marx, Engels and Lenin," after all, although undoubtedly they have been more shaped by the Sandinistas' experience than by their reading. Like Engels, the statement observes that religion has historically served the function of justifying exploitation but that on certain occasions it can be a revolutionary force. Like Lenin, it holds that religious believers, including priests, have the right to participate in the revolutionary party if they accept its program, but, like Lenin, it prohibits religious proselytism within the party. Like Lenin, it calls for complete separation of church and state. This means that the state does not in any way subsidize the church, that it does not intervene in its internal affairs, that none, including priests, are exempted from civil duties on religious grounds, and that all, including priests, have the right to hold public office, not as representatives of religious bodies but as individuals.

To be sure, Lenin evidently did not envisage the participation of religious believers and priests in the revolutionary process to the extent it has taken place in Nicaragua. He was aware, however, that revolutionary currents affected the lower clergy. Also, the Sandinistas, who do not hide the fact that many in their ranks and leadership are Marxists and atheists, do not publish educational material on religion, as Lenin demanded. However, Lenin qualified his statement by saying that the revolutionary party will subordinate the struggle against religion to the class struggle and "must be able to judge the concrete situation as a whole." What is true about not dividing the workers along religious lines in a strike situation is even more true in a revolutionary situation.

Religion and the Struggle for Socialism

Revolutionary Marxists can work with religious believers for common political objectives. They have joined with Muslims, Hindus, and Buddhists in anti-imperialist actions, with the persecuted Catholics of Northern Ireland against the dominant Protestants and British imperialism, and with liberal sections of the Protestant and Catholic churches in Europe and the United States in the struggle against nuclear weapons and war preparations.

In doing so, they have subordinated, without hiding their materialistic philosophy, the ideological struggle against religion to the concrete demands of the class struggle. This is not at all the same as the opportunist policy of reformist parties such as the Italian Communist Party, which has temporized on the liberalization of divorce and of abortion, and holds back the class struggle in order to grasp the hand of the church.[59] There is a world of difference between "Don't let the fight be lost by enemy-fostered divisions in your ranks" and "Don't antagonize the enemy: live and let live."

As long as religion remains a force to be reckoned with, Marxists have to know how to deal with it and be able to draw the masses under its influence into the struggle for socialism. The problem is especially acute in the underdeveloped countries and, paradoxically, in the United States, where religion is strongest. The principles of Lenin furnish a guide for Marxists to follow.

The victory of world socialism will bring the gradual demise of religion. The state, a strong prop for religion even in countries where there is an alleged separation of church and state, will no longer give it support. Indeed, the state itself, like religion, will come to cease existence. Humanity, being able to control its own destiny, will not need to believe in a God of its own creation, before whom it must prostrate itself in fear and trembling. It will at last be free.

But humanity will not only be intellectually free: it will be able to experience more fully the two greatest joys of life, creative work and love. In contemporary society human beings are alienated from their work, which is for most people drearily monotonous, not at all a means of self-expression. Work only means regimentation and the transformation of the products of one's labor into commodities in which one takes neither pride nor satisfaction.

So too are human beings alienated from each other. Under the conditions of an economy of commodity production, people tend to regard each other as things to which one is related only by the "cash nexus." They are the members of a "lonely crowd," to borrow the title of the sociologist David Riesman's book, where it is everyone for himself: we are all alone.

Things will be far otherwise in a socialist society, toward which the various post-capitalist societies, many of them suffering from bureaucratic deformation or degeneration as a result of having been born in backward countries subjected to the pressure of world capitalism, are only struggling. "Under socialism," says Trotsky,

> solidarity will be the basis of society. All the emotions which we revolutionists, at the present time, feel apprehensive of naming— so much have they been worn thin by hypocrites and vulgarians— such as disinterested friendship, love for one's neighbor, sympathy, will be the mighty ringing chords of socialist poetry.[60]

"Love thy neighbor" will not be a hollow phrase used to justify passivity in the face of oppression, but a reality.

Notes

Chapter 1

1. I have throughout regarded Marx and Engels as being in common agreement, as the evidence shows they were. As George Novack says (*Polemics in Marxist Philosophy* [New York: Monad Press, 1978], 87):

   > Although Engels modestly assigned himself the role of "second fiddle" to Marx, the development of the dialectical method and historical materialism was a collective creation.... Marx and Engels elaborated its fundamental principles together in the 1840s. Most of what they wrote thereafter, whether in the form of newspaper articles, manifestos, pamphlets, or books, was either discussed beforehand or submitted to each other's searching critical scrutiny. Whatever differences of opinion they had on this or that minor matter, there is no record of disagreement on any important theoretical or political question during their forty-year collaboration.

2. *Reader in Marxist Philosophy From the Writings of Marx, Engels, and Lenin*, ed. Howard Selsam and Harry Martel (New York: International Publishers, 1973), 27. Hereafter referred to as *Reader*.

3. *Karl Marx and Friedrich Engels on Religion* (New York: Schocken Books, 1977), 142–43. Hereafter referred to as *On Religion*.

4. Cf. 42–45, 77–79, 100, 101, 106, 191–93.

5. Cf. 45, 83, 280 (n.12).

6. Baron D'Holbach, *Good Sense: or Natural Ideas as Opposed to Supernatural* (New York: G. Vale, 1856), viii–ix. For the convenience of the reader, I have modernized the spelling and punctuation of all quotations before the twentieth century.

7. Since I am not here concerned with literary values, I have for the sake of clarity used throughout the Good News Bible of the American Bible Society, which "seeks to state clearly and accurately the meaning of the original texts in words and forms that are widely accepted by people who use English as a means of communication."

8. Cf. E.E. Kellet, *A Short History of Religions* (London: Victor Gollancz, 1933), 45. Cf. also 567 below.

9. Richard Watson, *An Apology for the Bible* (New York, 1796), 54.

10. Quoted by Reinhold Niebuhr, "Christian Politics and Communist Religion," *Christianity and the Social Revolution*, ed. John Lewis et al. (New

York: Charles Scribner's Sons, 1936), 452.

11. Cf. Herbert E. Morais, *Deism in Eighteenth Century America* (New York: Russell & Russell, 1960). Among others Jefferson, Franklin, Paine, and Ethan Allen were deists, and George Washington and James Madison were freethinkers with deistic tendencies. Jefferson, who was identified with the French Revolution, was attacked by the Congregational ministry in 1800 as "the arch-apostle of the cause of irreligion and free thought," (Morais, 117).

12. Bernard Bailyn, *The Ideological Origins of the American Revolution* (Cambridge, Mass: Harvard University Press, 1967), 26–27.

13. Cited by F.N. Robinson, ed., *The Works of Geoffrey Chaucer* (Boston: Houghton Mifflin, 1957), 662.

14. Bertrand Russell, *Religion and Science* (New York: Henry Holt, 1935), 34.

15. Quoted by Bertrand Russell, *A History of Western Philosophy* (New York: Simon and Schuster, 1945), 528.

16. Corliss Lamont, "The Illusion of Immortality," *Critiques of God,* ed. Peter Angeles (Buffalo, N.Y.: Prometheus Books, 1976), 264.

17. H.R. Trevor-Roper, *The European Witch-Craze of the Sixteenth and Seventeenth Centuries* (New York: Harper & Row, 1967), 107–08.

18. Thomas Szasz, *The Manufacture of Madness* (New York: Harper & Row, 1970), 82–94.

19. The same text had been cited by Luther and Calvin to justify the burning of witches. Cf. Trevor-Roper, 137.

20. L. Sprague de Camp, *The Great Monkey Trial* (Garden City, N.Y.: Doubleday, 1968), 406–407.

21. Cf. Cliff Conner, *Evolutionism vs. Creationism: In Defense of Scientific Thinking* (New York: Pathfinder Press, 1981), 5–11.

22. Russell, *Religion and Science,* 45.

23. Cf. Bertrand Russell, *Why I Am Not a Christian* (New York: Simon and Schuster, 1957), 8–9.

24. Hans Reichenbach, *The Rise of Scientific Philosophy* (Berkeley and Los Angeles: University of California Press, 1951); 208, quoted by Peter A. Angeles, *The Problem of God: A Short Introduction* (Buffalo, N.Y.: Prometheus Books, 1980), 42.

25. Ernest Nagel, "Malicious Philosophies of Science," *Critiques of God,* 362.

26. Reichenbach, *The Rise of Scientific Philosophy,* 207, quoted by Angeles, 42.

27. Angeles, 65.

28. This belief was anticipated by Engels. Cf. *On Religion,* 174.

29. *Hume on Religion,* ed. Richard Wollheim (New York: World Publishing Co., 1964), 38.

30. For refutation of contemporary versions of the argument from design, see Wallace I. Matson, "The Argument From Design," *Critiques of God,* 69–81.

31. Cf. H.J. McCloskey, "God and Evil," *Critiques of God,* 203–23.

32. Cf. John Stuart Mill, *Three Essays on Religion* (London: Longmans, Green, 1874), 179–80.

33. *Hume on Religion,* 239.

34. Cf. Russell, *Why I Am Not a Christian,* 90.

35. Cf. Sigmund Freud, "The Future of an Illusion," *The Standard Edition of the Complete Psychological Works* (London: Hogarth Press, 1962), vol. 21, 28.

36. Denis Diderot, *Thoughts on Religion* (London, 1819), 5.

37. Homer W. Smith, *Man and His Gods* (Boston: Little, Brown, 1952), 202.

38. Kellett, 118.

39. Smith, 183.

40. Cf. Robert G. Olson, *Ethics: A Short Introduction* (New York: Random House, 1978), 127.

41. Cf. Russell, *Religion and Science*, 185–95.

42. J.H. Leuba, *The Psychology of Religious Mysticism* (New York: Harcourt, Brace, 1925), ix.

Chapter 2

1. Twentieth century physics sees the atom as a miniature solar system within which negative electrons move around a positive nucleus. Instead of saying that motion is inherent in matter, it says that matter and energy are one. The so-called disappearance of matter and its reduction to electricity, said Lenin, does not contradict materialism, for the materialist is not committed to any kind of structure of matter, only to the concept of matter as an objective reality existing outside of the mind. On the contrary, it corroborates dialectical materialism, which "insists on the approximate, relative character of every scientific theory of the structure of matter and its properties" and "on the absence of absolute boundaries in nature" (*Reader*, 88–90).

2. One of the foremost contemporary authorities on biological evolution, George Gaylord Simpson, emphasizes its dialectical character. There are, he asserts, two "interwoven patterns" of "constant occurrence and major importance" in evolution, the "pattern of trend," which is "progressive," and the "pattern of change in adaptive type," which is "more rapid and sporadic, recurrent rather than continuous." "The times of rapid expansion...are the 'explosive phases' of evolution." Such an explosive phase, "the adoption of a new and distinct way of life," occurred when reptiles left the water for land. Cf. George Gaylord Simpson, *The Meaning of Evolution* (New Haven: Yale University Press, 1950), 238–39.

3. *Diderot, Interpreter of Nature: Selected Writings*, ed. Jonathan Kemp (New York: International Publishers, c. 1943).

4. Franklin L. Baumer, *Religion and the Rise of Skepticism* (New York: Harcourt, Brace, 1960), 47–48.

5. George Novack, *Pragmatism Versus Marxism* (New York: Pathfinder Press, 1975), 9.

6. The preceding six paragraphs are drawn from my "Marxism and Shakespearean Criticism," *Shakespeare Newsletter*, 24 (September–November 1974), 37, in which I presented as simply and concisely as I could the basic tenets of Marxism and the way they can be used in the study of literature. The essay is reprinted in *Shakespeare's English and Roman History Plays: A Marxist Approach* (London and Madison, N.J.: Fairleigh Dickinson University Press, 1986).

7. George Peter Murdock, *Our Primitive Contemporaries,* (New York:

Macmillan 1946), 11, 126, 183, 253, 313, 502, 585–86.

8. Ibid., 78, 127, 185, 346–47, 502, 545, 586.

9. Quinter Marcellus Lyon, *The Great Religions* (New York: Odyssey Press, 1957), 28–29.

10. Weston La Barre, *The Ghost Dance: Origins of Religion* (Garden City, NY: Doubleday, 1970), 562.

11. Marx, The Eighteenth Brumaire of Louis Napoleon," Marx & Engels, *Basic Writings on Politics and Philosophy,* ed. Lewis S. Feuer (Garden City, N.Y.: Doubleday, 1959), 321–22.

12. Cf. Christopher Hill, "Science and Magic in Seventeenth Century England" (mimeographed text of a lecture given to the J.D. Bernal Peace Library, October 19, 1976), 6, 9: in rejecting "the magical elements in medieval Catholicism"—"holy water, relics, incantations, crucifixes, exorcisms"— Calvinism "prepared for the reception of the mechanical philosophy."

13. Marx, *Capital* (London: George Allen & Unwin, 1957), 155 (vol. 1, ch. 6).

14. Russell, *Religion and Science*, 64.

15. Arnold Toynbee, "Traditional Attitudes Towards Death," *Man's Concern With Death* (New York: McGraw-Hill, 1968), 127.

16. See 218–19, 222, 245-47, 270–72.

17. Concerning the reaching out toward religion by scientists, the English scientist Lancelot Hogben comments (*The Nature of Living Matter*, 1930, 28):

    The apologetic attitude so prevalent in science today is not a logical outcome of the introduction of new concepts. It is based upon the hope of reinstating traditional beliefs with which science was at one time in open conflict. This hope is not a by-product of scientific discovery. It has its roots in the social temper of the period.... Contemporary philosophy has yet to find a way out of the intellectual discouragement which is the heritage of a World War. (Quoted by Bertrand Russell, *The Scientific Outlook* [Glencoe, Ill.: Free Press, 1931], 132.)

    For a devastating analysis of the religious yearnings of Eddington and Jeans, of religionists' use of Heisenberg's Principle of Indeterminacy to deny natural law, and of their finding a divine purpose in biological evolution, see 101–33 of *The Scientific Outlook*.

18. *The Interpreter's Bible*, ed. George A. Buttrick, Nolan B. Harmon, et al. (New York: Abingdon Press, 1952–57), vol. 1, 439–40, 465; Vol. 7, 242, 630.

19. Quoted by S.S. Prawer, *Karl Marx and World Literature* (New York: Oxford University Press, 1978), 291.

20. James Frazer, *The Golden Bough* (London, 1911), vol. 3, vi.

21. Cf. Leon Trotsky *Their Morals and Ours* (New York: Merit Publishers, 1969), 36–39.

22. Vilhjalmur Stefansson, "Lessons in Living From the Stone Age," *A Treasury of Science,* ed. Harlow Shapley et al. (New York: Harper & Brothers, 1946), 508–10.

23. It should be noted, however, that there are indications in the New Testament of a different Christ than the one who is represented as delivering the Sermon on the Mount, the Christ who drove the money-changers out of the temple and who probably was the authentic historical figure before he was enveloped by legend and myth. (See 100).

24. Sigmund Freud, *The Standard Edition of the Complete Psychological Work* (London: Hogarth Press, 1962), vol. 21, 18.

25. Freud, vol. 21, 53.

26. Ibid., 50.

27. Ibid., 49.

Chapter 3

1. For a devastating critique of a recent book purporting to show that Marxism is a religion, James H. Billington's *Fire in the Minds of Men: Origins of the Revolutionary Faith*, see Peter Singer, "Revolution and Religion," *New York Review of Books*, November 6, 1980, 51–54.

2. Writing in 1844, Marx is referring to a communism that antedates the scientific socialism he was shortly to enunciate in the *Communist Manifesto*. So Engels writes:

   > To our three social reformers ["the three great Utopians": St. Simon, Fourier, and Owen, "who worked out his proposals...in direct relation to French materialism"] the bourgeois world, based upon the principles of these [French materialist] philosophers, is quite as irrational and unjust and, therefore, finds its way to the dust hole quite as readily as feudalism and all the earlier stages of society. (*Basic Writings on Politics and Philosophy*, 70–71)

3. George Novack, *Empiricism and Its Evolution: A Marxist View* (New York: Pathfinder Press, 1973), 83–84.

4. Quoted by Engels in *Herr Eugen Dühring's Revolution in Science* (New York: International Publishers, 1939), 142.

5. Karl Marx, *Selected Works,* (New York: International Publishers, n.d.) vol. 1, 28.

6. Loren R. Graham, *Science and Philosophy in the Soviet Union* (New York: Knopf, 1972), 430, 6.

7. Quoted in preface to Marx, *Selected Works,* vol. 1, xviii.

8. *The Age of Permanent Revolution; A Trotsky Anthology,* ed. Isaac Deutscher (New York: Dell 1964), 290.

9. Leon Trotsky, *In Defense of Marxism* (New York: Pioneer Publishers, 1942), 175.

10. V.I. Lenin, *The State and Revolution* (Moscow: Foreign Languages Publishing House, n.d.), 9–10.

11. Leon Trotsky, *The History of the Russian Revolution* (New York: Simon and Schuster, 1937), vol. 3, 355.

12. Isaac Deutscher, *Stalin: A Political Biography* (New York: Oxford University Press, 1949), 269.

13. Leon Trotsky, *The Revolution Betrayed* (Garden City, N.Y.: Doubleday, 1937), 277.

14. Deutscher, *Stalin,* 271–72.

15. *Quotations from Chairman Mao Tse-tung* (Peking: Foreign Languages Press, 1966).

16. Isaac Deutscher, *The Prophet Outcast: Trotsky 1929–1940* (New York:

Random House, 1963), 521.

17. Quoted by George Novack, *Humanism and Socialism* (New York: Pathfinder Press, 1973), 136.

18. Isaac Deutscher, *The Prophet Armed: Trotsky 1879–1921* (New York: Random House, 1965), 54.

19. Leon Trotsky, *Their Morals and Ours* (New York: Merit Publishers, 1969), 39.

20. Deutscher, *The Prophet Outcast*, 479–80.

21. Leon Trotsky, *Stalin: An Appraisal of the Man and His Influence* (New York: Stein and Day, 1967), 54.

Chapter 4

1. Christopher Hill, "The English Civil War Interpreted by Marx and Engels," *Science and Society*, 12 (1948), 154.

2. For objections to Weber's thesis, see R.H. Tawney, *Religion and the Rise of Capitalism* (New York: Penguin Books, 1947), 261–63.

3. Marx and Engels, *Basic Writings*, 39.

4. Robert H. Pfeiffer, *Religion in the Old Testament* (New York: Harper, 1961), 15, 24–25.

5. Ibid., 54–55.

6. Ibid., 57.

7. Ibid., 68, 71.

8. Salo W. Baron, *A Social and Religious History of the Jews* (New York: Columbia University Press, 1937), vol. 1, 86–87.

9. Robert H. Pfeiffer, *History of New Testament Times* (New York: Harper, 1949), 8.

10. Karl Kautsky, *Foundations of Christianity* (New York: S.A. Russell, 1953), 169.

11. Ibid., 193.

12. Ibid., 195–96.

13. Ibid., 196.

14. Kautsky in *Neue Zeit,* cited by Abram Leon, *The Jewish Question: A Marxist Interpretation* (New York: Pathfinder Press, 1970), 68–69.

15. Lujo Brentano, *Die Anfange des Modernen Kapitalismus* (Munich, 1916), 15. Cited by Leon, 69n.

16. "Armenia," *Encyclopedia Britannica*, 11th ed.

17. *A History of Europe,* 1939, quoted by Leon, 74n.

18. "On the Jewish Question," *Selected Essays by Karl Marx* (London: Leonard Persons, 1926), 92.

19. Leon, 80–81. Leon's quotation is from the Zionist sociologist Arthur Ruppin, *The Jews in the Modern World* (London, 1934), 132.

20. Kautsky, 217–19.

21. Baron, vol. 2, 33–34.

22. Ibid., 35–36.

23. Ibid., 153–57.

24. Isaac Deutscher, *The Non-Jewish Jew and Other Essays* (New York: Oxford University Press, 1968), 26–27.

25. Baron, vol. 2, 285.

26. Ibid., 290.

27. Leon Trotsky, "What is National Socialism?" *The Age of Permanent Revolution: A Trotsky Anthology,* ed. *Isaac Deutscher* (New York: Dell, 1964), 180–81, 178–79.

28. Deutscher, 66–67.

29. Karl Kautsky, *Are the Jews a Race?* (New York: International Publishers, 1926),

30. Norman L. Zucker, *The Coming Crisis in Israel: Private Faith and Public Policy* (Cambridge, Mass: MIT Press, 1973), 76.

31. Deutscher, 130.

32. Zucker, 207.

33. Maxime Rodinson, *Israel A Colonial-Settler State?* (New York: Monad Press, 1973), 79.

34. Zucker, 141.

35. Ibid., 94–95.

36. Ibid., 149–50.

Chapter 5

1. Ernst Troeltsch, *The Social Teaching of the Christian Churches* (New York: Macmillan, 1950), I, 39.

2. Archibald Robertson, *The Origins of Christianity* (New York: International Publishers, 1962), 96.

3. Quoted by Erich Fromm, *The Dogma of Christ* (New York: Rinehart & Winston, 1963), 30, 29.

4. Robertson, 93.

5. Ibid., 80.

6. Ibid., 50–51.

7. Ibid., 56.

8. Ibid., 69–70.

9. Homer W. Smith, 199.

10. Robert H. Pfeiffer, *History of New Testament Times* (New York: Harper, 1949), 164–65.

11. Smith, 199.

12. Troeltsch, vol. 1, 65–68.

13. Kellett, 207.

14. James Westfall Thompson, *An Economic and Social History of the Middle Ages (300-1300)* (London: Century, 1928), 81–82.

15. Troeltsch, vol. 1, 133; Thompson, 85–86.

16. Troeltsch, 132–33.

17. Ibid., 296.

18. Ibid., 136–37.

19. V.I. Lenin, *On Religion* (New York: International Publishers, 1933), 7.

20. Quoted by Thompson, 681.

21. Kautsky, *Foundations of Christianity,* 395.

22. Quoted by Thompson, 681.

23. Kautsky, 396. Cf. Thompson, 623, 629.

24. Wallace K. Ferguson, "The Church in a Changing World: A Contribution to the Interpretation of the Renaissance," *Renaissance Studies* (New York: Harper & Row, 1970), 163–64.

25. "Alexander VI," *Encyclopedia Britannica,* 11th ed.

26. Karl Kautsky, *Thomas More and His Utopia* (London: A. & C. Black, 1927), 58–59.

27. Preserved Smith, *The Age of the Reformation* (New York: Henry Holt, 1920), 392.

28. Ibid., 402.

29. Albert Soboul, *A Short History of the French Revolution 1789–1799* (Berkeley: University of California Press, 1977), 9–10.

30. Gerald R. Cragg, *The Church and the Age of Reason* (Grand Rapids, Mich. Eerdmans, 1967), 206.

31. Alec R. Vidler, *The Church in an Age of Revolution* (Baltimore: Penguin Books, 1976), 19.

32. Frederick B. Artz, *Reaction and Revolution 1814–1832* (New York: Harper, 1934), 10–11.

33. Vidler, 151.

34. Ibid., 154.

35. Ibid., 153.

36. Parker Thomas Moon, *The Labor Problem and the Social Catholic Movement in France* (New York: Macmillan, 1921), 131.

37. Marx and Engels, *Basic Writings,* 31.

38. Ibid., 30.

39. Moon, 123.

40. Ibid., 195.

41. Ibid., 158.

42. Ibid., 160.

43. Ibid., 158, 162.

44. Quoted by Guenter Lewy, *The Catholic Church and Nazi Germany* (New York: McGraw-Hill, 1965), 328.

45. Lewy, xiv.

46. Ibid., 310–11.

47. Ibid., 226.

48. *New York Times,* November 19, 1964, quoted by Paul Blanshard, *Paul Blanshard on Vatican II* (Boston: Beacon Press, 1966), 141.

49. Saul Friedlander, *Pius XII and the Third Reich: A Documentation,* (New York: Knopf, 1966), 236.

50. Robert D. Cross, *The Emergence of Liberal Catholicism in America* (Cam-

bridge, Mass.: Harvard University Press, 1958), 6.

51. Vidler, 189.

52. Blanshard, 332–33.

53. Vidler, 189.

54. *New York Times*, September 3, 1980.

Chapter 6

1. Christopher Hill, *Change and Continuity in Seventeenth-Century England* (Cambridge, Mass.: Harvard University Press, 1975), 83.

2. Ibid., 84.

3. Ibid., 86–87.

4. Roy Pascal, *The Social Basis of the German Reformation* (New York: Augustus M. Kelley, 1971), 134, 138.

5. Quoted by Hill, 84.

6. Pascal, 193.

7. Quoted by ibid., 146.

8. Quoted by R.H. Tawney, *Religion and the Rise of Capitalism* (New York: Penguin Books, 1947), 96.

9. Ibid., 200.

10. Steele, quoted by Tawney, 202, 203.

11. Christopher Hill, *Puritanism and Revolution* (New York: Schocken Books, 1964), 235.

12. Christopher Hill, *Society and Puritanism in Pre-revolutionary England* (London: Seeker and Warburg, 1964), 226.

13. Hill, *Change and Continuity in Seventeenth-Century England,* 96.

14. Tawney, 209.

15. Quoted in Hill, *Puritanism and Revolution*, 199.

16. Marx and Engels, *Basic Writings*, 55.

17. Quoted in Hill, *Puritanism and Revolution,* 207.

18. David W. Petegorsky, *Left-Wing Democracy in the English Civil War* (New York: Haskell House, 1972), 67.

19. Quoted in H. Richard Niebuhr, *The Social Sources of Denominationalism* (Hamden, Conn: Shoe String Press, 1954), 49.

20. Petegorsky, 73 and n.

21. Ibid., 86.

22. Werner Stark, *The Sociology of Religion: A Study of Christendom*, vol. 2. *Sectarian Religion* (London: Routledge and Kegan Paul, 1967), 19.

23. Christopher Hill, *The World Turned Upside Down: Radical Ideas During the English Revolution* (New York: Penguin Books, 1976), 361.

24. Hill, *Puritanism and Revolution,* 145.

25. Isabell Grub, *Quakerism and Industry Before 1800* (London: Williams & Norgate, 1930), 175.

26. Wellman J. Warner, *The Wesleyan Movement in the Industrial Revolution* (New York: Longmans, Green, 1930), 165.

27. Stark, 22.

28. Warner, 171.

29. Ibid., 178.

30. Ibid., 127.

31. Marx and Engels, *On Religion*, 309.

32. R.M. Cameron, *Methodism and Society in Historical Perspective*, quoted by Stark, 294.

33. Warner, 190.

34. Quoted by Niebuhr, 171.

35. Warner, 196.

36. Ibid., 200.

37. Ibid., 201.

38. Ibid., 190.

39. K.S. Inglis, *Churches and the Working Classes in Victorian England* (London: Routledge and Kegan Paul, 1963), 1.

40. Ibid.

41. Ibid., 60, 117.

42. Ibid., 5.

43. Vidler, 92.

44. Tawney, 103.

45. Niebuhr, 131.

46. Vidler, 95.

47. Ludlow's account in F. Maurice's biography of him, quoted by Vidler, 95–96.

48. Vidler, 96; Inglis, 261.

49. Quoted by Inglis, 272.

50. Quoted by ibid., 268.

51. Marx and Engels, *Basic Writings*, 35–36.

52. Inglis, 34.

53. Inglis, 260.

54. Carlton J. Hayes, *A Generation of Materialism: 1871–1900* (New York: Harper, 1941), 133.

55. Hayes, 140.

56. Inglis, 323.

57. Michael Argyle and Benjamin Beit-Hallahmi, *The Social Psychology of Religion* (Boston: Routledge & Kegan Paul, 1975), 161.

58. Ibid., 163.

59. Ibid., 28.

60. Koppel Z. Pinson, *Pietism as a Factor in the Rise of German Nationalism* (New York: Columbia University Press, 1934), 104, 109.

61. William O. Shanahan, *German Protestants Face the Social Question: The Conservative Phase, 1815–1871* (South Bend, Ind.: University of Notre Dame Press, 1954), 388, 379.

62. Shanahan, p. 402.

63. Ninian Smart, "Death and the Decline of Religion in Western Society," *Man's Concern With Death*, ed. Arnold Toynbee (New York: McGraw-Hill, 1968), 138.

64. Vidler, 262.

Chapter 7

1. Larzer Ziff, *Puritanism in America* (New York: Viking Press, 1973), 177.

2. George Novack, "A Suppressed Chapter in the History of American Capitalism: The Conquest of the Indians," *Marxist Essays in American History*, ed. Robert Himmel (New York: Merit Publishers, 1966), 23.

3. Ziff, 90–91.

4. Ibid., 91.

5. Quoted by H. Richard Niebuhr, *The Social Sources of Denominationalism* (Hamden, Conn: The Shoe String Press, 1954), 104.

6. Alexis De Tocqueville, *Democracy in America* (New York: Vintage Books, 1959), bk. 2, ch. 9.

7. V.F. Calverton, *The Passing of the Gods* (New York: Charles Scribner's Sons, 1934), 220.

8. *New York Times*, September 22, 1980.

9. Charles A. Beard and Mary R. Beard, *The Rise of American Civilization* (New York: Macmillan, 1961), vol. 1, 212–13.

10. Eric Foner, *Tom Paine and Revolutionary America* (New York: Oxford University Press, 1976), 115–16.

11. G. Adolf Koch, *Republican Religion: The American Revolution and the Cult of Reason* (New York: Henry Holt, 1933).

12. Quoted by William G. McLoughlin, *Revivals, Awakenings, and Reform: An Essay on Religion and Social Change in America, 1607–1977* (University of Chicago Press, 1978), 44.

13. William G. McLoughlin, "The American Revolution as a Religious Revival: 'The Millenium in One Country,'" *New England Quarterly,* 40 (1967), 107.

14. Foner, 111–12.

15. Ibid., 112–17.

16. Beard, vol. 1, 271.

17. Koch, 10–11.

18. J. Franklin Jameson, *The American Revolution Considered as a Social Movement* (Boston: Beacon Press, 1956), 94.

19. Clement Eaton, *Freedom of Thought in the Old South* (Durham, N.C.: Duke University Press, 1940), 15.

20. Koch, 71.

21. Cf. 278 n. 11 above and Koch, 284n.

22. Calverton, 235.

23. Koch, 290–91.

24. Calverton, 234.

25. Koch, 252–55.

26. Ibid., 258–59.

27. Henry F. May, *Protestant Churches and Industrial America* (New York: Octagon Books, 1963), 9.

28. Koch, 275, 277.

29. McLoughlin, *Revivals, Awakenings, and Reform*, 126.

30. Tocqueville, bk. 2, ch. 12.

31. Jeremy Rifkin and Ted Howard, *The Emerging Order: God in the Age of Scarcity* (New York: G.P. Putnam's Sons, 1979), 153.

32. Ibid., 154.

33. H. Richard Niebuhr, 170.

34. Beard, vol. 2, 9.

35. Niebuhr, 192–93.

36. Ibid., 193.

37. Ibid., 193–94.

38. Calverton, 247.

39. H. Richard Niebuhr, 196.

40. Russel B. Nye, *William Lloyd Garrison and the Humanitarian Reformers* (Boston: Little, Brown, 1955), 108.

41. Ibid., 33–34.

42. Ibid., 108.

43. Niebuhr, 248–49.

44. Ibid., 242.

45. Albert J. Raboteau, *Slave Religion: The "Invisible Institution" in the Antebellum South* (New York: Oxford University Press, 1978), 163.

46. Gayraud S. Wilmore, *Black Religion and Black Radicalism* (Garden City, N.Y.: Doubleday, 1972), 54, 55.

47. Ibid., 56, 58–59.

48. Raboteau, 247.

49. Ibid., 311–12.

50. Wilmore, 69.

51. Ibid., 100.

52. Raboteau, 314.

53. Wilmore, 196.

54. Quoted in Ibid., 115.

55. Quoted in Arthur Huff Fauset, *Black Gods of the Metropolis: Negro Religious Cults in the Urban North* (Philadelphia: University of Pennsylvania Press, 1971), 7.

56. Wilmore, 234–35.

57. Fauset, 100.

58. Wilmore, 243.

59. Ibid., 244, 245.

60. Ibid., 245.

61. Ibid., 272.

62. Malcolm X, *By Any Means Necessary*, ed. George Breitman (New York:

Pathfinder Press, 1970), 91.

63. May, 15.

64. J. Milton Yinger, *Religion in the Struggle for Power: A Study in the Sociology of Religion* (Durham, N.C.: Duke University Press, 1946), 132.

65. Matthew Josephson, *The Robber Barons: The Great American Capitalists 1861–1901* (New York: Harcourt, Brace, 1934), 322–23.

66. William W. Sweet, *The Story of Religion in America* (New York: Harper, 1939), 500–04.

67. May, 92, 93, 101.

68. Yinger, 134.

69. Ibid.

70. Ibid., 153.

71. Argyle and Beit-Hallahmi, 162.

72. Robert D. Cross, *The Emergence of Liberal Catholicism in America* (Cambridge, Mass.: Harvard University Press, 1958), 34–35.

73. Ibid., 35, 34.

74. Ibid., 48.

75. Yinger, 148.

76. Cross, 117.

77. Blanshard, 13.

78. *New York Times*, January 29, 1979.

79. Will Herberg, *Protestant-Catholic-Jew* (Garden City, N.Y.: Doubleday, 1960), 175.

80. Ibid., 200, n. 8.

81. Stanley Feldstein, *The Land That I Show You: Three Centuries of Jewish Life in America* (Garden City, N.Y.: Doubleday, 1978), 250.

82. Ibid., 106, 157, 158n.

83. Ibid., 158.

84. Ibid., 460.

85. Tocqueville, bk. 1, ch. 1.

86. Ibid.

87. Herberg, 60.

88. Ibid., 82–83.

89. Peter L. Berger, *The Noise of Solemn Assemblies: Christian Commitment and the Religious Establishment in America* (Garden City, N.Y.: Doubleday, 1961), 59.

90. Thomas F. O'Dea, *The Mormons* (Chicago: University of Chicago Press, 1957), 124.

91. The founder of Mormonism, Joseph Smith, a man with a charismatic personality and fluent imagination, stated that an angel led him to hidden gold tablets which, with the help of "seer stones" given him by the angel, he deciphered and transcribed. Fawn Brodie, the Pulitzer Prize–winning historian, in her meticulously researched biography of Smith, shows that he had a reputation as a liar when a young man and that church records prove that he married at least forty women in the two years before his death while he was denying that he was practicing polygamy. Yet while

Smith undoubtedly fabricated fictions he no doubt thought of himself as an agent of God, a self-made prophet who through his own efforts had founded a new religion in the service of the deity.

92. O'Dea, 189.

93. *New York Times*, March 30, 1980.

94. On the class composition of the evangelicals, see Rifkin and Howard, 178, 240.

95. *New York Times*, January 6, 1980.

96. Lowell D. Streiker and Gerald S. Strober, *Religion and the New Majority: Billy Graham, Middle America and the Politics of the 1970s* (New York: Association Press, 1972), 30.

97. *New York Times,* October 8, 1984.

98. Ibid., August 18, 1980.

99. Ibid., December 16, 1977.

Chapter 8

1. D.D. Kosambi, *Ancient India: A History of Its Culture and Civilization* (New York: Pantheon Books, 1965), 87, 102.

2. Ibid., 78.

3. In this and the following chapter I have sought to avoid the Indian and Arabic words that besprinkle scholarly works, using instead approximate English equivalents. For the spelling of such Indian and Arabic words and names as I have used, I have employed those most likely to be familiar to general readers rather than those employed by scholars.

4. Kosambi, 15.

5. Debiprasad Chattopadhyaya, "Social Function of Indian Idealism," *Essays in Honor of Prof. S.C. Sarkar* (New Delhi: People's Publishing House, 1976), 82.

6. Max Weber, *The Religion of India: The Sociology of Hinduism and Buddhism,* (Glencoe, Ill.: The Free Press, 1960), 122.

7. Chattopadhyaya, 96.

8. Quinter Marcellus Lyon, *The Great Religions* (New York: Odyssey Press, 1957), 134–35.

9. Kosambi, 127.

10. Romila Thapar, *A History of India,* (Baltimore: Penguin Books, 1968), vol. 1, 46.

11. Debiprasad Chattopadhyaya, *Lokayata* (New Delhi: People's Publishing House, 1959), 174.

12. Ibid., 481–82.

13. Edward Conze, *Buddhism: Its Essence and Development* (New York: Harper & Row, 1959), 55.

14. Thapar, 252.

15. Kosambi, 9.

16. Weber, 234; Romila Thapar, *Ancient Indian Social History* (New Delhi: Orient Longman, 1978), 44; D.N. Jha, "Temples and Merchants in South

India c. AD 900–AD 1300," *Essays in Honor of Prof. S.C. Sarkar*, 116.

17. Thapar, *A History of India*, 130.

18. Weber, 215.

19. Thapar, *Ancient Indian Social History*, 71.

20. Thapar, *A History of India*, 86.

21. Ibid., 87.

22. Ibid., 63–64.

23. Edward Conze, *A Short History of Buddhism* (London: George Allen & Unwin, 1981), 12.

24. George Novack, *The Origins of Materialism* (New York: Merit Publishers, 1965), particularly his summary, 283–84.

25. Novack, 284–86.

26. Chattopadhyaya argues that Buddhism is indebted to what he calls (*Lokayata*, xvii) the "proto-materialism" of the primitive tribes and what Novack calls (30) "the instinctive materialism of primitive peoples." This "proto-materialism," which antedated the concept of the supernatural, consisted of an identification of humanity with nature. The savage sought to command nature by mimetic magic (for instance, a dance imitating a cloudburst to bring about rain), not, as in religion, to propitiate a supernatural being by prayer or sacrifice. The indebtedness that Chattopadhyaya finds may be real, but Buddhist atheism could not have come into existence without the speculative philosophy of an advanced civilization, which Chattopadhyaya slights. Religion grew out of magic, and philosophy grew out of religion, each retaining vestiges of the previous stages, but each stage represented something radically new. Cf. Novack (48–49) on the contribution of F.M. Cornford, the Marxist student of ancient Greek society, in "uncovering the extremely primitive background out of which the pre-Socratics emerged" even though Cornford failed to appreciate that the "remnants of the past" in Greek philosophy were "not so decisive and important as the new ideas and methods."

27. Novack, 286.

28. Novack notes (97–100) that the Greek materialist philosophers, particularly Heraclitus, anticipated dialectics. The same is true of Buddha. Cf. Rahul Sankrityayan, "Buddhist Dialectics," *Buddhism: The Marxist Approach* (New Delhi: People's Publishing House, 1970), particularly 5–6.

29. *Buddhism in Translations*, tr. and ed. Henry Clarke Warren (New York: Atheneum, 1963), 234.

30. Sir Charles Eliot, *Hinduism and Buddhism: An Historical Sketch,* (New York: Barnes & Noble, 1957), vol. 1, liii.

31. Lyon, 147.

32. Eliot, vol. 1, 227.

33. Ibid., 235.

34. Ibid., 230–31.

35. Kosambi, 176–77.

36. Eliot, vol. 2, 123.

37. Kosambi, 179.

38. Ibid., 180. Outside India, one of the Asian rulers designated a bodhisattva (to be sure, not by himself but by his heirs a century after his death) was

none other than the Mongol emperor Genghis Khan, notorious for the carnage he visited upon Europe and Asia. Cf. Conze, *Buddhism: Its Essence and Development*, 75.

39. Weber, 16–17.

40. Human sacrifices, of course, are no longer legal, but cf. Kosambi, 21: "Indian newspapers announce every few years the arrest and trial of tribal men and women in a group, on suspicion of ritual murder (human sacrifice)."

41. Eliot, vol. 1, xvii.

42. Ibid., vol. 2, 164.

43. Ibid., 165.

44. Kosambi, 175.

45. Thapar, *A History of India*, 252.

46. Kosambi, 185–87. Cf. Weber, 292: "They [the princes] revived the ties with the Brahminical intellectual strata and the caste organization over and against the ancient Buddhistic monkdom and the guilds.... As the inscriptural sources indicate throughout, the power of the kings was decisive for the restoration of the new [Hindu] orthodoxy."

47. Murray T. Titus, *Indian Islam: A Religious History of Islam in India* (New York: Oxford University Press, 1930), 22–26. It should be noted that the Christians who sought to supersede the Muslim merchants in the overseas trade were no better than the Muslims in their treatment of the Indians. "As the first discoverer of the direct sea-route between Europe and India, Vasco da Gama occupies a unique place in the history of the modern world. But in his treatment of the Indians he may be described almost as a monster in the disguise of human form, a worthy compeer of Sultan Mahmud and Tamerlane, though on a much smaller scale."—*History and Culture of the Indian People,* ed. R.C. Majumdar et al. (Bombay: Bharatiya Vidya Bhava, 1960), vol. 6, 422. On capturing an Indian fleet, da Gama had the hands, ears, and noses of the 800 crewmembers cut off. He then had their feet tied together, their teeth knocked out to prevent them from biting through the cords, and, finally their bodies stacked on top of each other before burning them alive.

48. However, the Muslims adapted to the Indian caste system, the Persian, Turkish, and Afghan nobles placing themselves at its pinnacle. After all, if the Muslim rich and the Muslim poor wore the same kind of robe on pilgrimage in Mecca, symbolizing their equality in the service of Allah, when they doffed their pilgrimage robes, the rich wore their splendid garments and the poor their rags. Muslim brotherhood, harking back to the egalitarian tribalism of the origin of Islam, was superficial and readily discarded by arrogant Muslim nobles. Nevertheless the observance of caste was not as rigid among Muslims, who did not have a religious concern for ritual purity, as among Hindus.

49. Peter A. Pardue, *Buddhism: A Historical Introduction to Buddhist Values and the Social and Political Forms They Have Assumed in Asia* (New York: Macmillan, 1971), 84.

50. Ibid., 87.

51. Donald E. Smith, *Religion and Politics in Burma* (Princeton, N.J.: Princeton University Press, 1965), 136.

52. Trevor Ling, *Buddhism, Imperialism and War: Burma and Thailand in*

Modern History (London: George Allen & Unwin, 1979), 138–39.

53. Pardue, 98.

54. Ibid., 100–02.

55. Ibid., 111.

56. Kenneth S. Chen, *The Chinese Transformation of Buddhism* (Princeton, N.J.: Princeton University Press, 1973), 90–92.

57. Chen, 109.

58. Pardue, 78.

59. Ibid., 117.

60. Masaharu Anesaki, *History of Japanese Religion* (Rutland, Vt.: Charles E. Tuttle Co., 1963), 145–47.

61. Pardue, 124.

62. Anesaki, 170.

63. Pardue, 129.

64. Anesaki, 262.

65. H. Neill McFarland, *The Rush Hour of the Gods: A Study of New Religious Movements in Japan* (New York: Macmillan, 1967), 51.

66. Samir Amin, *Unequal Development: An Essay on the Social Formations of Peripheral Capitalism* (New York: Monthly Review Press, 1976), 33.

67. Ibid., 13, 16.

68. Ibid., 33–34.

69. Ibid., 34.

70. Ibid., 55–56.

71. Michael Löwy, *The Politics of Combined and Uneven Development: The Theory of Permanent Revolution* (London: New Left Books, 1981), 164.

72. Sri Lanka under the influence of India is the one predominantly Buddhist country that has the caste system.

73. Jerrold Schecter, *The New Face of Buddha: Buddhism and Political Power in South East Asia* (New York: Coward-McCann, 1967) 143.

74. Ernst Benz, *Buddhism or Communism: Which Holds the Future of Asia?* (Garden City, N.Y.: Doubleday, 1965), 69.

75. Smith, 321.

76. Schecter, 236.

77. Ling, 121.

78. *History and Culture of the Indian People*, ed. R.C. Majumadar et al. (Bombay: Bharatiya Vidya Bhava, 1963), vol. 9, 424–33, 501–02, 630.

79. Hirendranath Mukerjee, *India's Struggle for Freedom* (Calcutta: National Book Agency, 1962), 57.

80. Mukerjee, 68.

81. Donald E. Smith, *India as a Secular State* (Princeton, N.J.: Princeton University Press, 1963), 168–72.

82. Donald E. Smith, "Gandhi, Hinduism, and Mass Polities," *Religion and Political Modernization*, ed. Donald E. Smith, (New Haven: Yale University Press, 1974), 137.

83. B.K. Roy-Burman, "The Problem of Untouchables," *Tribe, Caste and Reli-

gion in India, ed. Romesh Thapar (Meerut, India: Macmillan Co. of India, 1977), 90.

84. Smith, "Gandhi, Hinduism, and Mass Polities," 138.

85. Ibid., 139.

86. Mukerjee, 157–58.

87. Ibid., 158–59.

88. Gautam Chattopadhyay, "The Almost Revolution, February 1946" *Essays in Honor of Prof S.C. Sarker*, 442.

89. Ibid., 446.

90. Mukerjee, 288.

91. "Communalism—Its Causes and Consequences: Statement by the Revolutionary Communist Organization (Indian Section of the Fourth International)," *International Viewpoint*, No. 60, October 1, 1984, 18.

92. Now the official name of the Congress Party; the "I" stands for Indira (Gandhi).

93. M. Navid, "The Threat of Hindu Communalism," *International Viewpoint*, No. 66, December 24, 1984), 9.

94. "Communalism—Its Causes and Consequences," 21.

Chapter 9

1. Maxime Rodinson, *Muhammad* (New York: Pantheon Books, 1980), 12–13.

2. Cf. Bryan S. Turner, *Marx and the End of Orientalism* (London: George Allen & Unwin, 1978), 51–52.

3. Bryan S. Turner, *Weber and Islam: A Critical Study* (London: Routledge & Kegan Paul, 1974), 29.

4. W. Montgomery Watt, *Muhammad: Prophet and Statesman* (New York: Oxford University Press, 1980), 39.

5. Maxime Rodinson, *Islam and Capitalism*, tr. Brian Pearce (London: Allen Lane, 1974), 14.

6. Turner, *Weber and Islam*, 35.

7. Jane Idleman Smith and Yvonne Yazbeck Haddad, *The Islamic Understanding of Death and Resurrection* (Albany: State University of New York Press, 1981), 164.

8. Turner, *Weber and Islam*, 35.

9. Rodinson, *Muhammad*, 244.

10. Ibid., 267.

11. E. Ashtor, *A Social and Economic History of the Near East in the Middle Ages* (London: Collins, 1976), 11.

12. Maurice Lombard, *The Golden Age of Islam* (New York: American Elsevier, 1975), 3.

13. Rodinson, *Muhammad*, 297.

14. Maxime Rodinson points out (*Marxism and the Muslim World* [New York: Monthly Review Press, 1981], 316, n. 19) that the Koran actually says (x, 99–100), "Would thou compel men until they are believers? It is

not for any soul to believe save by the permission of Allah." This, he says, is only one of a number of such statements, but he adds that there are contradictory passages. In later centuries Islam became increasingly less flexible, but as late as 1697 the philosopher Pierre Bayle wrote (Rodinson, *Marxism and the Muslim World*, 316, n. 19): "There are the Turks who tolerate all sorts of religions although the Koran orders them to persecute the infidels; and there are the Christians who do nothing but persecute although the Scriptures prohibit persecution."

15. Bernard Lewis, *The Arabs in History* (London: Hutchinson's University Library, 1950), 140. Christians, on the other hand, were engaging in forcible baptism. The thinking of many of the time is illustrated by the story of the Elizabethan mariner who, observing forcibly baptized captured Moors turning to Mecca to pray, remarked naively that the poor fools did not know that they were now Christians.

16. Lombard, 4.

17. Rodinson, *Muhammad*, 294.

18. It is salutary for the intellectual representatives of a dominant civilization, arrogant in its ascendancy, to see how it was regarded when positions were the reverse of what they are today. The tenth century geographer Masudi said (Lewis, 164) of the western Europeans that "their bodies are large, their natures gross, their manners harsh, their understanding dull and their tongues heavy.... [T]heir religious beliefs lack solidity.... [T]hose of them who are farthest to the north are most subject to stupidity, grossness and brutishness."

19. Perry Anderson, *Lineages of the Absolutist State* (London: New Left Books, 1974), 502.

20. Lombard, 10.

21. William Osier, *The Evolution of Modern Medicine* (New Haven, 1922), 98, quoted by Philip K. Hitti, "America and the Arab Heritage," *The Arab Heritage*, ed. Nalub Amin Faris (Princeton University Press, 1946), 3.

22. Rodinson, *Marxism and the Muslim World*, 64.

23. Ibid.

24. Ibid.

25. Anderson, 509.

26. The Crusades were the Christian counterpart of the Islamic jihads or "holy wars" and brought the same kind of booty, which was likewise attributed to the beneficence of God. Lewis (150–51) quotes Fulcher of Chartres, a chronicler of the First Crusade: "For those who were poor there [in Europe] has God made rich here. Those who had a few pence there, have numberless gold pieces here; he who had not a village there possesses, with God as giver, a whole town here." Cf. John L. La Monte, "Crusade and Jihad," *The Arab Heritage*, ed. Paris, 196: "In the twelfth and thirteenth centuries, in the age of the crusades and of the *jihads*, religion...was an important and valuable stimulant; it was seldom a prime cause or dominant motive." In fact, not infrequently it was so far from being the dominant motive that both Christian crusaders against the heathen and the Muslim warriors against the unbelievers were, where the promise of plunder was greater, diverted from their holy wars to fight against their own coreligionists even making unholy alliances with their religious antagonists for that purpose.

27. Anwar H. Syed, *Islam and the Dialectic of National Solidarity in Pakistan* (NewYork: Praeger, 1983), ch. 2, quoted by Eqbal Ahmad, "Islam and

Polities," *The Islamic Impact*, ed. Yvonne Yazbeck Haddad et al. (Syracuse, N.Y.: Syracuse University Press, 1984), 16.

28. William H. McNeill, *The Rise of the West: A History of the Human Community* (Chicago: University of Chicago Press, 1963), 632.

29. For a study of scholarly apologetics for imperialism, see Edward W. Said, *Orientalism* (New York: Pantheon Books, 1978) and the review-article of Said's book by Stuart Schaar, "Orientalists in the Service of Imperialism," *Race and Class*, 21 (1979), 67–80.

30. Rodinson shows (*Islam and Capitalism*, 35–46 and 261, n. 52) that the Islamic prohibition of interest was circumvented from the very beginning and that there were similar prohibitions of interest by Judaism and Christianity, which were likewise circumvented.

31. *Shorter Encyclopedia of Islam* (Ithaca, N.Y.: Cornell University Press, 1953), vol. 1, 248.

32. Lewis, 81.

33. *Shorter Encyclopedia of Islam*, vol. 1, 311.

34. Ibid.

35. Rodinson, *Marxism and the Muslim World*, 66.

36. Cf. Lewis, 107–10.

37. Bernard Lewis, *The Assassins* (New York: Octagon Books, 1980), 70. The word "assassin" comes from the word "hashish," which an underground, terroristic branch of the Ismailis was said to use before undertaking its terroristic acts.

38. *Marx and Engels on Religion*, 317n. Possibly Engels got this idea from the fourteenth century Arab historian ibn Khaldun, part of whose history was translated into French in 1862.

39. Turner, *Weber and Islam*, 66.

40. Rodinson, *Marxism and the Muslim World*, 170–71.

41. Thomas Hodgkin, "The Revolutionary Tradition in Islam," *Race & Class*, 21 (1980), 228.

42. Hodgkin, 229.

43. Rodinson, *Marxism and the Muslim World*, 170–71.

44. G.H. Jansen, *Militant Islam* (New York: Harper & Row, 1979), 97.

45. Jansen, 51.

46. Wilfred Cantwell Smith, *Islam in Modern History* (Princeton, N.J.: Princeton University Press, 1957), 176.

47. Jansen, 136.

48. Ibid., 190.

49. Jean and Simonne Lacouture, *Egypt in Transition* (London: Methuen, 1958), 441.

50. Ahmad, 16.

51. So too for Qadafi's regime in Libya and the Ba'athist regimes in Syria and Iraq. Cf. Omar I. El Fathaly and Monte Palmer, *Political Development and Social Change in Libya* (Lexington, Mass: D.C. Heath, 1980), 58–59 and John Obert Voll, *Islam: Continuity and Change in the Modern World*, (Boulder, Colo.: Westview Press, 1982), 319.

52. Fathaly and Palmer, 59.

53. Edward Mortimer, *Faith and Power: The Politics of Islam* (New York: Random House, 1982), 264.

54. Jansen, 147.

55. Wilfred Cantwell Smith, 187.

56. Noam Chomsky and Edward S. Herman, *The Washington Connection and Third World Fascism* (Boston: South End Press, 1979), 207–09.

57. The Muslim Brotherhood, which exists in many countries, is a fundamentalist reactionary organization based on the traders and artisans who suffered from the changes in commerce and industry, white collar professionals, lower-level bureaucrats in the state apparatus, students, and a section of the peasantry. It first supported Nasser and then turned against him.

58. Derek Hopwood, *Egypt: Politics and Society 1945–1981* (London: George Allen & Unwin, 1983), 117.

59. Mortimer, 219.

60. Ibid., 221, 229.

61. Löwy, 164.

62. Eric Wolf, *Peasant Wars of the Twentieth Century* (London, 1973), 297, quoted by Löwy, 174.

63. David and Marina Ottaway, *Algeria: The Politics of a Socialist Revolution* (Berkeley: University of California Press, 1970), 179.

64. Ibid., 179.

Chapter 10

1. V.I. Lenin, *On Religion* (New York: International Publishers, 1935), 12.

2. Marx and Engels, *Basic Writings*, 356.

3. Lenin, *On Religion*, 8.

4. Ibid., 18.

5. Ibid., 12.

6. Ibid., 16.

7. Ibid., 14–15.

8. Ibid., 15.

9. Ibid., 16.

10. Ibid., 17.

11. Marx and Engels, *Basic Writings*, 41.

12. Quoted by Bohdan R. Bociukiw, "Lenin and Religion," *Lenin: The Man, the Theorist, the Leader*, ed. Leonard Schapiro and Peter Reddaway (New York: Praeger, 1967), 113.

13. Leon Trotsky, *Problems of Everyday Life* (New York: Monad Press, 1973), 117–18.

14. Bociukiw, 115.

15. Julius F. Hecker, *Religion Under the Soviets* (New York: Vanguard Press, 1927), 68.

16. Program of the Communist Party of Russia, March 1919, quoted in "Introduction," Lenin, *On Religion*, 6.

17. Ibid.

18. John Shelton Curtiss, *The Russian Church and the Soviet State 1917–1950* (Boston: Little, Brown, 1965), 243.

19. Ibid., 293–94.

20. Ibid., 309.

21. Gerhard Simon, *Church, State and Opposition in the U.S.S.R.* (London: C. Hurst, 1974), 70.

22. Ibid., 84.

23. Ibid., 124–25.

24. Ibid., viii.

25. Ibid., 126. Simon thinks (88) that "the opposition has not realized that a self-ruling Church in a Communist state is completely alien to Lenin's total concept," but it is he who is mistaken. He does not present any evidence for his statement about Lenin's "total concept," simply taking it for granted that Lenin shared Stalin's belief in a one-party state and in a totalitarian society so that if Lenin said that the party must propagandize against religion this must mean that it will be free to use the state against religion when it so wishes, guarantees of freedom to the contrary. He would have benefited from reading Marcel Liebman's closely documented analysis of the development of Lenin's ideas in *Leninism Under Lenin* (London: Merlin, 1975), published in French in 1973.

26. Simon, 128–29.

27. *Detente and Socialist Democracy: A Discussion with Roy Medvedev*, ed. Ken Coates (New York: Monad Press, 1976), 159.

28. Donald E. MacInnis, ed., *Religious Policy and Practice in Communist China: A Documentary History* (New York: Macmillan, 1972), 8–9. Cf. Holmes Welch, *Buddhism Under Mao* (Cambridge, Mass.: Harvard University Press, 1972), 1–2.

29. MacInnis, 23.

30. Ibid., 19.

31. Ibid., 125.

32. Welch, 25. The Chinese Buddhist Association actually depended on a direct government subsidy (Welch, 23).

33. Ibid., 20.

34. MacInnis, 345. There has been a continuing propaganda battle between the Western supporters of the exiled Dalai Lama and the Chinese Communists over what has happened in remote and isolated Tibet. The most balanced account seems to be Bina Roy Burman's *Religion and Politics in Tibet* (New Delhi: Vikas Publishing House, 1979), which originated as a doctoral dissertation and makes analytical use of New China News Agency coverage, interviews with Tibetan refugees in India, including the Dalai Lama, and the writing of foreign visitors and scholars. In brief, Burman finds that from the occupation in 1951 until the rebellion of 1959, the Chinese sought to govern through the traditional ruling class, leaving the social structure unchanged, but the rebellion made this method of governance impossible. The rebellion was largely limited to the capital city and was an attempt by the monastic and lay elite to free itself of Chinese reins. However, many ordinary people joined in the revolt. After the rebellion there were sweeping social changes, which were, however, bureaucratically administered, with the

masses being drawn into them only to a very limited degree. Moreover, there seems to have been much looting of the monasteries and temples, with the loot making its way to China. Nevertheless there has been a significant rise in the standard of living and in civil rights as compared to what existed under the theocratic state of the lamas. The younger generation is being won over to the new way of life, and the influence of lamaism is fast fading. There still remains a question, however, of how much a sense of national identity is in conflict with Chinese overlordship.

35. MacInnis, 300.

36. *New York Times*, June 15, 1983.

37. Alice L. Hageman, "Introduction," *Religion in Cuba Today: A New Church in a New Society*, ed. Alice L. Hageman and Philip E. Wheaton (New York: Association Press, 1971), 20.

38. Ibid., 21–22.

39. Herbert L. Matthews, *Revolution in Cuba: An Essay in Understanding* (New York: Charles Scribner's Sons, 1975), 353.

40. Aldo J. Büntig, "The Church in Cuba: Toward a New Fronter," *Religion in Cuba Today: A New Church in a New Society*, ed. Alice Hageman and Philip Wheaton (New York: Association Press, 1971), 107. Büntig also says (97) that in the last years of Batista, which were marked by a general discontent, "the opposition swelled its ranks in all social classes." He adds: "While today we wish that it had emphasized its denunciation more vehemently, nevertheless it would be unjust to say that the hierarchy kept quiet during this emergency."

41. Ibid., 29. The proclamation unconsciously echoed the United States Protestant churches that had clamored for United States intervention in the Cuban fight for independence. As a Congregationalist magazine wrote in 1898 (Hageman and Wheaton, 21), "The Churchmen of our land should be prepared to invade Cuba as soon as the army and navy open the way, to invade Cuba in a friendly, loving Christian spirit, with bread in one hand and the Bible in the other, and win the people to Christ by Christlike service."

42. Ibid., 108.

43. Ibid., 110.

44. Ibid., 116.

45. Ibid., 114–15.

46. Ibid., 115.

47. The letters are in ibid., 288–94 and 298–308.

48. The irony is that it is the dictators supported by the United States who have persecuted a sector of the Catholic Church. Between 1968 and 1978, says Penny Lernoux (*Cry of the People* [Garden City, N.Y.: Doubleday, 1980], 13), "over 850 priests, nuns, and bishops have been arrested, tortured, murdered, or expelled, and thousands of the Catholic laity have been jailed and killed. 'Nowadays it is dangerous...and practically illegal to be an authentic Christian in Latin America,' said Salvadoran Jesuit Rutilio Grande a month before he was shot dead by right-wing assassins in El Salvador."

49. *New York Times*, April 6, 1980.

50. Ibid., January 21, 1979.

51. Ibid.

52. V.I. Lenin, *Collected Works*, (Moscow: Foreign Languages Publishing

House, 1962), vol. 15, 27.

53. Lenin, *On Religion*, 8–9.

54. Cf. ibid., 158.

55. *Intercontinental Press*, July 21, 1980.

56. *Sandinistas Speak*, ed. Bruce Marcus (New York: Pathfinder Press, 1982), 20.

57. There is conclusive evidence that in ten Latin-American countries (and we may assume that it is true of Nicaragua), although the causes of the divisions lie within the Church, "malicious outside influences" have not been absent: CIA has worked with right-wing forces in the Latin American church to smear and harass "subversives" among the clergy. Cf. Lernoux, 142–46.

58. The statement is printed in full in *Sandinistas Speak*, 105–11.

59. Cf. David I. Kertzer, *Comrades and Christians: Religion and Political Struggle in Communist Italy* (New York: Cambridge University Press, 1980), 264–66.

60. Leon Trotsky, *On Literature and Art*, ed. Paul N. Siegel (New York: Pathfinder Press, 1970), 60.

Bibliography

Ahmad, Eqbal. "Islam and Polities," The Islamic Impact, ed. Yvonne Yazbeck Haddad et al. Syracuse N.Y.: Syracuse University Press, 1984.

"Alexander VI," Encyclopedia Britannica, 11th ed.

Amin, Samir. Unequal Development: An Essay on the Social Formations of Peripheral Capitalism. New York: Monthly Review Press, 1976.

Anderson, Perry. Lineages of the Absolutist State. London: New Left Books, 1974.

Anesaki, Masaharu. History of Japanese Religion. Rutland, Vt.: Charles E. Tuttle Co., 1963.

Angeles, Peter A. The Problem of God: A Short Introduction. Buffalo, N.Y.: Prometheus Books, 1980.

"Armenia," Encyclopedia Britannica, 11th ed.

Argyle, Michael, and Benjamin Beit-Hallahmi, The Social Psychology of Religion. Boston: Routledge & Kegan Paul, 1975.

Artz, Frederick B. Reaction and Revolution 1814–1832. New York: Harper, 1934.

Ashtor, E. A Social and Economic History of the Near East in the Middle Ages. London: Collins, 1976.

Bailyn, Bernard. The Ideological Origins of the American Revolution. Cambridge, Mass.: Harvard University Press, 1967.

Baron, Salo W. A Social and Religious History of the Jews. Vols. 1 and 2. New York: Columbia University Press, 1937.

Baumer, Franklin L. Religion and the Rise of Skepticism. New York: Harcourt, Brace, 1960.

Beard, Charles A., and Mary R. The Rise of American Civilization. Vol. 1. New York: Macmillan, 1961.

Benz, Ernest. Buddhism or Communism: Which Holds the Future of Asia? Garden City, N.Y.: Doubleday, 1965.

Berger, Peter L. The Noise of Solemn Assemblies: Christian Commitment and the Religious Establishment in America. Garden City, N.Y.: Doubleday, 1961.

Good News Bible: The Bible in Today's English Version. New York: American Bible Society, 1976.

The Interpreter's Bible, ed. George A. Buttrick, Nolan B. Harmon et al. Vols. 1 and 7. New York: Abingdon Press, 1952 and 1957.

Blanshard, Paul. Paul Blanshard on Vatican II. Boston: Beacon Press, 1966.

Bociukiw, Bohdan. "Lenin and Religion," Lenin: The Man, the Theorist, the   Leader, ed. Leonard Schapiro and Peter Reddaway. New York: Praeger, 1967.

Büntig, Aldo J. "The Church in Cuba: Toward a New Frontier," In Religion in Cuba Today: A New Chruch in a New Society, ed. Alice Hageman and Phillp Wheaton. New York: Association Press, 1971.

Burman, Bina Roy. Religion and Politics in Tibet. New Delhi: Vikas Publishing House, 1979.

Calverton, V.F. The Passing of the Gods. New York: Charles Scribner's Sons, 1934.

Chattodpadhyay, Gautam. "The Almost Revolution, February 1946," Essays in Honor of Professor S.C. Sarkar. New Delhi: People's Publishing House, 1976.

Chattodpadhyay, Debiprasad. Lokayata. New Delhi: People's Publishing House, 1959.

"Social Function of Indian Idealism," Essays in Honor of Professor S.C. Sarkar. New Delhi: People's Publishing House, 1976.

Chaucer, Geoffrey. The Works, ed. F.N. Robinson. Boston: Houghton Mifflin, 1957.

Chen, Kenneth S. The Chinese Transformation of Buddhism. Princeton, N.J.: Princeton University Press, 1973.

Chomsky, Noam, and Herman, Edward S. The Washington Connection and Third World Fascism. Boston: South End Press, 1979.

"Communalism—Its Causes and Consequences: Statement by the Revolutionary Communist Organization (Indian Section of the Fourth International)," International Viewpoint, No. 60 (October 1, 1984), 18–24.

Conner, Cliff. Evolutionism vs. Creationism: In Defense of Scientific Thinking. New York: Pathfinder Press, 1981.

Conze, Edward. Buddhism: Its Essence and Development. New York: Harper & Row, 1959.

———A Short History of Buddhism. London: George Allen & Unwin, 1981.

Cragg, Gerald R. The Church and the Age of Reason. Grand Rapids, Mich.: Erdmans, 1967.

Cross, Robert D. The Emergence of Liberal Catholicism in America. Cambridge, Mass.: Harvard University Press, 1958.

Curtiss, John Shelton. The Russian Church and the Soviet State 1917–1950. Boston: Little, Brown, 1965.

De Camp, L. Sprague. The Great Monkey Trial. Garden City, N.Y.: Doubleday, 1968.

Diderot, Denis. Diderot, Interpreter of Nature: Selected Writings, ed. Jonathan Kemp. New York: International Publishers, c. 1943.

———Thoughts on Religion. London: n.n., 1819.

Deutscher, Isaac. The Non-Jewish Jew and Other Essays. New York: Oxford University Press, 1968.

———The Prophet Armed: Trotsky 1879–1921. New York: Random House, 1965.

———The Prophet Outcast: Trotsky 1929–1940. New York: Random House, 1963.

———Stalin: A Political Biography. New York: Oxford University Press, 1949.

Eaton, Clement. Freedom of Thought in the Old South. Durham N.C.: Duke University Press, 1940.

El Fathaly, Omar I., and Palmer, Monte. Political Development and Social Change in Libya. Lexington, Mass.: D.C. Heath, 1980.

Eliot, Sir Charles. Hinduism and Buddhism: An Historical Sketch. Vols. 1 and 2. New York: Barnes & Noble, 1957.

Engels, Frederick. Herr Eugen Dühring's Revolution in Science. New York: International Publishers. 1939.

Fauset, Arthur Huff. Black Gods of the Metropolis: Negro Religious Cults in the Urban North. Philadelphia: University of Pennsylvania Press, 1971.

Feldstein, Stanley. The Land That I Show You: Three Centuries of Jewish Life in America. Garden City, N.Y.: Doubleday, 1978.

Ferguson, Wallace K. "The Church in a Changing World: A Contribution to the Interpretation of the Renaissance," Renaissance Studies. New York: Harper & Row, 1970.

Foner, Eric. Tom Paine and Revolutionary America. New York: Oxford University Press, 1976.

Frazer, James. The Golden Bough. Vol. 3. London: Macmillan, 1911.

Freud, Sigmund. "The Future of an Illusion," The Standard Edition of the Complete Psychological Works. Vol. 21. London: Hogarth Press, 1962.

Friedlander, Saul. Pius XII and the Third Reich: A Documentation. New York: Knopf, 1966.

Fromm, Erich. The Dogma of Christ. New York: Rinehart & Winston, 1963.

Graham, Loren R. Science and Philosophy in the Soviet Union. New

York: Knopf, 1972.

Grub, Isabell. Quakerism and Industry Before 1800. London: Williams & Norgate, 1930.

Hageman, Alice L., and Philip E. Wheaton (eds.). Religion in Cuba Today: A New Church in a New Society. New York: Association Press, 1971.

Hayes, Carlton J. A Generation of Materialism: 1871–1900. New York: Harper, 1941.

Hecker, Julius F. Religion Under the Soviets. New York: Vanguard Press, 1927.

Herberg, Will. Protestant-Catholic-Jew. Garden City, N.Y.: Doubleday, 1960.

Hill, Christopher. Change and Continuity in Seventeenth-Century England: Cambridge, Mass.: Harvard University Press, 1975.

———"The English Civil War Interpreted by Marx and Engels," Science and Society, 12 (1948).

———Puritanism and Revolution. New York: Schocken Books, 1964.

———"Science and Magic in Seventeenth Century England," J.D. Bernal Peace Library, October 19, 1976 (mimeo.).

——— Society and Puritanism in Pre-revolutionary England. London: Seeker and Warburg, 1964.

———The World Turned Upside Down: Radical Ideas During the English Revolution. New York: Penguin Books, 1976.

Hitti, Philip K. "America and the Arab Heritage," The Arab Heritage, ed. Nalub Amin Faris. Princeton University Press, 1946.

Hodgkin, Thomas. "The Revolutionary Tradition in Islam," Race & Class, 21 (1980).

Holbach, Paul Henri Thiry, Baron d'. Good Sense: or Natural Ideas as Opposed to Supernatural. New York: G. Vale, 1856.

Hopwood, Derek. Egypt: Politics and Society 1945–1981. London: George Allen & Unwin, 1983.

Hume, David. Hume on Religion, ed. Richard Wollheim. New York: World Publishing Co., 1964.

Inglis, K. S. Churches and the Working Classes in Victorian England. London: Routledge & Kegan Paul, 1963.

Jameson, J. Franklin. The American Revolution Considered as a Social Movement. Boston: Beacon Press, 1956.

Jansen, G.H. Militant Islam. New York: Harper & Row, 1979.

Jha, D.N. "Temples and Merchants, in South India c. AD 900–AD 1300," Essays in Honour of Professor S.C. Sarkar. New Delhi: People's Publishing House, 1976.

Josephson, Matthew. The Robber Barons: The Great American Capitalists 1861–1901. New York: Harcourt, Brace, 1934.

Kautsky, Karl. Are the Jews a Race? New York: International Publishers, 1926.

——Foundations of Christianity. New York: S.A. Russell, 1953.

——Thomas More and His Utopia. London: A. & C. Black, 1927.

Kellett, E.E. A Short History of Religions. London: Victor Gollancz, 1933.

Kertzer, David I. Comrades and Christians: Religion and Political Struggle in Communist Italy. New York: Cambridge University Press, 1980.

Koch, G. Adolf. Republican Religion: The American Revolution and the Cult of Reason. New York: Henry Holt, 1933.

Kosambi, D.D. Ancient India: A History of Its Culture and Civilization. New York: Pantheon Books, 1965.

La Barre, Weston. The Ghost Dance: Origins of Religion. Garden City, N.Y.: Doubleday, 1970.

Lacouture, Jean and Simonne. Egypt in Transition. London: Methuen, 1958.

Lamont, Corliss. "The Illusion of Immortality," Critiques of God, ed. Peter Angeles. Buffalo, N.Y.: Prometheus Books, 1976.

La Monte, John L. "Crusade and Jihad," The Arab Heritage, ed. Nalub Amin Faris. Princeton, N.J.: Princeton University Press, 1946.

Lenin, V.I. Collected Works. Vol. 15. Moscow: Foreign Languages Publishing House, 1962.

——On Religion. New York: International Publishers, 1935.

——The State and Revolution. Moscow: Foreign Languages Publishing House, n.d.

Leon, Abram. The Jewish Question: A Marxist Interpretation. New York: Pathfinder Press, 1970.

——The State and Revolution. Moscow: Foreign Languages Publishing House, n.d.

Lernoux, Penny. Cry of the People. Garden City, N.Y.: Doubleday, 1980.

Leuba, J.H. The Psychology of Religious Mysticism. New York: Harcourt, Brace, 1925.

Lewis, Bernard. The Arabs in History. London: Hutchinson's University Library, 1950.

——The Assassins. New York: Octagon Books, 1980.

Lewy, Guenter. The Catholic Church and Nazi Germany. New York: McGraw-Hill, 1965.

Liebman, Marcel. Leninism Under Lenin. London: Merlin, 1975.

Ling, Trevor. Buddhism, Imperialism and War: Burma and Thailand in Modern History. London: George Allen & Unwin, 1979.

Lombard, Maurice. The Golden Age of Islam. New York: American Elsevier, 1975.

Löwy, Michael. The Politics of Combined and Uneven Development: The Theory of Permanent Revolution. London: New Left Books, 1981.

Lyon, Quinter Marcellus. The Great Religions. New York: Odyssey Press, 1957.

McCloskey, H.J. "God and Evil," Critiques of God, ed. Peter Angeles. Buffalo, N.Y.: Prometheus Books, 1976.

McFarland, H. Neill. The Rush Hour of the Gods: A Study of New Religious Movements in Japan. New York: Macmillan, 1967.

MacInnis, Donald E. (ed.). Religious Policy and Practice in Communist China: A Documentary History. New York: Macmillan, 1972.

McLoughlin, William G. "The American Revolution as a Religious Revival: 'The Millenium in One Country,'" New England Quarterly, 40 (1967).

————Revivals, Awakenings, and Reform: An Essay on Religion and Social Change in America, 1607-1977. Chicago: University of Chicago Press, 1978.

McNeill, William H. The Rise of the West: A History of the Human Community. Chicago: University of Chicago Press, 1963.

Majumdar, R.C., et al. (eds.). History and Culture of the Indian People. Vols. 6 and 9. Bombay: Bharatiya Vidya Bhava, 1960 and 1963.

Malcolm X. By Any Means Necessary. Ed. George Breitman. New York: Pathfinder Press, 1970.

Mao Tse-tung. Quotations from Chairman Mao Tse-tung. Peking: Foreign Languages Press, 1966.

Marcus, Bruce (ed.). Sandinistas Speak. New York: Pathfinder Press, 1982.

Marx, Karl. Capital. London: George Allen & Unwin, 1957.

————"On the Jewish Question," Selected Essays by Karl Marx. London: Leonard Parsons. 1926.

————Selected Works. Vol. 1. New York: International Publishers, 1939.

Marx, Karl, and Friedrich Engels. Basic Writings on Politics and Philosophy, ed. Lewis S. Feuer. Garden City, N.Y.: Doubleday, 1959.

Karl Marx and Friedrich Engels on Religion. New York: Schocken Books, 1977.

Matson, Wallace I. "The Argument from Design," Critiques of God, ed. Peter Angeles. Buffalo, N.Y.: Prometheus Books, 1976.

Matthews, Herbert L. Revolution in Cuba: An Essay in Understanding. New York: Charles Scribner's Sons, 1975.

May, Henry F. Protestant Churches and Industrial America. New York: Octagon Books, 1963.

Medvedev, Roy. "Problems of General Concern," Detente and Socialist Democracy: A Discussion with Roy Medvedev, ed. Ken Coates.

New York: Monad Press, 1976.

Mill, John Stuart. Three Essays on Religion. London: Longmans, Green, 1874.

Moon, Parker Thomas. The Labor Problem and the Social Catholic Movement in France. New York: Macmillan, 1921.

Morais, Herbert E. Deism in Eighteenth Century America. New York: Russell & Russell, 1960.

Mortimer, Edward. Faith and Power: The Politics of Islam. New York: Random House, 1982.

Mukerjee, Hirendranath. India's Struggle for Freedom. Calcutta: National Book Agency, 1962.

Murdock, George Peter. Our Primitive Contemporaries. New York: Macmillan, 1946.

Nagel, Ernest. "Malarious Philosophies of Science," Critiques of God, ed. Peter Angeles. Buffalo, N.Y.: Prometheus Books, 1976.

Navid, M. "The Threat of Hindu Communalism," International Viewpoint, No. 66 (December 24, 1984).

Niebuhr, H. Richard. The Social Sources of Denominationalism. Hamden, Conn.: Shoe String Press, 1954.

Niebuhr, Reinhold. "Christian Politics and Communist Religion," Christianity and the Social Revolution, ed. John Lewis et al. New York: Charles Scribner's Sons, 1936.

——"Introduction," Karl Marx and Friedrich Engels on Religion. New York: Schocken Books, 1977.

Novack, George. Empiricism and Its Evolution: A Marxist View. New York: Pathfinder Press, 1973.

——Humanism and Socialism. New York: Pathfinder Press, 1973.

——The Origins of Materialism. New York: Merit Publishers, 1965.

——Polemics in Marxist Philosophy. New York: Monad Press, 1978.

——Pragmatism Versus Marxism. New York: Pathfinder Press, 1975.

——"A Suppressed Chapter in the History of American Capitalism: The Conquest of the Indians," Marxist Essays in American History, ed. Robert Himmel. New York: Merit Publishers, 1966.

Nye, Russel B. William Lloyd Garrison and the Humanitarian Reformers. Boston: Little, Brown, 1955.

Olson, Robert G. Ethics: A Short Introduction. New York: Random House, 1978.

O'Dea, Thomas F. The Mormons. Chicago: University of Chicago Press, 1957.

Ottaway, David, and Marina. Algeria: The Politics of a Socialist Revolution. Berkeley: University of California Press, 1979.

Pardue, Peter A. Buddhism: A Historical Introduction to Buddhist Values and the Social and Political Forms They Have Assumed in Asia. New York: Macmillan, 1971.

Pascal, Roy. The Social Basis of the German Reformation. New York: Augustus M. Kelley, 1971.

Petegorsky, David W. Left-Wing Democracy in the English Civil War. New York: Haskell House, 1972.

Pfeiffer, Robert H. History of New Testament Times. New York: Harper, 1949.

————Religion in the Old Testament. New York: Harper, 1961.

Pinson, Koppel Z. Pietism as a Factor in the Rise of German Nationalism. New York: Columbia University Press, 1934.

Prawer, S.S. Karl Marx and World Literature. New York: Oxford University Press, 1978.

Raboteau, Albert J. Slave Religion: The "Invisible Institutions" in the Antebellum South. New York: Oxford University Press, 1978.

Rifkin, Jeremy, and Ted Howard. The Emerging Order: God in the Age of Scarcity. New York: G.P. Putnam's Sons, 1979.

Robertson, Archibald. The Origins of Christianity. New York: International Publishers, 1962.

Rodinson, Maxime. Islam and Capitalism, tr. Brian Pearce. London: Allen Lane, 1974.

————Israel A Colonial-Settler State? New York: Monad Press, 1973.

————Marxism and the Muslim World. New York: Monthly Review Press, 1981.

————Muhammad. New York: Pantheon Books, 1980.

Roy-Burman, B.K. "The Problem of Untouchables," Tribe, Caste and Religion in India, ed. Romesh Thapar. Meerut, India: Macmillan Co. of India, 1977.

Russell, Bertrand. A History of Western Philosophy. New York: Simon and Schuster, 1945.

————Religion and Science. New York: Henry Holt, 1935.

————The Scientific Outlook. Glencoe, Ill.: Free Press, 1931.

————Why I Am Not a Christian. New York: Simon and Schuster, 1957.

Said, Edward W. Orientalism. New York: Pantheon Books, 1978.

Sankrityayan, Rahul. "Buddhist Dialectics," Buddhism: The Marxist Approach. New Delhi: People's Publishing House, 1970.

Schaar, Stuart. "Orientalists in the Service of Imperialism," Race and Class, 21 (1979).

Schecter, Jerrold. The New Face of Buddha: Buddhism and Political Power in Southeast Asia. New York: Coward-McCann, 1967.

Selsam, Howard and Harry Martel (eds.). Reader in Marxist Philosophy From the Writings of Marx, Engels, and Lenin. New York: International Publishers, 1973.

Shanahan, William O. German Protestants Face the Social Question: The Conservative Phase, 1815–1871. Notre Dame, Ind: University of Notre Dame Press, 1954.

Shorter Encyclopedia of Islam. Vol. 1. Ithaca, NY: Cornell University Press, 1953.

Simon, Gerhard. Church, State and Opposition in the USSR. London: C. Hurst, 1974.

Simpson, George Gaylord. The Meaning of Evolution. New Haven, Conn.: Yale University Press, 1950.

Singer, Peter. "Revolution and Religion," New York Review of Books, November 6, 1980.

Smart, Ninian. "Death and the Decline of Religion in Western Society," Man's Concern With Death, ed. Arnold Toynbee. New York: McGraw-Hill, 1968.

Smith, Donald E. "Gandhi, Hinduism, and Mass Politics," Religion and Political Modernization, ed. Donald E. Smith. New Haven, Conn.: Yale University Press, 1974.

———India as a Secular State. Princeton, N.J.: Princeton University Press, 1963.

———Religion and Politics in Burma. Princeton, N.J.: Princeton University Press, 1965.

Smith, Homer W. Man and His Gods. Boston: Little, Brown, 1952.

Smith, Jane Idleman, and Yvonne Yazbeck Haddad. The Islamic Understanding of Death and Resurrection. Albany: State University of New York Press, 1981.

Smith, Preserved. The Age of the Reformation. New York: Henry Holt, 1920.

Smith, Wilfred Cantwell. Islam in Modern History. Princeton, N.J.: Princeton University Press, 1957.

Soboul, Albert. A Short History of the French Revolution 1789–1799. Berkeley: University of California Press, 1977.

Stark, Werner. The Sociology of Religion: A Study of Christendom. Vol. 2: Sectarian Religion. London: Routledge & Kegan Paul, 1967.

Stefansson, Vilhjalmur. "Lessons in Living from the Stone Age," A Treasury of Science, ed. Harlow Shapley et al. New York: Harper, 1946.

Streiker, Lowell D., and Gerald S. Strober. Religion and the New Majority: Billy Graham, Middle America and the Politics of the 1970s. New York: Association Press, 1972.

Sweet, William W. The Story of Religion in America. New York: Harper, 1939.

Szasz, Thomas. The Manufacture of Madness. New York: Harper & Row, 1970.

Tawney, R.H. Religion and the Rise of Capitalism. New York: Penguin Books, 1947.

Thapar, Romila. Ancient Indian Social History. New Delhi: Orient Longman, 1978.

——A History of India. Vol. 1. Baltimore: Penguin Books, 1968.

Thompson, James Westfall. An Economic and Social History of the Middle Ages (300–1300). London: Century, 1928.

Titus, Murray T. Indian Islam: A Religious History of Islam in India. New York: Oxford University Press, 1930.

Tocqueville, Alexis de. Democracy in America. New York: Vintage Books, 1959.

Toynbee, Arnold. "Traditional Attitudes Towards Death," Man's Concern With Death, ed. Arnold Toynbee. New York: McGraw-Hill, 1968.

Trevor-Roper, H. R. The European Witch-Craze of the Sixteenth and Seventeenth Centuries. New York: Harper & Row, 1970.

Troeltsch, Ernst. The Social Teaching of the Christian Churches. Vol. 1. New York: Macmillan, 1950.

Trotsky, Leon. The Age of Permanent Revolution: A Trotsky Anthology, ed. Isaac Deutscher. New York: Dell, 1964.

——The History of the Russian Revolution. Vol. 3. New York: Simon and Schuster, 1937.

——In Defense of Marxism. New York: Pioneer Publishers, 1942.

——On Literature and Art, ed. Paul N. Siegel. New York: Pathfinder Press, 1970.

——Problems of Everyday Life. New York: Monad Press, 1973.

——The Revolution Betrayed. Garden City, N.Y.: Doubleday, 1937.

——Stalin: An Appraisal of the Man and His Influence. New York: Stein and Day, 1967.

——Their Morals and Ours. New York: Merit Publishers, 1969.

Turner, Bryan S. Marx and the End of Orientalism. London: George Allen & Unwin, 1978.

——Weber and Islam: A Critical Study. London: Routledge & Kegan Paul, 1974.

Vidler, Alec R. The Church in an Age of Revolution. Baltimore: Penguin Books, 1976.

Voll, John Obert. Islam: Continuity and Change in the Modern World. Boulder, Colo.: Westview Press, 1982.

Warner, Wellman J. The Wesleyan Movement in the Industrial Revolution. New York: Longmans, Green, 1930.

Warren, Henry Clarke (tr. and ed.). Buddhism in Translations. New York: Atheneum, 1963.

Watson, Richard. An Apology for the Bible. New York: n.n., 1796.

Watt, W. Montgomery. Muhammad: Prophet and Statesman. New

York: Oxford University Press, 1980.

Weber, Max. The Religion of India: The Sociology of Hinduism and Buddhism. Glencoe, Ill.: Free Press, 1960.

Welch, Holmes. Buddhism Under Mao. Cambridge, Mass.: Harvard University Press, 1972.

Wilmore, Gayraud S. Black Religion and Black Radicalism. Garden City, N.Y.: Doubleday, 1972.

Yinger, Melton J. Religion in the Struggle for Power: A Study in the Sociology of Religion. Durham, N.C.: Duke University Press, 1946.

Ziff, Lazer. Puritanism in America. New York: Viking Press, 1973.

Zucker, Norman L. The Coming Crisis in Israel: Private Faith and Public Policy. Cambridge, Mass.: MIT Press, 1973.

Index

ABOUT HAYMARKET BOOKS

Haymarket Books is a nonprofit, progressive book distributor and publisher. We believe that activists need to take ideas, history, and politics into the many struggles for social justice today. Learning the lessons of past victories, as well as defeats, can arm a new generation of fighters for a better world.

We take inspiration and courage from our namesakes, the Haymarket Martyrs, who gave their lives fighting for a better world. Their 1886 struggle for the eight-hour day, which gave us May Day, the international workers' holiday, reminds workers around the world that ordinary people can organize and struggle for their own liberation. These struggles continue today across the globe—struggles against oppression, exploitation, hunger, and poverty.

ALSO FROM HAYMARKET BOOKS

SUBTERRANEAN FIRE: A HISTORY
OF WORKING-CLASS RADICALISM IN THE UNITED STATES
Sharon Smith   1 931859 23 X   February 2006

This accessible, critical history of the U.S. labor movement examines the hidden history of workers' resistance from the nineteenth century to the present.

THE DISPOSSESSED: CHRONICLES OF
THE DESTERRADOS OF COLOMBIA
Alfredo Molano   1 931859 17 5   April 2005

Here in their own words are the stories of the Desterrados, or "dispossessed"—the thousands of Colombians displaced by years of war and state-backed terrorism, funded in part through U.S. aid to the Colombian government. With a preface by Aviva Chomsky.

LITERATURE AND REVOLUTION
Leon Trotsky, edited by William Keach 1 931859 21 3 May 2005

A new, annotated edition of Leon Trotsky's classic study of the relationship between politics and art.

WHAT'S MY NAME, FOOL?
SPORTS AND RESISTANCE IN THE UNITED STATES
Dave Zirin   1 931859 20 5   July 2005

Edgeofsports.com sportswriter Dave Zirin provdes a no-holds-barred commentary on the personalities and politics of American sports.